From East to West

Memoirs of a Finance Professor on Academia, Practice, and Policy

From East to West

Memoirs of a Finance Professor on Academia, Practice, and Policy

Cheng-Few Lee
Rutgers University, USA

World Scientific
NEW JERSEY • LONDON • SINGAPORE • BEIJING • SHANGHAI • HONG KONG • TAIPEI • CHENNAI • TOKYO

Published by

World Scientific Publishing Co. Pte. Ltd.
5 Toh Tuck Link, Singapore 596224
USA office: 27 Warren Street, Suite 401-402, Hackensack, NJ 07601
UK office: 57 Shelton Street, Covent Garden, London WC2H 9HE

British Library Cataloguing-in-Publication Data
A catalogue record for this book is available from the British Library.

FROM EAST TO WEST
Memoirs of a Finance Professor on Academia, Practice, and Policy

ISBN 978-981-3146-12-9
ISBN 978-981-3146-13-6 (pbk)

Printed in Singapore

I dedicate this book to my family
for their devotion and support.

This book also celebrates the 250th anniversary
of the founding of Rutgers University.

Contents

Introduction

I started teaching at the University of Georgia in the fall of 1973. In the fall of 2016, I finished my 43rd year of teaching. I decided to translate and update my Chinese autobiography, which was originally published in January 2000. Based on the Chinese edition, I updated some of the chapters. I have also added seven new chapters in this English edition of my autobiography. These seven chapters are: Chapter 8, "Experience in Training Ph.D. Students in Finance and Accounting," and Chapter 9, "Innovative and Active Approach to Teaching Finance," which was expanded from Chapter 7 of my Chinese autobiography; Chapter 10, "World Records in Academic Achievements," Chapter 12, "Editing Journals and Writing Books," Chapter 15, "Contributions to Taiwan's Economic and Financial Policies," Chapter 17, "Forty Three Years of a Challenging and Rewarding Academic Career," and Chapter 18, "Life Begins at 70." These topics present my academic achievements, review my career in academia, and reflect on my life, respectively.

In my original Chinese autobiography, there were three chapters related to the economic policy for Taiwan, China, and the Pacific Basin region; in this version I kept the chapter entitled, "Contributions to Taiwan's Economic and Financial Policies," which is related to the economic policies for Taiwan. However, I have updated and expanded some of the other chapters to discuss my academic activities and contributions during the last 43 years.

Since I left Taiwan in 1968, I have been living in the United States for 48 years and have been teaching here for 43 years. Before taking a teaching position at Rutgers University in 1988, I taught at the University of Georgia from 1973 to 1976 and before that the University of Illinois at Urbana-Champaign from 1976 to 1988. In 1982, I was awarded the IBE distinguished professor of finance at the University of Illinois. After my time at the University of Illinois at Urbana-Champaign, Rutgers University hired me as special professor II and set up a department of finance at its New Brunswick campus. At present, I am the distinguished professor of the Department of Finance and Economics at Rutgers University in New Jersey. I am also the chief editor of two internationally known journals and three annual academic journals, and the chairman of three important international conferences. In addition, I also presided over the Foundation of Pacific Basin Financial Research and Development.

During my 43 years of teaching, I have advised more than 100 Ph.D. students, published more than 225 academic papers, and completed more than 26 books. Since 1992, I have also devoted myself to do research concerning the financial markets and policies in Taiwan and the Pacific Basin countries. I am constantly providing my opinions to the government, academic institutes, and the industries.

The main objectives of this autobiography are (i) to share with my readers the stages of my academic training, (ii) to show the growth over my 43-year academic career in research, teaching, and service, and (iii) to share my experience of journal editing and conference organizing.

For the last 43 years, I have been very fortunate to have the opportunity to teach at three flagship universities, namely, University of Georgia, University of Illinois at Urbana-Champaign, and Rutgers University. I would especially like to express my appreciation to the University of Illinois and Rutgers University since they gave me enough resources to create my academic legacy, which includes paper publishing, journal editing, and conference organizing.

Now, I will briefly discuss the overview of this book. There are 18 chapters in this book. The first 17 chapters have been divided into three parts, they are: "Childhood, Education Experience, and Family Life," which covers Chapters 1 through 6; "Teaching, Service, and Research Activities," which covers Chapters 7 through 12; and "Contributions to Academia and Policy Making in Taiwan," which covers Chapters 13 through 17. The first three chapters cover my early life and education in Taiwan and in the U.S., and my working experience in the Bank of China (BOC). Chapter 4 describes my happy family life. Chapters 5 and 6 explain my relationship with President Lee Teng-hui and with ex-Governor of the Central Bank, Dr. Kuo-shu Liang, and their assistance to me.

Chapter 7 discusses my teaching methods and education philosophy. Chapter 8 talks about my experience in training Ph.D. students in finance and accounting, and Chapter 9 discusses my innovative approach to teaching finance. Overall, these three chapters can be useful for finance and accounting professors in training their undergraduate, master's, and Ph.D. students.

Chapter 10 explains how I achieved world records in academic activities that include the achievements in teaching, research, journal editing, book writing, and international conference organizing.

Chapter 11 illustrates my experience and gains in participating in various organizations as well as teaching and traveling through different countries. Chapter 12 discusses my experiences in writing books and editing journals.

Chapters 13 through 15 describe what I had gone through in researching and teaching Taiwan's financial markets and policies and in providing my viewpoints to help draft governmental financial policies. Chapter 13 discusses why I joined the democratic movements. Chapter 14 explains my extensive networks in the government, the academic instititutitions, and the industries. It also describes how the Foundation of Pacific Basin Financial Research and Development was founded and its funding principles. Chapter 15 details my contributions and participation in the planning and developing of Taipei as a financial center. In Chapter 16, my influence on the management of education in Taiwan is detailed. In Chapter 17, I review my 43 years of a challenging and rewarding academic career. Finally, in Chapter 18, I reflect on my life and discuss my future plans.

I appreciate the comments and suggestions of Governor Fai-nan Perng from the Central Bank of China, R.O.C., Professor Ben Sopranzetti, Rutgers University, Joe Schaffer, Associate Dean of Rutgers Business School and Professor Hong-Yi Chen, National Chengchi University. Finally, I would like to show my great appreciation to Governor Fai-nan Perng, Dean Lei Lei, Professor Richard E. Kihlstrom, Professor Ivan Brick, and Professor Yong Shi for their kind and thoughtful words. I am honored. Finally, I appreciate Natalie Krawczyk for her help in editing and writing this book.

Foreword I

I was surprised when my good friend, Prof. Cheng-Few Lee, known as CF to friends and colleagues, told me that he was going to write an autobiography. My first reaction was how he could possibly fit this challenging project into his already grueling schedule. When I got the first draft two weeks ago, I could not help but admire him. He really did finish it, and with efficiency and flair. The book even includes several illustrations showing the seating plans of various courses he taught in Taiwan. As soon as I received CF's draft I started reading and couldn't put it down "till the midnight oil burned out." This book is full of fascinating anecdotes and useful insight.

CF's knowledge in the field of finance is immense. He obtained full professorship within five years of completing his Ph.D. program, a rarity among United States academic institutions. He has since devoted himself not only to teaching but also to writing, with 225 academic papers and 26 books currently in his portfolio. CF is a great teacher, too. He has advised more than 90 Ph.D. students. His former students are scattered all over the world, some of whom are valued employees of Taiwan's central bank.

Although CF is a naturalized American citizen and has lived in the United States for 48 years, Taiwan is never far from his mind. He would often call me from the United States at his own great expense to discuss issues that concerned him. He has frequently flown back to Taiwan to teach short courses and to provide policy advice whenever he is available. He is also popular with Taiwan's media. In the summer of 1994, CF and a team from the central bank coauthored the report "Suggestions and Directions on Developing Taiwan as a Regional Financial Center." We both advocated the gradualist approach to the opening of capital accounts. This viewpoint was later vindicated following the 2007 Asian Financial Crisis. CF never transplanted policies that worked well in the United States directly to Taiwan without giving due consideration to local idiosyncrasies. Before introducing a new policy, he would make the necessary modification to meet the specific needs of Taiwan.

Though CF is usually busy with research and teaching there is also an easy side to his character. He loves dogs. When I visited him in New Jersey a few years ago I was impressed by the affection he showered on his dog, Snoopy, who is actually on the cover of CF's statistics textbook.

CF's new book is a labor of love and well worth reading. It should be of particular interest to those who care about finance in general and Taiwan in particular.

Fai-nan Perng
Governor of the Central Bank of China, R.O.C.

Foreword II

During 1979, shortly after China launched the transformational economic reform toward its role in the world economy, a delegation from the U.S. Department of Commerce traveled to Beijing to discuss how the United States could help the reformists spur economic development. As part of this effort, the National Center for Industrial Science and Technology was formed and was housed at Dalian Institute of Technology. The center became the first management executive training facility in China to operate with the cooperation of a foreign government. When I was a student of Dalian Institute of Technology, I learned the name of Cheng-Few Lee, who was one of the 40 distinguished U.S. professors selected to teach in this prestigious program offered to high-level Chinese government officials.

I did not actually meet him until many years later when I became his colleague at Rutgers University's business school. As an academic and researcher with a career spanning over 40 years, his scholarly record in the field of finance is unparalleled. He is the editor of many prestigious journals, including *Review of Quantitative Finance and Accounting*, *Review of Pacific Basin Financial Markets and Policies*, *Advances in Financial Planning and Forecasting*, and *Advances in Quantitative Analysis of Finance and Accounting*, and he has chaired many conferences on Financial Economics and Accounting and on Pacific Basin Business, Economics and Finance. He has published more than 225 articles in peer-reviewed journals such as: *Journal of Finance*, *JFQA*, *The Accounting Review*, *Journal of Accounting Research*, *Review of Economics and Statistics*, and *Management Science*. He has written several books on corporate finance, portfolio management, business statistics, and urban econometrics, and has made numerous speeches at various academic conferences both domestically and internationally. A whole generation of finance students has had the privilege of taking his courses on Asset Price Analysis and Portfolio Theory, Corporate Finance, Derivatives and others. There is a well-known Chinese phrase that admires a master teacher who plants the seeds that lead to fields all over the world covered by the fruits of his students' contributions. To me, CF is this master in the field of finance.

CF is a colleague with an admirable personality. He is well known as a kind and humble person, with many friends and acquaintances. He has influenced countless faculty, students, and staff who have benefited from his wit and wisdom. I count myself among this fortunate group, and I am honored to call CF a great friend at Rutgers Business School.

Lei Lei, Ph.D.
Dean, Rutgers Business School

Foreword III

Readers of CF's autobiography will surely already know that, in an impressive variety of ways, he has been a tireless contributor to the finance profession. His most direct contributions have come through publication in numerous journals and books of the important scholarly contributions made by his research. He has also supervised the training of a large number of Ph.D. students, who have made numerous significant contributions to the literature of finance and accounting. He has, furthermore, created and edited journals that have provided an important outlet for significant work. Beyond this he has organized countless conferences that have been a stimulus to furthering research. Finally, there is his teaching at all academic levels. I can testify that he does all of this with an enthusiasm that never seems to diminish. His energy continually amazes me.

I am tempted to take this opportunity to recount in detail all of CF's contributions to the general progress of our field. I have chosen instead to briefly discuss the personal experiences I have had interacting with him for over 40 years. Most of that interaction took place in the years just after I first met CF in 1976. At that time, he had just arrived as Professor of Finance at the University of Illinois. Although I have now been a Professor of Finance at the Wharton School of the University of Pennsylvania for 37 years, then I was in the Economics Department at University of Illinois at Urbana-Champaign (UIUC) and my knowledge of finance literature was quite limited. During the three years we spent as colleagues at UIUC, my interest in finance developed and my own work evolved in that direction. In part that was due to my interaction with CF. As an economic theorist, I was familiar with a good part of the theoretical foundations of finance, but I really didn't know much about the broader literature of finance. It was CF who helped to introduce me to that literature and who kept me up to date on how the field was developing.

As I look back on those years, I regard this as all quite fortuitous. At that time, important advances had recently been made and were continuing to be made in both the theory of finance and the empirical testing of these new theories. The driving force in this progress was the application of the economic theory of uncertainty and the application of econometrics to finance. Both CF and I had been trained as economists; his training was primarily in econometrics. In fact, as a student I had also concentrated on theoretical econometrics and statistics. But in the years after finishing my graduate work at the University of Minnesota the focus of my work shifted primarily to economic theory, with a focus on the economics of uncertainty and information. CF and I had quite common backgrounds and shared interests. We spoke the same language, and we were both familiar with different aspects of a literature that was rapidly growing in important and diverse directions. The opportunity to learn from each other presented itself and we took advantage of it. I can say with certainty that I learned a lot from CF during that time. The discussions we had led me to think about finance from a new perspective and it helped to shape the direction of my work by informing me about the new results in the field.

I left UIUC in 1979, but since that time CF and I have stayed in touch and continued to interact. Much of this interaction has taken place at conferences he has organized at Rutgers University and elsewhere. I have on several occasions presented my work at Rutgers and I always appreciate the questions CF raises and his perspective on my ideas. It is a pleasure to be able to benefit from his expertise and knowledge. It is a joy to have him in the audience and I look forward to the next time.

Richard E. Kihlstrom, Ph.D.
Ervin Miller–Arthur M. Freedman Professor of Finance and Economics
Wharton School of the University of Pennsylvania

Foreword IV

I have personally known CF Lee since 1988 when he joined the faculty at Rutgers University. He was a ball of fire interested in ensuring that students received a top-notch education and his colleagues were engaged in quality teaching and research. A number of times, CF, as he is affectionately known, would come into my office to discuss how he would improve the department or suggestions for the finance curriculum at Rutgers. In most cases CF identified and analyzed potential problems correctly even when others thought that the issues might be politically too sensitive. But as hard-driven as he is, CF is generous to his colleagues and students alike. CF could not turn anyone down and often looks for ways to help a colleague who needs advice on how to publish a paper. Most impressive, is that at his age (I will only say he is older than me and I am 64 at the time of this writing) he is still going strong. Academically he is more active than most academicians who have less than half his time in academia.

CF Lee is a distinguished and highly visible scholar. He has published more than 225 articles. He is the editor of *Review of Quantitative Finance and Accounting*, *Review of Pacific Basin Financial Markets and Policies*, *Advances in Investment Analysis and Portfolio Management*, *Advances in Financial Planning and Forecasting*, and *Advances in Quantitative Analysis of Finance and Accounting*. He was an associate editor of *JFQA* (1977–1983), co-editor of the *Financial Review* (1986–1991) and *Quarterly Review of Economics and Finance* (1988–1992). He has published the *Encyclopedia of Finance* (2006, 2013), *Handbook of Financial Econometrics and Statistics* (2014), and the *Handbook of Quantitative Finance and Risk Management* (2010). In addition he has published many different textbooks: *Financial Analysis,*

Planning and Forecasting (1985, 2009, 2016), *Corporate Finance: Theory, Method, and Applications* (1990), *Statistics for Business and Financial Economics* (1993, 2000, 2013), *Foundations of Financial Management* (1997), *Security Analysis and Portfolio Management* (1990), *Portfolio Management, and Financial Derivatives* (2012), *Readings in Investment Analysis* (1980), and *Financial Analysis and Planning: Theory and Application, A Book of Readings* (1983). In sum, he is the most prolific researcher of articles and books in the finance field. Often, I would meet people at academic conferences and upon learning that I am from Rutgers, the inevitable question was: "What is CF up to now?"

In addition to his many publications, CF has organized many highly visible conferences. He initiated the Annual Conference on Financial Economics and Accounting beginning in 1990. A consortium of top research institutions including Rutgers University, NYU, UT-Austin, Indiana University, University of Maryland, Georgia State, University of Toronto, Temple University, and Tulane University sponsors the conference. Last fall, this conference took place at Rutgers. CF led the selection of papers and discussants and verified that all the logistics were in place. The participants were highly regarded researchers and helped promote our school, Rutgers Business School, as a top-notch business school. In 1993, Professor CF Lee initiated the Annual Conference on Pacific Basin Finance, Accounting, Economics, and Management. This conference has been held in Taiwan, Hong Kong, China, Thailand, Singapore, Vietnam, Australia, and at Rutgers University. He has also organized two conferences for Taiwan: the Annual Conference of Economic and Financial Policy, which began in 2005, and National Chiao Tung University International Finance Conference, which began in 2006. These conferences helped cement Professor Lee's reputation as an important and highly visible scholar in finance.

Besides teaching his normal course load, CF has been a very active dissertation advisor. He has supervised or served as a committee member for over 90 dissertations. Many of his students are highly successful academic faculty or government officials. However, it should be known that he was willing to supervise students who had a difficult time finding an advisor either because the subject was not of interest to any faculty member or the student failed to make a personal connection. CF is always ready to help.

As a result of his activity, I sought to nominate CF to receive the 2016 Dean's Award for the Nationally Prominent Professional Activities. The process of nomination required me to obtain external letters citing his many contributions. And to my surprise, CF is also sought after for counsel to numerous financial policymakers in Taiwan. Fai-nan Perng, Governor of the Central Bank of the Republic of China, writes in his letter: "Dr. Lee was regularly consulted by regulators and the financial industry in Taiwan. While addressing difficult issues, he readily defies conventional views and promotes policy that would specifically work in Taiwan." I am his Chair for almost 20 years and he never once mentioned to me his prominence in advising government officials. In many ways, CF can be very humble and modest about his impact.

I received a letter from one of the more prominent faculty members in finance, Kose John of New York University. He ably summarizes Professor Lee's achievements: "CF has a worldwide reputation as a highly prolific researcher, mentor to hundreds of students and professors, editor of multiple journals of high impact, and an active organizer of many national and international conferences. Through all these channels, CF has influenced generations of doctoral students, junior and senior faculty including myself."

I am, indeed very fortunate, to have CF as a colleague and friend for over 27 years.

Ivan Brick

Dean's Institutional Professor and Chair

Finance and Economics Department

Executive Director of the Whitcomb Center for Research in Financial Services

Rutgers University

Foreword V

It is my great honor to write this foreword for Professor Cheng-Few Lee's autobiography. I was his student in the China–U.S. joint MBA program at the National Center for Industrial Science and Technology Management Development, Dalian, China in 1983. Professor Lee taught a financial management course there. After 33 years, I still remember his great enthusiasm and sense of humor during his lectures. Given his educational background in both Taiwan and the U.S., my classmates and I respected Professor Lee a lot, especially for his outspoken view and suggestion about how China could speed up the open market economy policy. As an eager-to-learn young man, I have discussed with Professor Lee how to apply Fuzzy Sets techniques to remodel the Net Present Value (NPV) to reflect the uncertainty of Capital Budgeting problems in accounting. His supervision and encouragement triggered my research interest in accounting. From 1996 to 2010, I have coauthored four papers with Professor Lee in bankruptcy prediction, human resource allocation, capital budgeting, and transfer pricing. Even more important, our teacher–student relation has expanded to a lifetime of friendship. In Chapters 4 and 11 of this book, Professor Lee has recalled our meeting at Dalian in 1983.

Professor Lee is a very warm and helpful person to his students. In 1985, I was admitted by Professor Po-lung Yu at the University of Kansas as a visiting scholar, but did not know Professor Lee was a roommate of Professor Yu when they studied at the National Taiwan University during the 1960s. When I arrived at the Kansas City International Airport, Professor Yu told me that Professor Lee had called him to take good care of me. This made me feel comfortable on my first day in the U.S. In 1999, after 13 years, I asked my friends in the Development Research Center of the State Council of China to invite both Professor Lee and Professor Yu, two of my great mentors, to visit Beijing, Chengdu, and Lhasa. In addition to giving lectures on our respective areas to the Chinese audience, we traveled to many historic spots and visited a number of Buddhist temples. The best part of this trip was that I, as the observer, listened to Professor Lee and Professor Yu's conversations about their college life, including their personal stories from the 1960s. Their experiences, not only academically, but also personally demonstrated the beauty of our career as scholars.

After visiting China, we visited Taiwan together. During my stay in Taiwan, Professor Lee brought me to meet a number of his friends, including Fai-nan Perng, the Governor of the Central Bank of Taiwan. In 2010, Professor Lee and I co-organized the 18th Pacific Basin Finance, Economics, and Accounting (PBFEA) conference at the Graduate University of Chinese Academy of Sciences Beijing, China. In addition, I have joined together with Professor Lee at his academic conferences in various places, such as Bangkok, Taipei, and Nagoya.

In 2007, Professor Siwei Cheng, father of China's Venture Capital, and I jointly established the Research Center on Fictitious Economy and Data Science at the Chinese Academy of Sciences, Beijing, China. Professor Lee was invited to serve as a member of the board of advisors with four other Nobel Prize winners in Economics. In 2013, Professor Lee was presented the first "Siwei Cheng Award in Quantitative Management" by the First International Conference on Information Technology and Quantitative Management (ITQM 2013), Suzhou, China for his outstanding academic contributions in accounting and quantitative finance (http://www.iaitqm.org/honorhall.html). Professor Lee is definitely a world-class scholar and my teacher forever. And I think he is my teacher for my lifetime. I would like to congratulate him for completing the meaningful autobiography.

Yong Shi
Bai-Ren Distinguished Professor and
Director of Key Laboratory of Big Data Mining and Knowledge Management
Chinese Academy of Sciences, China
and
Union Pacific Chair of Information Science and Technology
University of Nebraska at Omaha, U.S.A.

Chapter 1

Happy Childhood of Kites and Geese

My ancestors came from Shao-An County, Fujian Province, China. I was the 15th generation to be born in Wu Chuan Tsun, Ta Yuan Township, Tao Yuan County, Taiwan in 1939. My grandfather, Kun-hao Lee, married my grandmother, Cha Chen, and gave birth to my father, Wan-cheng Lee, who married my mother, Chu-mei Chang. There are four boys and three girls in my family and I am the oldest.

The 9th generation of my family went across the Taiwan Strait and settled in Taiwan. My family has been in Taiwan ever since. There is a 32-character family poem in which each character used in the beginning of our first name specifies our generation, from the 2nd to the 33rd generation. It was quite a shame that the tradition was interrupted during my grandfather's generation. My brothers and I have decided that we will continue the tradition by naming our grandsons according to the character sequence of our family poem.

My grandfather had five brothers. In the year I was born, my grandfather and his brothers built five beautiful brick houses named Lung-Si Tang at Ta Yuan Township of Tao Yuan City. Lung-Si (means west of Gansu Province) Tang might have indicated that our ancestors relocated from Gansu Province of Mainland China many years ago.

My grandfather and father, who were both farmers, worked by themselves on about five acres of rice fields and rented out the other five acres. Typically, we harvested twice a year. At that time, according to the status of a farmer's life, we were classified as a well-to-do family. Every year, at the beginning of rice planting or harvesting, we celebrated by holding worship ceremonies. On this day, we had the opportunity to have excellent meals. The rice noodles and the red, colored, and stuffed turtle-shaped cakes that were prepared by my mother and grandmother in the summer harvest were so delicious that they made my mouth water.

When I was a little boy, my grandmother took me to the local temples to worship the gods. There were lots of various celebrations to entertain the gods, such as the performance by the Taiwanese opera troupe, which touched me deeply. Part-time farmers performed Taiwanese opera and the performances were closely related to a farmer's daily life. Therefore, a small kid like me got really excited when I would see these types of performances. Soaked in this environment, the spirit of Taiwanese religions more or less influenced my beliefs. Overall, Buddhism, Taoism, and Confucianism influence me. This kind of influence affected my education, philosophy, and my career decisions.

When I was a small child, I loved the Chinese New Year and other festivals very much. They were thc only occasions that we could wear new dresses and eat pork, chicken, duck, or goose. I always looked forward to sweeping our ancestors' tombs on Tomb Sweeping Day, eating wrapped bamboo leaves and glutinous rice tamales during the Dragon Boat Festival, or having delicious moon cakes for the Mid-Autumn Festival. In particular, the Chinese New Year was my favorite. I loved receiving new clothes, new shoes, lucky money, and juicy red oranges.

Right at the time of World War II, when I was about four or five years old, I became painfully acquainted with the outside world. Americans bombed our town every day. Whenever I was frightened to tears by the bombings, my father or my uncle, Ke-ming Lee, would take me to the bunkers to hide. Although life was difficult at that time, I lived quite happily. I recalled that the Japanese garrisoned their army nearby our home for a while. I did not like them because they treated the Taiwanese poorly. The daily food supply, which consisted of thin rice porridge and pickles, was distributed in rations at that time. Rice and meat were very rare. When I was six years old, I couldn't go to school because the bombings never stopped. I could only study in a private tutor's house nearby and learn from some old Chinese books, such as the *Three-Character Odes*.

We lived on the hill that was not far away from an anti-aircraft artillery unit at the Tao Yuan Air Force Base. Whenever the American bombers came, the artillery would fire. Sometimes, from the bunker we could see the fighting between American and Japanese aircraft. Japanese fighter planes would usually hide themselves whenever they could not beat the Americans. Therefore, I had some chances to observe the Japanese fighters at a very short distance since they were hidden nearby our house. When American fighters were hit and the pilots who jumped out were captured, the Japanese would have a jubilant celebration.

During World War II, the American artillery shells spread over the fields. In the fall of 1945 when the Japanese lost the war, my family and I picked up the artillery shells in our rice paddy and sold them. I felt sorry for the Japanese who looked upset when their army left Taiwan. On the other hand, I along with all the Taiwanese people looked forward to welcoming home our soldiers with excitement and joy. However, we were disappointed when we finally saw our soldiers, poorly equipped and lacking training and moral discipline.

Another large part of my childhood consisted of listening to folk stories told by my grandparents. My grandfather told me that when the Japanese first invaded Taiwan, every family killed their fowls and ate them before they escaped from their homes. My grandmother told stories about the Grandaunt Tigress who ate children. Her stories really scared me. Of all the stories I heard, I liked the myth, "Eight Immortals Crossing the Sea" the most. When I taught at the American Training Center at the Engineering College of Dalian, China, in 1983, I took the chance to visit Yentai of Shantung Province by boat to see where that story took place.

Bamboo was a main product in the countryside. Even though

bamboo stems are sturdy, bamboo shoots need to be treated delicately. They can be used to make cradles and high chairs. The simple handmade bamboo toys were my favorite and since there were no commercial toys available for us, they were the only toys at that time. When I was about six years old, I would try to catch crickets, tadpoles, and frogs in the field. While I was studying in elementary school, my favorite games were playing cards with Chinese zodiac drawings, playing marbles, jumping rope, and hide-and-seek. I also enjoyed the bamboo flutes made by my father.

I also enjoyed fishing and flying kites. The streams and ponds were clear of industrial pollution, so we could easily catch fish and shrimp. This was a lot of fun especially because what we caught would become a delicious addition to our dinner. Another pleasant fall pastime was flying kites in the open wilderness under the blue sky.

I also helped my family herd our water buffalo and remove the weeds in the rice paddy. When I took care of the buffalo, I would let them wander and graze by themselves as I rode on their back, watching the beautiful sights, enjoying the high soaring eagles and elegantly gliding egrets. As for the weeding, it was a tough job, which I believe no modern kid will have the chance to experience.

Sometimes, I helped my grandmother guide geese to the wilderness. I could not let them get lost. On the way home, I had to cut some grass to feed our buffalo and geese. Another one of my jobs involved catching frogs and rice field shells for our ducks. I would also catch mud snails and eels in the winter for our supper. My father would often go to the streams to catch crabs and shrimp in the winter. I think of this as the perfect memory of my father, because it shows just how hard he worked for his family.

When I was a little kid, both Chinese herbs and western medicine were used to treat diseases. My grandmother and mother usually worried when I was sick, especially when my fever lasted for a long time. They would sit by me, and stay up to take care of me. When my tooth was loose, my grandfather would pull it out and throw it on top of the roof because it was said that in doing so, the new tooth would grow out sooner.

By 1946, Taiwan had recovered from Japan's occupation and I had started my elementary school education. I was one of the first students to attend the official Chinese schools. The Pu-shin Elementary School where I studied was far from my home. I walked about one and half hours to and from school every day. Walking on the unpaved country road, without wearing shoes, was like a foot massage and it set up an excellent foundation for my health. To have a bike to ride to school was our dream. There were no electric lights then, so I read under the kerosene lamps. There were no radios or televisions at that time either; therefore, I could spend much more time than kids today, focusing on my studies.

Winters during my childhood were tough. I had to walk to and from school with bare feet, and my hands and feet were always freezing when I arrived home in the evening. I had to read with a quilt to warm up my body. My grandfather and my father usually stuffed hay under the mattresses to make us warmer. We called it the hay spring bed in winter. When it rained, I had to wear the straw raincoat and hat to herd our buffalo and to chase geese. However, the experience of such a tough life made me stronger and more prepared for the future.

At a young age, I was extremely fond of reading. I brought my books with me when I herded our buffalo and geese. Every night I would stay up late and study until my grandfather urged me to go to bed. People in the village never understood why I studied so hard. My relatives, Ke-da Lee and Ke-hsiung Lee, were in my class at that time. We always went to school and studied together.

Ms. Yen Lee was my homeroom teacher in the first grade. She appointed me as the class leader because of my excellent academic performance. Being the class leader made me more confident of my ability and cultivated my leadership. For all of my six years in elementary school, I was the class leader and was always at the top of the class. My teachers included Mr. A-chang Liu, Ms. A-hsiang Wu, Mr. Jen-tang Huang, Mr. Chiu-hsun Wu, Mr. Chao-ming Kuo, and Mr. Ching-hui Chen.

In our elementary school, labor services for the school, such as gardening, were required. During our second reunion in 1999, under the guidance of Principal Ching-chun Huang, we were very proud to see the tall eucalypti, which my classmates and I planted during our time at Pu-Shin.

During my elementary school years, dodgeball and basketball were my favorite sports. I tried high jump, long jump, and track, but I was never good at them. Since I served as class leader during elementary school, I led my class to the flag-raising ceremony and stood imposingly on the platform every morning. I am grateful for this experience because I can now speak confidently in front of crowds.

Everyone in elementary school would take part in the annual field day activities. My classmate, Chu-tsun Yu, was always the champion in racing contests. Most students in our school came from Wu Chuan, Pu-Shin, and Nei Hai villages. Every year, the chief of each village led their athletes to participate in the contests. As students from the Wu Chuan Village, we often won most of the contests. Because of this, our village chief won our utmost respect. At that time the current chief of Wu Chuan Village, Chung-wang Lu, was my brother-in-law. This was his second term as chief; he was also the chairman of the Farmers' Association at Ta Yuan Township. Although many farmers' associations suffered financial problems in Taiwan, my in-law's association held a sound financial structure, which ranked third in the country.

In the summer of 1986, when I went back to Taiwan, I called my classmate, Mr. Chao-hsiung Wang, manager of Nanking Branch of the Medium Business Bank of Taiwan. We returned to our elementary school to visit our teachers and took pictures in front of the school gate for old times' sake.

On April 25, 1998, we had our first reunion among our elementary classmates. All of the teachers joined us, except Mr. Chiu-hsun Wu, who passed away several years before. It was a precious moment. Forty-seven years after graduation, most of us were over 60 and had become grandparents. Everyone was joyous, but upset by the realization of how quickly time flied by. All of the classmates were so excited by this reunion that we decided to have another reunion the following year. We had another successful reunion on August 22, 1999 at our alma mater, Pu-Shin Elementary School.

Over the past 47 years, my classmates succeeded in different areas. Currently, Mr. A-cheng Lee, Mr. Ke-hsiung Lee, Mr. Cheng-shan Chiu, and I serve in the field of education. Mr. A-cheng Lee was the principal of Yang-Ming Senior High School at Tao Yuan County. Mr. Ke-hsiung Lee was the principal of Pei-Men Elementary School at Tao Yuan County and, Mr. Cheng-shan Chiu was the teacher of Wu Chuan Elementary School at Ta Yuan Township.

My aunt, Hsiu-ying Hsu, visited my home from time to time. She was very fond of me and often encouraged me to study harder in order to attend the better high schools in Taipei. Her encouragement was the main reason I participated in the entrance examination for high schools in Taipei. When I was a third grader, it was difficult for me to understand the snow scenes of northern China described in a textbook. My aunt explained them patiently to me and in the winter of 1957, when I was a sophomore at Chien Kuo Senior High, my aunt took me with her to see the rare snow scenes of Yang Ming Mountain in the Taipei suburb.

To help us to pass the junior high school entrance exams, our school offered supplemental learning classes for us. During the second semester of the sixth grade, we studied even harder than before. Many students succeeded in their entrance exams because of the encouragement we received at our school. I passed the exams of the local Ta Yuan Junior High School and also the junior high of Tao Yuan High School. More importantly, I also passed the entrance exam for the junior high of the famous Chien Kuo High School (C.K. High included three years of junior high and three years of senior high). My classmate, A-chung Wang, also gained admission to C.K. High while my other classmate, Chun-ching Wu, passed the exam for the Affiliated Junior High of National Normal University. Our success in the exams honored our school and encouraged our younger schoolmates to set higher expectations.

My grandmother insisted that I study at Ta Yuan Junior High to save money, but I was so eager to attend Chien Kuo Junior High (C.K. High) that I begged my aunt, teachers, and my friends to persuade my grandmother. After crying for several days and with the help from my grandfather, I finally got my grandmother's consent to study at C.K.

High. If I had not insisted and studied at Ta Yuan Junior High School or Tao Yuan High School, it would have been impossible for me to study at the best university in Taiwan, and my life would have been entirely different. From this experience, I realized that persistence is essential in achieving goals.

As well-to-do landlords, my family encountered some tenant farmers who humbled themselves and paid high respects to us because they were afraid of losing their lease on their farmland. I felt really sorry for the tenant farmers. Later, when Chiang Kai-shek retreated to Taiwan, to stabilize the society, he forced landlords to give up their farmland by executing the 37.5 percent Land-rent Discount Program and Land to the Tiller policies during the years of 1949 to 1953.

After executing the 37.5 percent Land-rent Discount Program, our family income decreased and our finances were affected. In the policy regarding farmers owning their own land, the government forced landlords to sell their farmland with a compensation of 70 percent of rice and 30 percent of stocks to one of the three big nationally owned companies. The landlords were not confident in stocks after the big depreciation of the old Taiwan dollar. Most landlords sold their land at the price of about 30 percent of the original. My family did the same. This policy really angered the farmers, but people kept quiet. After experiencing the terrible riot and massacre on February 28, 1947, caused by the corruption of government officers and misbehavior of soldiers, I believed, even more, that the only way to help and honor my family was to study hard.

During my elementary school days, I lived a happy childhood with a well-off family and love from my teachers. Having experienced World War II and the social reforms brought by the relocation of Nationalist Kuomintang after they retreated to Taiwan from the civil war, I understood that working hard and aggressively would be the only way to achieve success. Although suffering in an unstable society, I still graduated with excellent performance and gained admission to a prestigious high school, and became famous in the neighborhood areas. Even though it cost more money to attend Chien Kuo Junior High, I appreciated the understanding of my family, which was indeed the beginning of the happiness for the rest of my life. I guess this must be the good return of my frequent visits to temples and worshipping gods with my grandparents. Buddha blessed and brought happiness to me.

Chapter

2

Mathematics and Chemistry at Chien Kuo (C.K.) High School

In the summer of 1952, all of my relatives and friends congratulated me on my success in passing the entrance exam to Chien Kuo Junior High School (C.K. High), Taipei. It was a big deal since I was only the second one, in the history of my elementary school, to be admitted to C.K. High. All my relatives had great expectations for me because I was the first person to gain admission to such a good school since my family migrated to Taiwan. The pressure to succeed became a heavy burden on me.

Before I left home for Taipei, my grandfather and father expected me to help the family more. They wanted to have more abundant harvests and successful reproductions of livestock in order to collect enough money for me to pay the tuition.

In August before I started junior high, my mother took me to Taipei. We went by bus and then by train. Aunt Hsiu-ying Hsu let me stay at her home in Taipei, but the house she rented was so small that I could only settle down on a temporary bed in their living room. The landlords, Mr. and Mrs. Chin-ho Chen, were nice to me and took me to C.K. High to complete the registration. They also showed me the shortcut to school. For a young kid who came from the rural area, living in such a big city was a real dismay. I missed my family, but I knew I had to tolerate the strangeness of the big city because I wanted to pursue an academic career.

I lived with my aunt for the first two years of junior high and moved to the house of Mr. Yu-fong Hsu, who was a friend of my grandfather's, in Shu Lin Township for the last year. Shu Lin is a small town located in the suburbs of Taipei City. Although the commute into Taipei was troublesome, I had the opportunity to become friendly with more people, such as Mr. Yu-fong Hsu's family. I usually called Mr. Hsu, Uncle Hsu. Once, when chasing the train, I fell down and broke my right arm, Uncle Hsu found a famous doctor known for treating bone fractures to take care of me.

Uncle Hsu's family grew tomatoes on more than one acre of land. During the fall harvest, the Hsus always encouraged me to eat more tomatoes. Since then, I have learned to love tomatoes and thus am always supplied with an abundance of vitamin C.

C.K. High was located on Nan-Hai Road, Taipei, and was close to the Botanical Garden and the U.S. Information Service (USIS). There were some wooden and brick buildings on campus. The wooden buildings were poorly equipped and were occupied by the junior high school students. These buildings were located at the farthest end of campus. The brick buildings were located at the front of campus. A playground that belonged to the C.K. senior high students separated the brick buildings and wooden buildings. Our playground was barren and dusty so we would often go to the nearby Botanical Garden to enjoy the beautiful trees and flowers and to get a breath of fresh air. We, the juniors, all wished to get into the senior high some day and study in those brick buildings.

Not much time had passed since the Nationalist Kuomintang (KMT) retreated to Taiwan. Many outstanding scholars from Mainland China came with the KMT and taught at C.K. High. Our principal, Mr. Yi-Hsin Ho, always tried his best to attract good teachers to the school. C.K. High was considered the best male high school in Taiwan. Every day Principal Ho would inspect the campus and all kinds of school activities. The students at our school performed well in both academics and sports. Our basketball and rugby teams often won Taiwan's championships. I preferred basketball, but I played both basketball and rugby. Since junior high, I have always enjoyed a good game of basketball.

During junior high, I was not only good at Chinese and English, but also excelled in mathematics. The most famous geometry teacher on the island, Mr. Chia-pei Tan, taught us mathematics. Although he was recognized as one of the toughest teachers on campus, I learned a lot from him. Our drawing teacher, Mr. Dan-chen Chen, was famous for his paintings of roosters. Mr. Yi-hsien Yang instructed us in natural science, one of my favorite classes, which enlightened me. Once, I had even thought of focusing on research in natural science for my future. I also scored high in both my chemistry and physics classes, but for me, the most difficult class was music.

In junior high, my classmates included Cheng-nan Lin, Tsung-chang Lee, Ming-de Lin, Ming-hsien Lin, Shih-hsiung Hsieh, Chao-hsiung Chen, and Wen-hai Liu. I studied with Cheng-nan. I played basketball with Wen-hai. We would invite Yueh-ning Hsieh to join us too. Yueh-ning was my classmate and son of Mr. Ming-chu Hsieh, who is the brother of Mr. Tung-min Hsieh (Vice Governor of Taiwan Province). Yueh-ning came from a wealthy family. When he invited us over, we were honored. Being with my good friends lessened my homesickness and I learned to love Taipei.

Every summer, during junior high, I would go home to help my family with the rice paddy. During these trips, I would visit my elementary school teachers who were very satisfied and proud of my excellent academic performance in Taipei. The officers of Ta Yuan Township gave me an annual scholarship of NTD (New Taiwan Dollar) 200. This scholarship extended my fame within the township. Parents asked their children to follow me as an example. Despite the scholarship and the fame, the school's tuition was a heavy financial burden on my family. To collect money for my tuition, my mother sold vegetables at the market. I am truly sorry that these expenses affected the life of my younger brothers and sisters.

The Nationalist KMT government retreated to Taiwan in 1949 and the crisis was intense. When the Korean War commenced on June 25,

1950, U.S. President Harry Truman commanded the Seventh Fleet to protect and cruise the Taiwan Strait.

Taiwan suffered financially from taking care of the 600,000 soldiers and government officers that retreated from Mainland China. Many soldiers ate only two meals a day while students and teachers were no better off. The slogans of fighting back and re-taking Mainland China flooded Taiwan. Songs of anti-communism and praising of leaders became an obligatory part of our music classes in junior high. The song "Fighting Back at Mainland China" was the most popular song at the time.

Chiang Kai-shek ruled Taiwan as a dictator. The capture of communist spies was on the news all of the time. Public notices and frightening photos of the execution of communist spies were posted in the Taipei Train Station. It was not surprising to hear that a teacher or student disappeared from campus without any reason. Listening to radio programs from Mainland China was against the law since Mainland China was spreading propaganda about liberating the Taiwanese. On campus, students were frightened and we used our studies as a way to stay out of the mess that surrounded us.

On July 27, 1953, when the treaty that ended the Korean War was signed, I was in the eighth grade. Because the exchange of war prisoners was called upon in the treaty, many anti-communist soldiers came to Taiwan. This caused a big wave of anti-communism movements in Taiwan. The politics in Taiwan improved after Taiwan accepted U.S. financial assistance as defined by the Sino-American Mutual Defense Treaty on December 3, 1954. The nerves of the entire society gradually relaxed. However, in January of 1955, the people of Taiwan were again startled by the loss of Yi-Chiang-Shan Island, the army retreated from Ta-Chen Island, and the student movement to serve in the military and donate money to build warships and aircraft. Looking back, I experienced many reforms and changes that are impossible for current junior high students to imagine.

Despite all that was occurring in Taiwan and the effects it had on the Taiwanese people, I was able to remain focused on my studies. With my efforts and good fortune, I graduated from junior high as valedictorian and gained admission to Chien Kuo Senior High without having to take any exams. For the first year of senior high, I moved back home. It was very time consuming to get to school. I had to take a bus then transfer to the train to and from school every day. Sometimes the bus wouldn't stop for me because it was overcrowded. However, commuting provided me the opportunity to learn how to be patient and self-disciplined. The next year, I lived with my aunt in Taipei. My aunt's financial situation had greatly improved and she bought her own house. This time, I had a bedroom in her house. I biked to school every day and moonlighted to earn more money for tuition.

In senior high, I studied in the class nicknamed "directly getting admission into universities without taking the exams." This class consisted of the top five students from each class in the junior department of C.K. High. The competition among these excellent classmates was tremendous. At C.K. High, the teachers in the senior high school were even better than those in junior high. When I was a freshman, Mr. Huai-nien Yang, the best trigonometry teacher on the island, instructed me in mathematics. As a sophomore, I was taught by Mr. Chih-ming Wu, the most famous chemistry teacher in Taiwan. Mr. Rong Ding, the most marvelous Chinese teacher, taught me during my last year of senior high. Of course, being in the "directly admitted class," every teacher enjoyed teaching us.

Mr. Chih-ming Wu was my homeroom teacher when I was a sophomore. He was an excellent and famous teacher. Ever since I was in junior high I had been interested in chemistry and physics; Mr. Wu's teaching enriched my study in chemistry and made me decide to pursue an advanced study in the field of chemistry at a university. Mr. Wu was enthusiastic about student activities. He took us to the Green Grass Lake in Hsinchu for sightseeing and to visit the local fertilizer factory. He often led us in cleaning up our classroom.

My studying in Chinese literature was well founded by Mr. Rong Ding, my homeroom teacher in my last year of senior high school. Mr. Ding read us many beautiful Chinese poems and essays, such as "Man Ching Hong," "Song of Regrets Lasted Forever," "300 Gem Poems of Tang Dynasty," and so on. Occasionally, he would take us on picnics and sightseeing. We visited Shih-men Reservoir, in the Chiao-Hsi Township. Upon graduating, we traveled to Guantze Hill to see the rare scene of "Co-existence of Water & Fire." Mr. Wu won our high respects because he would describe the beautiful sights whenever he saw them, by writing poems. We respected him because he had to raise his two boys by himself since his wife failed to escape to Taiwan with them. In 1992 when I taught in Xi'an, Mainland China, I visited the tomb of Concubine Yang of Tang dynasty and thought of the days Mr. Wu read us the long poem "Song of Regrets Lasted Forever," and all of a sudden, the memory of my good old days came back to me.

Since C.K. High was close to the USIS, I borrowed English books from there very often. Reading these books improved my English. When I saw the beautiful colored pictures in American magazines I was shown a new world. I wished that one day I could have a chance to travel to the U.S.

In the second year of senior high, the incident of Liu Tzu-jan caused a big disaster to the USIS. People protested and attacked the USIS; they damaged their furniture and book collections.[1] After a long time, the USIS finally reopened. As students, we were very sad about this accident. The government executed martial law in Taipei and everyone was nervous under the circumstances. Many students from a number of schools joined the demonstration but none from our school.

In the senior high, I formed many friendships among my classmates. I often visited my classmates' homes. The families of my classmates, Yu-chen Lai and Cheng-chang Lin, owned a Chinese herb medicine business. Whenever I needed Chinese medicine, they would give me a discount. Hsiu-fu Wu's family owned a soap factory and I went to him whenever I needed soap. Cheng-yi Wang's home was located in Tan-shui Township, and they managed a woodselling business. His parents and sisters were very kind to me whenever I visited and we listened to classical music in their living room. Mr. Wang became the vice president of the Hospital of National Taiwan University and a

[1] Also known as the "May 24 Incident." Protesters staged violent demonstrations against the U.S. Embassy and other facilities, after an American military court acquitted Sgt. Robert G. Reynolds of unlawfully killing Liu Tzu-jan, an army major of the R.O.C. army.

famous specialist in gastroenterology. He served as a special doctor to former President Lee Teng-hui and former Vice President Lien Chan. During those days, we studied hard, but we also enjoyed normal young men's entertainment and always kept a good relationship with each other.

One day, in the spring of my sophomore year, to reward the hospitality of my classmates, I invited 16 classmates to my home in Wu Chuan Village, Tao Yuan County to join me in the banquet for worshipping the gods. My classmates were very satisfied with their meals and experienced a totally different lifestyle in the countryside. I guessed this gathering enhanced a good understanding between the urban and the rural people. My family was very happy seeing so many Taipeinese visiting us. Before saying good-bye, my classmates and my grandparents took a picture together to remember the visit. This picture was very precious to me since it was the only picture that I have taken with my grandparents. I love my grandparents and I will never forget how much they gave to me.

During my senior high school years, I tried my best to go home and help my family in the summer and during winter breaks. Besides planting, weeding, and harvesting in the rice paddy, I also caught fish and shrimp in the streams and ponds. At that time, it was popular to catch fish by transmitting electric power to water. In the summer when I was a sophomore, we got more than 20 pounds of fish and shrimp from an irrigating pond. The whole family not only enjoyed the delicious food, they also sold some of the catch.

In summary, I lived a very happy and normal life during my senior high days. We did not use drugs, smoke, or drink alcohol in those days. I really doubt whether the modern teaching methods used on our youth are good since there are so many misbehaved young kids. I do not think it was a good idea to abandon the Joint Entrance Exams for senior high schools and the system of "Repeating the Year's Work" (where a second year in the same grade is established) will be very effective in Taiwan. I would like to suggest that if there are too many side effects, the Education Ministry should stop these policies right away.

Before graduating from the senior high, many of my classmates were admitted to National Taiwan University (NTU) or National Cheng Kung University (NCKU) without taking entrance exams. Wu-yi Chang, our valedictorian, was admitted to the Medical School of NTU. Yi-hsiung Kuo, the salutatorian, was admitted to the Department of Agricultural Engineering of NTU. Cheng-yi Wang, who was ranked third, was admitted to the Medical School of NTU. Yi-yi Fu ranked fourth and was admitted to the Department of Physics of NTU. Yu-jen Lai, ranked fifth, was admitted to the Department of Politics of NTU. I was ranked twelfth and was admitted to the Department of Chemical Engineering at NCKU.

However, less than one year before the universities' joint entrance exam was held, the Minister of Education, Dr. Chen-hsing Yen, announced that the exam would not be divided into four different sections as before and all students would take all of the exams. That meant all students had to take the history and geography exams, including students who planned to study engineering and science.

Meanwhile, taking the suggestions and encouragement from the C.K. High alumni at NTU, most C.K. High students put different departments at NTU as one of their top 10 choices on their application form. I gave up the opportunity to enter the Department of Chemical Engineering at NCKU without taking exams and I participated in the Joint Entrance Exam. Because of my poor scores in history, geography, and Three Principles of the People, I received the first big shock in my life. I was allocated to the Department of Economics at NTU, which was my eighth choice. The result of the exam affected me poorly and ended my happy high school years.

In the next chapter, I detail how I kept my hope despite deep disappointment and how I made efforts to keep advancing. Through this, I was able to regain a happy and self-confident life.

Chapter

3

Misfortune May Be a Blessing in Disguise

In high school, my biggest aspiration was to study chemical engineering or chemistry. When I graduated from the senior high in 1958, I was admitted to the Department of Chemical Engineering at National Cheng Kung University (NCKU) in Tainan, Taiwan without taking the entrance exams. However, because Tainan was too far away from my home, I gave up the opportunity and decided to take the Joint Entrance Exam for the university instead. Unfortunately, the Minister of Education at that time, Dr. Chen-hsing Yen, who supported the idea of education for all-round talent, suddenly announced that the exam would not be divided into the traditional different fields. Thus, every student could fill in any department on their school wish list, but had to take all of the subject exams.

At the time, many Chien Kuo High alumni studying at National Taiwan University (NTU) came back to persuade us, the upcoming graduates of C.K. High, to put more departments at NTU on our wish list. Since many C.K. High students studied at NTU, C.K. High would be allocated a larger quota of students to NTU without taking the exams in the following years. This would further extend the fame of C.K. High. Therefore, I put various departments at NTU as my top 15 choices. That year the exams in mathematics, physics, and chemistry were quite easy. Those, like me, who were good at these subjects and formerly planned to take the first division to study in engineering or science, could not take any of the advantages from this exam. On the contrary, we had the chance of failing history, geography, and Three Principles of the People, which were previously not supposed to be on the first division test. As a result of the exam, I was admitted to the Department of Economics at NTU, which was my eighth choice.

I was depressed and planned to transfer to another department, but my aunt's landlord, Mr. Chin-ho Chen, advised me not to do so. He explained that once industry and commerce became prosperous, I would have great opportunities and would become marvelous and outstanding by studying business-related fields. He encouraged me to take more courses in accounting. During my college years, I took all the courses provided by the Accounting Division of the Department of Business at NTU. The courses totaled 28 credits in Elementary Accounting, Inter-medium Accounting, Advanced Accounting, Cost Accounting, Auditing, Governmental Accounting, and Analysis of Financial Reports. Professor Kuo-chang Chu instructed these courses. Prof. Chu was famous in the field of accounting in Taiwan. It was well known that he set a very high standard for his classes.

Besides accounting courses, I took a lot of courses in my own major. These courses included Economics, Money and Banking, International Trading, Elementary Statistics, Advanced Statistics, National Accounting, Input-Output Analysis, Calculus, Western Economic History, Chinese Economic History, Economic Policies, and so on. Among my teachers at that time, Professors Kuo-wei Chang, Kuo-shu Liang, Han-yu Chang, and Chien-sheng Shih affected me the most. Prof. Kuo-wei Chang was not only my teacher in Advanced Statistics during my undergraduate years and Statistics during graduate school, but also my advisor for my master's thesis.

When I was in college, students enjoyed playing sports, having picnics, and traveling. I visited many famous attractions, such as Yang-Ming Mountain, Sun Moon Lake, Shih-Men Reservoir, East-West Cross-Island Highway, and the Yen-Liu seashore. Occasionally I would also go to my classmates' homes. In 1959, I invited 20 classmates to my home in Wu Chuan Village to enjoy the god worship banquet. My classmates were excited by this reunion. We still recall some of the funny things that happened at the banquet.

In the second semester of my second year, my friend Jeffrey Lee patiently taught me how to dance in the dormitory for my first party. Although I learned right before the party, I danced to three songs. The following week, I was infatuated with the beautiful memory of the party. This must have been the result of having studied at an all-boys high school for six years and rarely socializing with girls.

My classmates were very active in college. Both Yu-hao Chen and Hsiu-chiang Pan were elected as Chairmen of the Association of Student Representatives. Of course, when they were the chairmen, our classmates had to be a part of their supporting team. Hsiu-chiang asked me if I would join the Kuomintang (KMT). I thanked her for her kindness and after thorough examination of the pros and cons, I rejected her offer. Up to this date, I have never belonged to any political parties.

Life in college was both bitter and joyful. To collect part of my tuition, I worked as a private tutor and I would deliver fresh milk. In 1961, I was the representative of food supply for the 4th Dormitory in the law school, while Mr. Rong-yi Wu represented the 16th Dormitory. Our daily food expense was NTD 6.00. Being young and bold, Wu and I looked over the expending accounts recorded by the military officer in charge of our dining service. We discovered and pointed out to the student body for the dormitories that he was misusing money paid by the students. Under the circumstances of that time, our disrespectful behavior annoyed some of the faculty. However, with the school policy to keep a liberal and open academic environment advocated by the president of NTU, the officer apologized and returned more than NTD 5,000. We forgave him and did not ask for further punishment to him because his wife begged pardon for him. Both Wu and I became well known in the law school because of this incident.

Reunions were the best way to communicate with schoolmates after graduation. The leading members in organizing our reunions were Rong-yi Wu, Ching-yun Wong, Jeffrey Yu-ly Lee, Yu-hao Chen, and

Ming-shan Fang. For our 30-year reunion, we stayed at the Hilton Hotel in Los Angeles, for five days during July of 1992. Yu-hao owned the hotel and paid for all of the expenses. Including spouses, there was a total of more than 80 people. We had a wonderful time. In a special collection of papers for this reunion I wrote a piece entitled, "Exclamation and Review of the Past 30 Years." Below is an excerpt:

> I am very happy to have the opportunity to celebrate our 30th anniversary of our graduation from the Department of Economics, NTU, with 40 classmates in the luxurious hotel owned by Yu-hao Chen in Los Angeles. It looks to me as if our college days have come back during this joyful five-day reunion. It reminds me of how much fun we had in our good old days. Though it is regretful that time flies, we are very proud of the successful careers our classmates have achieved up to date.
>
> In this short essay, I have reviewed my working experience, graduate training, and teaching career during the last 30 years (1962–1992). First, I discussed my five-year working experience in Bank of China (1963–1968) and my part-time study at Department of Economics, National Taiwan University to get my master's degree in economics in 1966. Then, I also discussed my graduate training at West Virginia University (1968–1970) and SUNY at Buffalo (1970–1973). Finally, I reported my successful teaching career at the University of Georgia (1973–1976), University of Urbana-Champaign (1976–1988) and Rutgers University (1988–1992).

In 2012, our college classmates held a 50-year reunion in Taipei. We visited the Economic Department's new building. Our classmate, Chin-son Ho, Chairman of Ton Ho Steel Corporation, donated about half of the money for this new building. In the dinner of the 50-year reunion, every one of us said something about their experiences and achievements during the past five decades. After that, our classmate Yu-hao Chen treated most of the classmates by paying the cost of traveling to several famous cities of China, such as Jiuzhaigou, Chengdu,

Hangzhou, and Guilin. Since then, our classmates frequently had small group reunions and had a good time.

For two months during the summer break of my junior year in college, I completed my first military training, which was conducted in Chengkung Hill, Taichung. It was an unforgettable experience and good for my health. However, I was quite poor at target practice. When I served as a reserve officer, the Army sent me to the Regiment Control District at Hsin Ying, Tainan, to handle administrative affairs. Without any more opportunities in target practice, my shooting has never improved. Completing more training was part of my duty as a citizen; thus, I had many opportunities to travel around Tainan County.

At that time my barrack was close to Ming-shan Fang's home, so I visited his parents frequently and was welcomed with hospitality. I also had the opportunity to visit the parents of Chung-tao Hsin and Cheng-hsiung Ho since their homes were not too far away from my barrack either.

When I finished the R.O.C. military service required by the government in 1963, I took the special entrance exam for the Bank of China (currently the International Commercial Bank of China, ICBC) and the entrance exam for the Graduate Institute of Economics, NTU. Fortunately, I got both, the job offer from the Bank of China and admission to the Graduate Institute of Economics, NTU. I decided to work and study part-time for my master's degree. I started my bank job in August of that year. The monthly wage was about NTD 4,000, which was much more than my family's income from working on eight acres of rice paddy.

My grandfather was really grateful for the blessing from our ancestors, which made me successful. However, he passed away just one year later in 1964. I highly appreciated my supervisor at the Bank of China for allowing me to work at the bank while studying at the Institute of Economics. During my five years at the bank, I served in the divisions of Import, Accounts Payable, and the Economic Research Office. My colleagues included Chairman Ching-yi Wang, Principal Ting-wang Cheng, and President Rong-yi Wu. The current Deputy General Manager of ICBC, Mr. Chi-hsiung Lee, was one of our colleagues at the time too. I worked with Mr. Kuang-hwa Lo and Mr. Lien-song Koo in the Import Division. In 1966, I started my new position in the Economic Research Office where Mr. Chun Chien was my supervisor. At the time, I was quite lucky to get involved in the research of Taiwan's tax reform under the guidance of Prof. Ta-chung Liu and Prof. P.B. Musgrave. This experience enhanced my understanding of Taiwan's financial policies in 1994, which will be explored in a later chapter.

I completed 30 credit hours at the Graduate Institute of Economics, NTU. My instructors included Prof. Kuo-wei Chang, Prof. Lee Teng-hui, Prof. Wan-rong Kuo, Prof. Han-yu Chang, Prof. Meng-wu Sa, etc. My advisor, Prof. Kuo-wei Chang, had a great effect on me, as did Prof. Lee Teng-hui and Prof. Meng-wu Sa. (Chapter 5 will illustrate Prof. Lee Teng-hui's influence on me.) By way of Prof. Sa's History of Chinese Political and Society class, I finally understood why so many Chinese did not obey laws and why most social reforms failed in Chinese history. It was very helpful to have this understanding when I participated in drafting Taiwan's financial policies.

When I studied in graduate school, I took Prof. Kuo-wei Chang's statistics courses and asked him to be my advisor for my thesis. I was pretty good at mathematics since my previous aspiration for undergraduate study was engineering and science. Thus, I was attracted to Prof. Chang's statistics classes. Prof. Chang graduated from Berlin University, Germany and his expertise was in the statistics of survey sampling. From time to time I visited his home on the weekends to discuss the title of my thesis. In 1964, the Director-General of Budget, Accounting and Statistics (DGBAS), (Executive Yuan, R.O.C.) invited Prof. H.L. Jones of the University of Chicago to give a lecture about the Jackknife Method used in the analysis of sampling statistics. Although most people could not understand what Prof. Jones talked about, I found a title for my thesis from his lecture. Later, I found more relative information about the Jackknife Method in the Biological Statistics Office, NTU and completed my thesis in the field of sampling statistics.

In 1964, Prof. Ming-min Peng and Mr. Tsung-min Hsieh delivered the Taiwan Independence Declaration and many people involved were arrested. Mr. Hsieh's brother, Shih-chia Hsieh, was one of my classmates at the Graduate Institute of Economics, NTU. To save his brother, Shih-chia posted many posters in NTU's law school. Many names, including mine, were put on the posters. The officers from Taiwan Garrison Command investigated this incident and even checked and compared the handwriting on the poster with my handwriting filed at the Bank of China. When Shih-chia was finally put in jail, the atmosphere of Taiwan changed. I was terrified.

In December 1966, I earned my first master's degree. This thesis not only helped me get a master's degree at NTU, but it also set me up with the foundational research I needed for my second thesis to finish my second master's degree at West Virginia University in 1970 and my Ph.D. dissertation, from SUNY-Buffalo in 1973.

It should be mentioned here that my thesis committee members included three of the most famous statistics professors in Taiwan at the time. They were Prof. Kuo-wei Chang of the Department of Economics, NTU, Prof. Chao-chen Chen of the Department of Agricultural Economics, NTU, and Prof. Nao-pan Cheng of the Department of Statistics, National Chengchi University. I was very honored to have their advice on my thesis.

In addition to my thesis of sampling statistics, I also translated a German textbook on the same subject under the encouragement of Prof. Chang. This translated copy has more than 200 pages and was published in the *China Statistics Journal* and the *Quarterly Review of the Land Bank*. My wife spent a lot of time transcribing it by hand. This was the first time in my life that I was paid for my writing. Because I learned German as my second foreign language in college and learned even more by translating this book, Prof. Chang strongly recommended that I pursue an advanced academic degree in Germany. If I had done that, my career would have been completely different.

Upon completing my master's degree, I had more leisure time. I used this time to think of ways to make more money. In 1967, I proposed a plan to six of my good friends, including Pang-chung Lin, Cheng-hsiung Cheng, and Che-hsiung Chen, to set up a sweater-processing factory in Sanchung, Taipei County. We signed the business partner contract and every partner contributed NTD 20,000, giving us a total of NTD 120,000 to start our business. At the time, Che-hsiung and I worked at the Bank of China, Cheng-hsiung at the Vegetable and Fruit Marketing Association of Taiwan Province, and Pang-chung at the Central Trust of China. No one paid a great deal of attention to this business since we were caught up in our own lives. As a result, the factory closed in 1968. It was disappointing. If one of us jumped out to run the business, the factory might have been the biggest sweater-processing company in Taiwan.

In the meantime, both Chairman Kuo-hwa Yu and General Manager Wu Chang of the Bank of China subscribed to *TIME* magazine and I got a chance to read the issues. I was very confused with the future of Taiwan whenever I read the reports about Taiwan and Mainland China in the magazine.

To broaden my research and leave the unstable society of Taiwan, I made up mind to study overseas. I took the TOEFL exam and applied to several U.S. graduate schools. Finally, I gained admission and a scholarship to the Economics Ph.D. program at West Virginia University. I left for the U.S. in August 1968. I was 29 at the time. My son was two years old and my daughter was just a six-month-old baby. I was anxious about the future when I arrived in the U.S., but I found encouragement at the thought of Prof. Lee Teng-hui who left for Cornell University at the age of 42 and earned his Ph.D. in agriculture and economics in 1968.

I went abroad to study because of the strong support from my aunt, Hsiu-ying Hsu, her husband, Tsu-sheng Hsia, my wife, and her parents. Prof. Kuo-wei Chang suggested that I study statistics and Prof. Lee Teng-hui also gave me valuable advice. (Chapter 5 will explain all of their advice.)

Before leaving for the U.S., my colleagues at the Bank of China and classmates held a farewell party for me. My wife, grandmother, parents, in-laws, and other family members all came to say good-bye to me at the airport. I felt sad and confused about leaving when I held my daughter in the airport. Her innocent smile grew as she bit the paper wreath on my neck. It touched me deeply that Prof. Kuo-wei Chang spent the money and the time to take a taxi to the airport just to say good-bye to me. With the fear of an uncertain future, I left for the U.S.

by way of Tokyo, Japan.

My first stop in the U.S. was Seattle. My classmate Ming-san Fang picked me up at the airport and invited me and another classmate, His-san Lee, to dinner in Chinatown. My second stop was Chicago, where Jeffrey Yu-li Lee welcomed me. It was during the time of the Vietnam War and the Democratic National Convention was being held in Chicago. Riots between the protesting students and the policemen occurred. Here I saw the real life of a democratic country and I felt sorry for the people in Taiwan, who lived in fear under martial law. This was where the seeds for me to join the democratic movement were planted in my mind.

My classmate Teng-mei Yu was studying in the Department of Economics at West Virginia University when I arrived. With her help, I adjusted myself to the new school quickly. My cousin's husband, Dr. Chao-hsiung Chen, was teaching in the medical school there too. One year later, I transferred to the Department of Statistics. In the second year (1969), my wife brought my son to live with me. We could not afford to buy a car since my annual scholarship provided me with only USD 1,800. In 1970, I completed my second master's degree in statistics. My thesis was about the difference between sampling and non-sampling errors in sampling surveys. During my years studying at West Virginia University, my cousin, Yueh-jung Lee, and her husband, Dr. Chao-hsiung, helped us greatly.

In the spring of 1970, I applied to other graduate schools for Ph.D. programs and luckily got a scholarship from the Economics Department at SUNY-Buffalo. I left for Buffalo in fall of that year. My good friend Wen-tsun Chang was teaching there as an associate professor and assisted me a great deal. Prof. Chang was one of my classmates in the Department of Economics, NTU. I took his classes in Microeconomics and International Trading Economics. He told his colleagues that I might be the best student they had in the department to date. That must have been the reason why Prof. M. Brown asked me about the topic of my doctoral dissertation just two months after my arrival at the school. I told Prof. Brown that I was planning to do research on econometrics. This was based on a concept that I developed from my thesis at NTU and West Virginia University. I planned to write my dissertation on the models of errors in variables. Prof. Brown approved the topic right away.

My in-laws wanted me to take my wife and kids to the U.S. as soon as possible. They were concerned for them because at the time Taiwan had been forced to leave the United Nations. Under such pressure, I studied harder and my wife found a job in Buffalo, U.S. It was easy to apply for a green card at that time. I obtained my green card easily as a student at West Virginia University in 1969, while my wife and my son got theirs in 1970. In 1971, my mother-in-law brought my daughter to the U.S. In order to take care of our two children, we had to buy a car. Fortunately, we bought a used car for USD 150. Though it looked ugly, it worked pretty well. Compared to my friend Ching Chi, who spent more than two thousand dollars on a much nicer looking car and had to spend a fortune on fixing it, I thought we were really lucky.

In the winter of 1971, I invited Prof. Brown and his wife to dine at my house. My mother-in-law, who was an excellent cook, cooked our meal. Prof. Brown and his wife enjoyed the meal very much. Prof. Brown and his wife gave us an amazing clock with movable numbers on it. My kids loved this marvelous gift.

Prof. Brown always supported me. On the following day when I discussed with him my dissertation, he asked me if I would stay in the U.S. after graduation. I replied without any hesitation that I wanted to stay in the U.S. because the economic and political situation was so unstable in Taiwan. Prof. Brown told me that the markets for econometrics were quite poor and it might be difficult for me to financially support my family after graduation. To have more opportunities in job-hunting, he suggested that I talk with Prof. Frank Chi-feng Jen in the College of Management and discuss how to relate my dissertation to financial management. I was deeply touched by his concern and was full of appreciation for him. He has been my role model for the way I deal with my own Ph.D. students.

I spoke with Prof. Jen in accordance with Prof. Brown's suggestion and decided to add one more chapter of financial applications to the original content of econometrics in my dissertation. Prof. Jen, who was the distinguished professor of the Department of Finance, promised to help me. Since I was the first economic student that came to the Department of Finance, Prof. Jen handled this case in a unique way. He asked me to do two things: first, I had to complete all courses required for the Ph.D. students by the Department of Finance and second, I had to immediately register for the Ph.D. seminar. I not only took the 16 credits asked by the Department of Finance, but also completed four credits on Analysis of Time Series, four credits on Stochastic Calculus and Differential Equation, and eight credits on Multi-Variables Statistical Analysis. Therefore, in comparison to the other students, I received significantly better academic training, which further helped me in establishing a solid foundation for future research. Though I was extremely busy working on my dissertation, I kept my spirits high. Unfortunately, I did not have as much time to spend with my family. Therefore, my wife and mother-in-law took care of the children.

All my classmates at the Department of Finance discussed various topics enthusiastically in our seminars and completed wonderful dissertations. They all obtained prestigious teaching jobs afterwards. I finished my Ph.D. program in two years and 10 months. My advisor for my dissertation was Prof. Brown. My dissertation committee members were Prof. Frank Chi-feng Jen, Prof. Andrew H. Chen, and Prof. N. Revankar. During less than three years of studying at Buffalo, Prof. Brown, Prof. Winston Chang, and Prof. Frank Chi-feng Jen always cared for my family and invited us to their homes for dinner. I will never forget their kindness.

Later, Prof. Jen helped me to find an ideal teaching job in finance and invited me to work with him on research and publishing papers. He trained me with his comprehensive financial knowledge. When my research and teaching ability met his standards, he did his best to help me get an assistant professor position in the Department of Finance, at the University of Georgia at Athens (UGA). In 1973, I drove my wife, my mother-in-law, and two kids to Athens, Georgia. This began my teaching career at UGA. I am one of the first econometricians devoted to research and teaching in finance. Therefore, I spent a lot of time promoting financial econometrics, which will be discussed in later chapters.

Recalling the tough training I'd been through in undergraduate and graduate schools, I was full of mixed feelings. However, because of the rigorous training, my independent thinking was enhanced and a solid foundation for research was established. I believe that graduate students should never give up and never hesitate to ask questions while working on their theses or dissertations. They should enjoy their learning. No matter how many difficulties they see ahead of them, they should be able to reach their goal at the end. In Chapter 8, entitled "Experience in Training Ph.D. Students in Finance and Accounting," I will share my experience in teaching and research and give more advice to Ph.D. students and young faculty. Finally, I would like to discuss how an economics major has helped me and my classmates to be successful for the last 54 years.

First, most of my classmates have gone on to have very successful careers. Mr. Yu-hao Chen is the President of Tuntex Group; Mr. Chen-hsiung Ho is the President of Tung Ho Steel Enterprise Corp.; Mr. Chien-chih Chen is the President of Syntex Semiconductor Co., Dr. Rong-yi Wu is the President of the Taiwan Institute of Economic Research; Mr. Yi-ping Chen is the Deputy General Manager of Shanghai Commercial Bank; Dr. Sheng-cheng Hu is the Director of the Institute of Economics, Academia Sinica; and Mr. Yi-jen Huang is the General Manager of South China Insurance Co.

Second, for myself, my 43-year teaching career has been successful. I have published more than 225 academic papers and 26 books, with topics including company financial management, stock analysis, business statistics, etc. I have also advised more than 100 Ph.D. students. Many of them are Chinese finance professors now. Twelve of my financial and accounting students went back to Taiwan and have been teaching in colleges for the past four decades. Many of my Ph.D. students have also taught in the U.S., China, Hong Kong, and Korea. Later chapters will discuss further about their successes. Over the past 43 years I have traveled to Taiwan, Japan, Europe, Hong Kong, and Mainland China where I have taught short courses and conducted lectures. Although my schedule is packed, my life is meaningful and fun. This chapter reviews my wish to study chemical engineering, but by chance why

I devoted myself to economics. It also describes how I completed all of the accounting courses offered by the Accounting Division of the Department of Business at National Taiwan University (NTU) so I could take the accountant license exam and how I worked for the Bank of China (BOC), studied at the Graduate Institute of Economics, NTU, and got my first master's degree in economics simultaneously. This chapter also illustrates how and why I studied overseas and received my second master's degree in statistics and Ph.D. in economics and finance in the U.S. Finally, it describes how finance economics became one of the most popular fields in the university for the last 40 years. The point where I was denied my wish to study chemical engineering and decided to study economics was a "misfortune that was a blessing in disguise."

Chapter

4

Happy Family Life

Having worked at the Bank of China for two years, I had saved enough money to marry Miss Schwinne C. Tseng, a high school teacher, who graduated from the Department of Economics, Soochow University, in Taipei in 1965. After getting married, my wife continued her teaching job in Ming Chuan Commercial High School. My son, John, and daughter, Alice, were born in 1966 and 1968, respectively. John was only two years old and Alice only six months old when I went abroad to the United States. When I was abroad, my wife and children returned to Fengyuan Township to live with my in-laws, Mr. Tzu-cheng Tseng and Mrs. Yun-ying Huang. I was very sorry that my wife had to work and take care of the kids at the same time.

In the summer of 1969, Schwinne and John moved to Morgantown, West Virginia, to live with me. At that time, I was a graduate student studying for a master's degree in statistics. Since I was busy with my studies, I left Schwinne with most of the responsibilities of taking care of John. In the meantime, Alice was left in Taiwan and taken care of by my in-laws. We missed her very much. John was cute and active and soon could speak enough simple English to chat with our neighbors. Once Schwinne bought him a picture book in which a bear was lying on the grass basking in the warm sunlight. John, mimicking the story, took off his clothes and lied down on the grass in our front yard.

Schwinne and John quickly established their own social circle. Mrs. Chin-li Huang, whose husband studied in the Department of Education, and Mrs. Shou-chung Yeh, whose husband was in the College of Engineering, took their kids to play with Schwinne and John very often. These friends enjoyed spending time together. Schwinne and John gradually adjusted themselves to the foreign environment.

In May 1970, I received my master's degree in statistics from West Virginia University and a scholarship for the Ph.D. program in economics from SUNY-Buffalo. Before going to SUNY-Buffalo, I took my family to New York City. While I worked there during the summer, we had the chance to see the Statue of Liberty, the Empire State Building, and other attractions. At the end of August 1970, when we arrived in Buffalo, John's English had greatly improved. My wife and I enjoyed his company. He was always so active, happy, and playful. In the following year, my mother-in-law brought Alice to live with us. Our two kids kept Schwinne busy all the time, so my mother-in-law agreed to stay with us for a while. Having her mother there to help gave Schwinne the time to work as an accountant at a local church to earn some money. Later on, we saved enough money to buy a used car and were able to take our kids for picnics. Niagara Falls was our favorite spot. Since I enjoyed fishing, we barbequed and fished in the Niagara Falls area quite often.

In the fall of 1970, John went to preschool at a local church. While I studied, he liked to climb on my back and shout out the numbers he knew. This is how I knew he was a smart kid and eager to learn. In 1971, we let Alice go to preschool with her brother. Although she just arrived in America and could speak little English, she bravely faced preschool. It was worth the hard work to watch our children grow up and learn more and more each day.

In May 1973, I received my Ph.D. degree in economics and was offered a job as an assistant professor in the Department of Finance at the University of Georgia at Athens (UGA). Our life was becoming better every day. On my way to Georgia, I visited my friends, Mr. Cheng-nan Lin in Oxford, Ohio, and Mr. Hui-tsiung Chang in Knoxville, Tennessee.

By using this opportunity, my family and my classmates' families got together and had nice parties. We enjoyed these visits a lot.

When we arrived in Athens, John was in second grade while Alice was in first grade. Their academic performance was excellent, as were their athletic skills and as a result they were grouped in the same baseball team. My wife and I participated in the PTA (parent–teacher association) activities and got in touch with the American style of educational methods and philosophy. Over our three years in Athens, I discovered that the way Americans taught their kids was to stimulate their thinking and creativity and not to push them to memorize things. Students did not bring books home. Parents were involved with their children's education and enthusiastically participated in their after-school activities.

"When in Rome, do as the Romans do" was our philosophy. In the spring of 1975, I organized a visit to Mekong Air Force Base for John's Boy Scouts troop. When we boarded a B52 bomber at the base, I was able to see the basic structure of American flights as well as the mighty power of the American military. The students learned a lot and enjoyed themselves on the field trip. The PTA also showed their appreciation for this arrangement.

While I taught at UGA, Schwinne began taking courses in accounting for her master's degree. She took care of the kids and studied at the same time. Although we were extremely busy, we made time to go on family trips. We took several trips to Disney World and during the weekends we would gather with members of the Taiwanese Association of America for picnics and baseball games. In the summer of 1974, we went with some members of the association and traveled to South Carolina to crab. We had a wonderful time, catching, cooking, and eating the fresh crabs.

At that time, there were only two Taiwanese professors teaching at UGA, Prof. Chia-ming Chen and I. Prof. Chen, some graduate students, and I myself took the responsibility upon ourselves to look after the Taiwanese students at UGA. We would get together with the Taiwanese students and discuss the political future of Taiwan. Everyone in our group hoped that Taiwan would become a real democratic country soon.

In 1976, Schwinne received her master's degree in accounting from

UGA. She was offered a job in Atlanta, but gave it up for me because I decided to transfer to the University of Illinois at Urbana-Champaign (UIUC). She took a trivial job in the Accounting Department at UIUC. I appreciate her for giving up such a great opportunity to work for a big company, for the sake of my career.

In the fall of 1976, we settled down in Urbana, Illinois. John and Alice studied at a local elementary school where they had good teachers and a well-equipped learning environment. Schwinne and I continued to participate in the PTA activities. To make some extra money, John and Alice delivered newspapers, mowed the neighbors' lawns, and babysat along with other odd jobs. Their hard work proves that children in America are not spoiled. After elementary school, Alice was accepted to the affiliated high school of UIUC by passing a tough written exam and oral test. However, due to limited space John was not accepted. He attended Urbana High School where he also received a good education.

In the spring of 1983, John and Alice were admitted to the Department of Economics and Department of Electrical Engineering, at UIUC, respectively. Before their college semester began, Schwinne and I traveled with them to Mainland China and Japan. We arrived in Dalian, China in June. I taught a financial management course at the Dalian American Chinese Center, which was run jointly by the U.S Department of Commerce and Dalian Institute of Technology.

In 1979, Deng Xiaoping, the most prominent political figure of the Communist Party of China, visited the U.S. and toured a lot of cities. When he visited the General Motors factory, he found out the productivity of American automobile workers is 50 times higher than their Chinese counterparts. He asked how this could happen and how American automobile workers could improve their productivity. The American representative told him that the capitalism method should be used, but it might not be applicable in a socialism system such as China. Deng Xiaoping replied that it's no problem to apply a capitalism ideology in China. He said, "As long as a cat can catch the mouse, it doesn't matter if this cat is white or black."

In 1980, the U.S. Department of Commerce sent a delegation to Beijing to discuss how the U.S. could help China improve its production technology. During the meeting, a U.S. representative told his Chinese counterpart they would need to improve the management skills of Chinese managers. Therefore, they would like to set up a training center in China. The Chinese counterparts asked what kind of topics were going to be taught to their students. The U.S. representative said they were going to teach courses similar to the courses offered to students working towards a master's in business administration. The Chinese replied that it was not appropriate to teach their managers capitalism. However, they could report to Deng to hear his opinion. Deng immediately decided to let the U.S. Department of Commerce set up a training program at the Dalian Institute of Technology in 1981. I was one of the faculty members who taught in this program in 1983 and 1984.[1]

After the program ended in August 1983, we took a group photo with the students and American professors.[2] In this photo, besides myself were the U.S. dean, Richard Van Horne from Carnegie Mellon University, and the Chinese dean, Tian-Yue Lei. Tian-Yue Lei was the father of our current dean, Dean Lei Lei of Rutgers Business School.

In 1983, China's economy was quite underdeveloped. Although we lodged at a so-called "Building for Experts," there were no televisions in the rooms and the refrigerator functioned poorly. It was very inconvenient for us and we needed to go to special "friendship stores" (the Chinese set up special stores for foreigner visitors) daily to buy many everyday items. During our stay, we toured the beach in Dalian and other attractions and historical spots. One of our hosts took us to visit the battlefield of the Japanese–Russian War of 1895. It overlooked the famous Lüshun Harbor (more popularly known as Port Arthur). At the time, this site was not open to the public so we were very lucky to be able to visit this famous historical site.

In mid-August, the training program in Dalian finished. Our hosts arranged a trip for us to Beijing, Xi'an, Shanghai, and Nanjing. Dr. Joe

[1] A list of the faculty and staff who participated in the Dalian U.S. Chinese Center can be found at http://www.worldscientific.com/worldscibooks/10.1142/10182#t=suppl.

[2] The article "Rutgers Professor Played a Role in China's Economic History," edited by Susan Todd and published in Rutgers Business School's IMPACT newsletter in Spring 2016 can be found at http://www.worldscientific.com/worldscibooks/10.1142/10182#t=suppl.

Alutto, the former dean at the Business School of Ohio State University, and some other people went with us. Although it was extremely hot and humid, I appreciated this opportunity to visit so many Chinese historical spots and attractions.

Before coming back to the U.S., by a special arrangement, we went to the hometown of my aunt's husband, Tsu-sheng Hsia. At that time, people from Taiwan could not freely travel to Mainland China. My Uncle Hsia could not go back to his hometown in Fuyang County, Zhejiang Province, so he asked us to visit him and check on his children. Although their life seemed tough, my uncle's children welcomed us. In Fuyang County we saw the beautiful Fuchun River and made sure my uncle's children were doing well. During our trip to Mainland China, my children experienced a bit of oriental culture and life. They also realized how lucky they were to be living in the U.S.

In the summer of 1986, I was invited by the World Bank to deliver short courses in Guangzhou and Lanzhou. I brought Schwinne and Alice with me. After completing the three-day lecture in Guangzhou, we toured the beautiful landscape of Guilin and Yangshuo. It is said that the scenery of Guilin is the most beautiful in the world. However, I think Yangshuo's scenery is more beautiful than Guilin. After a short period of sightseeing in Shanghai, Schwinne went back to the U.S. by herself and Alice traveled with me to Beijing to go shopping. Alice liked the cotton shirts in the department stores there. She said the shirts were cheap and stylish; she bought a total of 15 shirts in a single trip. I followed her example and bought some for myself. Two days later, we flew directly to Lanzhou. I taught short courses there for four days. In Lanzhou, we visited the First Iron Bridge over the Yellow River. Unfortunately, we missed the chance to visit Dunhuang, a famous historical site, due to the bad airline schedule. We then flew back to Beijing and Alice returned to the U.S. while I stayed and continued to teach in Dalian. This trip enriched our views of both ancient and modern China, and more importantly, it strengthened my relationship with my daughter, Alice.

On May 24, 1987, John and Alice graduated from UIUC. Schwinne and I attended Alice's graduation ceremony in the morning and John's in the afternoon. When I talked about this busy day with the president of UIUC, Dr. Dave O. Ikenberry, he said with a smile that he believed my kids must have broken a record at UIUC. For over 116 years of UIUC's history, he'd never heard of any two children from the same family graduating from UIUC on the same day.

On the day of their graduation, Schwinne and I thought back to four years ago when John was 17 and Alice was 15, and they were both ready for college. We did our best to persuade them to study at UIUC. We explained that it was convenient for them to study at UIUC since they could still have their mother and grandmother's delicious meals and could do their laundry at home. Moreover, we told them that UIUC was one of the top universities in the world and both the Department of Economics and Department of Electrical Engineering were known around the world. With very keen efforts, we finally got their consent to go to UIUC. This way we did not have to apply for loans for their college education and we could keep an eye on them. We feared they would get into bad habits if they lived too far from home.

Alice worked for IBM during the summer of her sophomore and junior years in college. John also worked for financial companies in the summer. After graduation, John stayed at UIUC and studied accounting. Alice decided to work for Digital Computer after thoroughly thinking about it and rejected many other offers. We were glad to see that both of our children had developed good and healthy careers based on their strong educational backgrounds.

In 1989, John received his accounting degree and worked for a few accounting firms and banks on the East Coast. He came back to UIUC in 1991 and got his master's in accounting two years later. He went on to work for Arthur Andersen, the accounting firm, on the East Coast. He met and fell in love with Miss Jennifer C. Huang, daughter of Mr. Hsin-yi Huang and Mrs. Hsiu-fong Cheng, during his studies for his master's degree and got married in 1993. Jennifer was a graduate of UIUC too. She received her bachelor's degree in accounting in 1993. Since I taught at UIUC for 12 years and three of my family members received their academic degrees from there, I really have a very close relationship with the university.

After working for Digital Computer for four years, Alice decided to go back to school in 1991 and studied at Wharton Business School, University of Pennsylvania, for her Ph.D. in insurance. She received her degree in 1995. She then taught at South Carolina University for a year and then Syracuse University for another year. She has since been a consultant for over 20 years at several accounting firms. She was a manager of the Washington branch of PricewaterhouseCoopers, the largest accounting firm in the U.S. Alice was also an assistant professor of finance at San Francisco State University and a director in the Model Validation Group, Enterprise Risk Management, at State Street Corporation. Currently, Alice is working at KPMG as a consultant in banking and risk management.

John has been a senior technology officer at the headquarters of Chase Manhattan Bank and assistant vice president at Merrill Lynch. He is currently working for Chase Bank in Manhattan. He has also written a book on how to use Microsoft Excel and MINITAB to do statistical and financial analyses. John and Alice are experts in their fields and both have successful careers. I am quite content with their achievements and my own as well. My wife was always patient with them and gave them her loving guidance. Indeed, I would not be able to have a successful career without her help. I would like to give her my sincere appreciation.

John and Alice have also both coauthored several books with me such as *Statistics for Business and Financial Economics, Third Edition,* and *Financial Analysis, Planning and Forecasting, Third Edition.* Alice has coauthored the books *Advances in Investment Analysis and Portfolio Management, Advances in Financial Planning and Forecasting,* and *Advances in Quantitative Analysis of Finance and Accounting* with me for almost six years.

Although most students hate it, statistics for business has been one of the major courses offered in American business schools. In the summer of 1985, Chicago University's business school organized a conference on how to improve the teaching of statistics for business. One of the many opinions suggested in the conference was to invite experienced business school professors to write textbooks on applied business statistics. Several publishers asked me to write a statistics book in terms of financial applications. I was hesitant and did not respond immediately to their requests. In August of the following year, the American Statistical Association held its annual convention in Chicago. I asked the attendants for their opinions about this matter. At the banquet specifically arranged for Chinese statistical scholars, the book proposal surprisingly got very positive feedback. Since this would be the first time a Chinese statistical scholar wrote a book of this kind, everyone at the banquet wanted me to write the book and promised to recommend and use it. With such wonderful support, I started writing statistics books for financial and banking applications.

In 1987, I signed a contract with a publisher with the intent of writing a statistics book for business majors. In the early part of 1992, I asked my children to help me compile materials for the book. John prepared the computer-assisted instructional materials while Alice wrote the test bank questions. D.C. Heath published the book in 1993. It was the first time that I completed a book with the help of my children. The outcome was quite encouraging. The book features a picture of Snoopy, my beloved dog, and me. This must have been the first time that an author of a book on statistics for business book was pictured with his pet in his book.

Snoopy was a favorite among all my family members. He was adopted from a pet shop near Princeton, New Jersey in 1990. He kept me company while I was writing the book; therefore, I decided that he deserved a place in the book. I walked Snoopy every morning and evening. He always stood by the window to watch me leave for work and greeted me at the front gate when I came home. When I promised to take him with me to my office on the weekends, he would get very excited, and jumped and dashed around the house.

Unfortunately, he passed away in 2005. In human years, he would have been 105 years old. Strangely enough, Schwinne and I rejected John and Alice's pleas for a dog when they were young. Yet now we could never imagine life without Snoopy. Even though John and Alice have grown up, they have accepted Snoopy as a member of the family. Since he passed away, my family has missed him a lot.

In August of 1997, my son's wife, Jennifer, gave birth to my handsome grandson, Michael. Even though they live about an hour away in North Jersey, we see them frequently. As I watched Michael grow, I recalled John and Alice's childhood. I was always so busy with academic work when they were very young that I missed many joyful moments in their lives. I regret that I cannot go back in time and capture those moments I missed.

Under the patient instruction of John and Jennifer, Michael was able to recognize the whole alphabet and all the numbers before he turned two. We are all very proud of him. My grandson, Michael Lee, is currently 18 years old and studies at the computer-engineering department at the Georgia Institute of Technology. Academically, he performs very well; he excels in mathematics, English, and music — in high school he played the saxophone in the school band.

During the same year, 1997, I decided to revise my statistics book. John, Alice, and I signed the contract. John spent a lot of time in correcting the computer-related content and improving the computer-assisted instructional materials. At last, the second version of the statistics book for business was published by World Scientific in 1999, with father, son, and daughter as coauthors. This became a family business. I guessed it might be considered another world record to have a father coauthor a book with his son and daughter.

The first version of the book has been one of the most popular statistics textbooks in the world. It was also available in Taiwan with Yeh Yeh Book Gallery as the consignee. The new version was available through the Hwatai Publishing Co. that had imported 1,500 copies in August 1999. They expected that many professors would use this book as their textbook. I do hope that the next edition will be even more popular than this edition.

In 2000, my granddaughter, Michelle, was born. I liked the idea to welcome the new millennium in this way. My granddaughter is currently 16 years old and is in the 11th grade at Newark Academy. Her academic performance is outstanding as well. In 2012, Kent Place School held a *pi* competition, she memorized more than 130 digits and earned first place. In 2013, in the same competition, she was able to memorize more than 170 digits and won first place again. I'm really proud of both of my grandchildren. One of the reasons they perform so well is because my daughter-in-law takes good care of them.

Looking back, Schwinne and I are content with how we have spent our 70 plus years on Earth. Since we married in 1965, we watched our kids study in kindergarten, elementary school, high school, college, and graduate school and then grow into two very successful adults. I appreciate the contributions, endeavors, and sacrifices of my wife, my parents-in-law, and my children. My family is still close and dear to me, and though 51 years have passed, Schwinne and I still love and respect each other as much as we did when we first met.

Chapter

5

Help from President Lee Teng-hui

At the end of the Sino-Japanese War, Mr. Lee Teng-hui came back to Taiwan in 1946 from Kyoto Imperial University, Japan and studied at the Department of Agricultural Economics at National Taiwan University (NTU), in Taipei. Three years later, he received his bachelor's degree in agricultural economics, after which he remained as a teaching assistant at the university. In 1951, Mr. Lee was awarded a scholarship from the Sino-American Fund for Economic and Social Development, and traveled to Iowa State University in the United States to do research in agricultural economics. He returned to Taiwan in 1953, resumed his teaching job as an instructor at the Department of Agricultural Economics, NTU, accepted a post as a specialist and section chief at the Taiwan Provincial Department of Agricultural and Forestry, and also took the post of research fellow at Taiwan Provincial Cooperative Bank. Being an agricultural economist, he was also appointed as a specialist in the U.S.–R.O.C. Joint Commission on Rural Reconstruction (JCRR).

When I studied at the Graduate Institute of Economics, NTU, Mr. Lee was invited by Prof. Han-yu Chang to start a course titled "Agricultural Economical Policies in Taiwan." Coming from a family of farmers, I was attracted by the name and took the course in the first semester of 1964. During the semester, in addition to taking notes and reading his handouts in class, I read a lot of his articles regarding agricultural policies in Taiwan, including one he coauthored with Dr. Sen-chung Hsieh.

At that time, Chiang Kai-shek accepted Mr. Lien-chun Lee's suggestion and applied the exchange system of grain for fertilizer, but this hurt farmers. Mr. Lee was strongly against this system and insisted that farmers should grow plants that boosted the economy, such as bananas and flowers, which could be exported to Japan or Hong Kong for more foreign reserve. Having grown up in a farmers' family, I was quite familiar with the situation in the rural area, so I strongly supported his idea. Besides, the analytical methods I learned from his classes set up a solid foundation for me to explore and analyze government policies in the future.

Mr. Lee became one of my favorite teachers in graduate school. Often I dropped by his office to ask for his opinion about Taiwan's agricultural problems.

In 1965, Mr. Lee was awarded an agricultural economics scholarship sponsored by the Rockefeller Foundation and Cornell University. Again, Mr. Lee traveled to the U.S. and this time studied at Cornell University. In 1968 he received his Ph.D. in agricultural economics. His doctoral dissertation, "Intersectoral Capital Flow in the Economic Development of Taiwan, 1895–1960" won a national award from the American Association for Agricultural Economics in 1968 for the best doctoral dissertation in his field. Soon after, Dr. Lee returned to Taiwan and I visited him in the JCRR. I asked for his advice on studying overseas. He told me that I would learn a lot in the U.S., even though the Americans were quite lavish. He inquired about what I was going to study. I responded that I would study statistics and quantitative economics. He praised my decision to learn more about economic methods and theories, but he suggested that I learn more about management and policies since it would help my growth as a leader. He did not want me to become a follower. His suggestions enlightened me.

As a side note, Dr. Lee added that girls in the engineering schools usually worked in the lab all day and night. They had no time to dress well and thus missed many opportunities to find good husbands. Therefore, he suggested to his daughter, who was studying at Taipei First Girls' High School, to major in literature or business. After a two-hour conversation with Dr. Lee, I decided that it would be worthwhile to study in the U.S. despite the difficulties that I might encounter in the coming years. Today I can still recall Dr. Lee's expression during that long conversation as vividly as I could back in 1964.

Eleven years later in 1979, when I was a full professor at the University of Illinois at Urbana-Champaign, I returned to Taiwan. The president of Tamkang University, Mr. Clement C.P. Chang, studied for his Ph.D. in education at UIUC in 1978. In October of that year, I invited him to my house for dinner. During his visit, he expressed his wish to invite me to Tamkang University for a special lecture. I explained that because of my participation in Taiwan's democratic movements, Taiwan's government would prevent my return. Mr. Chang did not think that this would be a problem. In July 1979, with the joint invitation from Tamkang University and the Tatung Institute of Technology, I returned to Taiwan and taught for more than two months. I delivered a course entitled "Corporate Financial Management" in the MBA program at Tatung and held a series of special seminars on Financial Planning and Analysis at Tamkang. Dr. Tai-ying Liu, who was then the dean of College of Management, introduced me at these special seminars. Through this great opportunity, I became acquainted with Professor Hsin-fu Tsai, who was the dean of College of Technology at Tamkang University and we became good friends. At the end of my time at Tatung, Chancellor Ting-shen Lin held a farewell party for me at the School Board Meeting Hall. Chancellor Lin's son, Mr. Wei-shan Lin, and my classmate, Prof. Jui-chen Chen, accompanied us. The 14 guests at the party signed their names on the menu and posed for a group photo.

During my stay in Taiwan, I planned to visit Prof. Lee Teng-hui, who was mayor of Taipei City, but I did not have the opportunity. I called his office in the municipal government several times, but I could not get in touch with him. I returned to the U.S. disappointed, but I was also very glad to see Prof. Lee's accomplishments in his tenure as mayor of Taipei City. His achievements had greatly improved Taipei compared to 11 years ago when I first left.

While in Taiwan, I visited many old friends and relatives. I called on the International Commercial Bank of China where I previously worked for five years. The general manager, Mr. Chih-Tao Wang, invited me to give a lecture on the topic of how to determine the interest rate in view of the risk premium. At that time, my old friend, Mr. Chi-hsiung Lee, and his colleagues thought that the ideas mentioned in my speech would be impossible to be carried out in Taiwan in a short time. However, I am very glad to hear that Taiwan's banks decided to carry out the interest rate for loans and manage banking systems.

Seven years later during the summer of 1986, Professor Hsin-fu Tsai of Tamkang University invited me back to Taiwan. This time I held seminars as a distinguished professor and taught Financial Theories and Applications. Prof. Tsai had been promoted to dean of the College of Technology. I made up my mind before the trip that this time I would visit Prof. Lee, who was then Vice President of the R.O.C. I mailed a letter to Prof. Lee before I left the U.S. and informed him that I would be teaching at Tamkang University for 10 days. I asked if he had the time to see me, if he would please leave a message with the president of Tamkang University, Dr. Clement C.P. Chang.

Surprisingly, soon after I arrived in Taiwan, Dr. Chang's secretary informed me that Vice President Lee Teng-hui would see me in the Office of the President at 10 a.m. on August 17, 1986. That morning, I nervously entered the building of the Office of the President to see Vice President Lee. I had not seen him for 18 years. No sooner after we greeted each other, he had said that he heard from President Chang of Tamkang University that I had an outstanding record of academic achievements in the U.S. and he was very happy for me. During our meeting, he suggested that I spend more time researching the economic problems in Taiwan and Asia.

Although we had not seen each other for a long time, Prof. Lee talked to me with the same kindness and concern that he expressed for me when I was his student. Prof. Lee inquired as to why I had waited so long before coming back to Taiwan. I explained that because of my participation in Taiwan's democratic movements in the U.S., my applications for Taiwanese visas were often rebuffed for different reasons. He nodded understandingly and said there shouldn't be any more problems. He promised to take care of that for me. Since then, I have been able to make many trips to Taiwan.

Under the suggestions and encouragements from Prof. Lee, I devoted myself to the research of financial issues in Taiwan and the Asia-Pacific region. I initiated the Annual Conference of Pacific Basin Finance, Economics, and Accounting (PBFEA) in 1993 and started the journal *Review of Pacific Basin Financial Markets and Policies* (RPBFMP) in 1998. Since I represented UIUC, the Department of Commerce, the U.S., and World Bank in delivering short courses in Mainland China, I was able to describe to Prof. Lee what I had seen in Mainland China, especially in terms of development in economic reforms. I explained to him why Taiwan should be alert to the economic development of Mainland China. I also made up my mind to go back to Taiwan every year and contribute my expertise in management education in Taiwan.

In the summer of 1987, Prof. Yu-tsung Lin invited me to teach a four-week course entitled "International Financial Management" for the graduate students of National Taiwan University and National Chengchi University. Prof. Gili Yen and Prof. Ching-liang Hsu also participated. Prof. Kuo-shu Liang arranged for me to visit Vice President Lee in the Office of the President again. We chatted about the economic development of Taiwan, Asia, and the U.S. Vice President Lee also asked my views regarding the impact of lifting the restrictions for Taiwanese residents to visit Mainland China. My answer was that people would not choose to stay there after their visits because of the poor economic condition and political restriction in Mainland China. Vice President Lee mentioned that he had discussed with President Chiang Ching-kuo about the removal of the ban on new political parties and expected to have a reasonable solution soon. He wanted me to deliver this message to all the Taiwanese in the United States.

In 1987, there were lots of large structural changes in the economy and politics in Taiwan, such as the lifting of the ban of Taiwanese residents to visit Mainland China, the end of martial law, and the free exchange of foreign currency. During this key moment, Vice President Lee held office and participated in these major decisions. With an abundance of experience at different academic institutions, manufacturers, and government offices, he finally had the opportunity to put his expertise to use. It also proved that Mr. Chiang Ching-kuo had made a smart decision to have Prof. Lee as Minister without the Portfolio of Executive Yuan, Mayor of Taipei City, Governor of Taiwan Province, and Vice President.

My third trip to Taiwan occurred in 1988. Unfortunately, President Chiang Ching-kuo passed away while I was in Taiwan on January 13, 1988. I went out for dinner with a friend that night and came back late to Mr. Ching-yun Wong's house where I was lodging. Mr. Wong told me that a reporter from the *China Times* called to ask my opinions regarding the presidency succession of Prof. Lee Teng-hui. I regretted not being present to tell the reporter my thoughts about Prof. Lee's contributions to Taiwan. At six o'clock on the evening of January 13, Prof. Lee succeeded the presidency in accordance with the constitution of the Republic of China. I remember dining with Prof. Chien-sheng Shih and friends on the evening of January 15; we had an enthusiastic discussion about the possibility of President Lee being elected as Chairman of KMT. Prof. Shih thought that President Lee should succeed to chair KMT. He used the old saying "monkeys scatter away when the big tree falls" to predict the reorganization of KMT and the new era of Lee Teng-hui. He was elected to the acting chair of KMT, the ruling party of Taiwan, on January 27 after some internal conflicts and compromises with the KMT members.

Between 1988 and 1994, I taught in Taiwan at least once a year. Each time, Prof. Kuo-shu Liang arranged for me to visit with President Lee. During our conversation, President Lee mentioned that American doctoral students in economics and finance lacked training on policy analysis. He suggested that I emphasize this when training my Ph.D. students. His suggestions and advice pushed me to make more of an effort in policy research. To further fulfill his expectations, I initiated the first Conference on Pacific Basin Finance, Economics, and Accounting at Rutgers University in the spring of 1993. We explored the business, economic, and financial issues of the Asia-Pacific countries. Prof. Ssu-meng Chen, who was a visiting scholar at the Department of Finance, at Rutgers University, presented his paper entitled "Evaluation of Domestic Economic Policies in Taiwan," which he coauthored with Mr. Pai-hsien Pang. My paper entitled "Capital Structures of Taiwan Enterprises" that I coauthored with Prof. Gili Yen and Prof. Chun-chiung Lin was also presented at the conference.

On August 11 and 12, 1990, the North American Taiwanese Professors' Association (NATPA) held its first convention in Taiwan. NATPA's chairman and staff planned a visit to President Lee in the president's office after the convention meeting on August 13. However, on the second day of the convention, news broke that Prof. Ying-yuan Lee illegally traveled from the U.S. to Taiwan. Because of this, the president's office notified us that President Lee could not see us that day. He went to Taiwan without the government's permission and therefore he was arrested. Fortunately for me, on the morning of the following day, President Lee, who was accompanied by Secretary-General Yen-shih Chiang, met me in his office. The first question that President Lee asked me was about the topics we discussed at the NATPA convention. He asked whether what we discussed was more about political or academic affairs. I responded that our discussions were 70 percent academic affairs and 30 percent political. He told me to encourage investors when I was giving a talk in Kaohsiung County Government that night, to invest smartly, but not to speculate on stocks. I was surprised that he had learned from the newspaper and knew I was going to give a speech in Kaohsiung County Government that night. I was impressed that President Lee read the newspaper every day in order to fully understand everything that happened in Taiwan.

In Kaohsiung, there was another speaker, Mr. Tien-tsai Hsu, who was to speak that night. Mr. Hsu addressed the labor policy while I discussed the stock markets in Taiwan. In this lecture, I became acquainted with the County Governor, Mrs. Yueh-ying Yu Chen. She later sent her son, Mr. Cheng-tao Yu, to Rutgers University to study. Cheng-tao told me how when President Lee came to visit his family after the death of Cheng Tao's grandfather, he applauded me as a marvelous student and scholar whom Cheng-tao would learn a great deal from.

From my experience with Prof. Lee, I can attest to his being a knowledgeable, kind, and friendly president. At that time I believed that the political and economic future of Taiwan would be enhanced under the leadership of President Lee. During his 12-year presidency, President Lee contributed a lot to Taiwan's democracy and improved Taiwan's economic condition significantly. People regarded him as founder of democracy for Taiwan.

In January 1992, Prof. Gili Yen invited me as a visiting distinguished professor sponsored by the National Science Council to give speeches at National Taiwan University (NTU) and National Central University (NCU). I addressed the intra-relationship in the research of economics and finance at NTU and the relationship of finance and other subjects at NCU. In Taiwan, I visited the president of Tamkang University, Dr. Clement C.P. Chang; Prof. Yu-tsung Lin; Vice Chairman Koong-lian Kao; President of Central Trust of China, Fai-nan Perng; Mr. Shen-hai Kuo; Mr. Po-tsuan Cheng; Prof. Yi-sheng Chen; and Mr. Chia-hung Kuo. Dr. Kuo-shu Liang, Governor of the Central Bank, arranged for me to visit President Lee in his office on the afternoon of January 13. President Lee mentioned that he just finished meeting with an American congressman. They talked about the Sino-U.S. relationship. President Lee wanted the Sino-U.S. military cooperation to be further strengthened. I spoke with President Lee regarding the necessity to upgrade technology in Taiwan and the possible political risks that Taiwanese investors might face in investing with Mainland China. Again, President Lee reminded me to encourage my Ph.D. students to pay more attention to policy research.

The 3rd Annual Conference on PBFEA was held on August 8–9, 1995. On August 8, my wife, Schwinne, and I along with 12 other foreign scholars visited President Lee at the Presidential Office. President Lee gave a long speech in which he praised Governor Hsu for his excellence in handling financial problems. During the conference, the famous economist Prof. Anna Schwartz asked President Lee how he planned to face the military threats and challenges from Mainland China. President Lee confidently responded that the Republic of China was well prepared. I suggested that in order to fight against the possible crisis of stock markets and banking systems caused by the military threats from Mainland China, we might be able to reduce the bank reserve rate. President Lee responded positively and asked Governor Hsu to think over my suggestion immediately.

Although President Lee could not attend the 3rd Annual Conference on PBFEA to deliver his welcome address, he asked Secretary-General Poh-Hsiung Wu to read the congratulatory message for him. However, due to some urgent issues, Secretary-General Wu was not able to attend either. As a result, I was asked to deliver President Lee's congratulatory message. In his speech, he welcomed the government officials, scholars, and business executives who made the trip to Taipei for the third annual conference. President Lee stated that in this conference, which focused on financial market developments and comparing major financial centers, he suggested that everyone in the region "work together to strengthen international collaboration, ensure sustained progress and prosperity of this region, and promote a balanced and stable development of the world economy."

On May 16, 1996, I went back to Taiwan to attend President Lee Teng-hui's inauguration ceremony. On the early morning of May 20, President Fai-nan Perng (Mr. Perng was president of Central Trust of China then) and I arrived at the baseball dome in Taoyuan County to participate in the inauguration ceremony for President Lee. President Lee's marvelous inaugural address was so encouraging that it gave me confidence of a bright future for Taiwan.

In June and July of that year, I was invited to be Shaw Foundation Professor at the School of Accountancy and Business, Nanyang Technological University in Singapore. One morning, while in Singapore, I learned from the *Lianhe Zaobao* that President Lee had proposed his "Slow Trading" policy on Mainland China investments. "Slow Trading" policy means economic relationships with Taiwan should have some restrictions and government approval. I was touched to hear the news and confident that the political risks in investing in Mainland China would be under appropriate control.

In the early part of 1998, I served as a consultant for the American

United Group and worked in Mainland China for 22 days. Then, I went back to Taiwan. On the morning of January 29, I, along with Dr. Kuang-sheng Liao, visited President Lee at the Presidential Office and reported to him the possibilities of the devaluation of Renminbi (RMB) and Hong Kong dollars. We also talked of other Taiwanese and Asia-Pacific financial problems. I updated him with the progress of my PBFEA conferences and the purpose of editing the journal *Review of Pacific Basin Financial Markets and Policies* (RPBFMP). He inquired if I could organize the 7th Conference on PBFEA in Taipei the following year and make the main theme of the conference the issues of the current financial problems in Taiwan. I promised that I would start at once to organize the materials in accordance with his suggestion.

In September, I went back to Taipei and discussed with President Lee the difficulties that Taiwan encountered in stock markets and banking systems. I invited President Lee to give an opening remark on May 28 and 29, 1999 for the opening ceremony of the 7th Conference on PBFEA, which was held at the Grand Hotel, Taipei. He immediately accepted and mentioned again that he hoped to discuss more of the current financial and economic issues of Taiwan at this conference. Upon returning to the U.S., I decided to invite the College of Management, NTU to co-organize the conference. Dean Hong-chang Chang agreed to co-chair the conference with the support of NTU President Wei-jao Chen.

Upon the introduction of NTU President Wei-jao Chen, President Lee gave his welcome speech and expressed his concerns on the risk of the hot money flooding all over the world. When he finished his speech, Dean Hong-chang Chang, Chairman Yung-ching Chang, and I escorted him out of the Grand Hotel. He told us that he was going to suggest the creation of a national security fund. He wanted me to further discuss the national security fund with Minister Paul C.H. Chiu and Governor Fai-nan Perng. With President Lee's support and the support of many government offices, this conference was a success.

On May 31, my wife, Schwinne, my daughter, Alice, Dean Hung-chung Chang of National Taiwanese University, Prof. Kuang-sheng Liao, a representative of Legislative Yuan and I accompanied the foreign scholars attending the conference to visit President Lee. President Lee's 40-minute lecture about Taiwan's economic condition and diplomatic relationships with foreign countries helped to indicate the direction of Taiwan's future.

In May 1999, President Lee had the opportunity to deliver the welcome address in person for the 7th Conference on Pacific Basin Finance, Economics, and Accounting. Since this conference was less than a year after the beginning of the Asian Financial Crisis, President Lee used his welcome address to speak on the crisis and its impact on the global economy.

"The Asian Financial Crisis is related to the inadequately developed capital markets in some countries," said President Lee. "Therefore, knowing how to set up a financial development scope by matching its basic financial structure and situation is an important issue that deserves the sincere attention of every country."

He also mentioned how important it was for countries around the world to have a working financial relationship. President Lee used the example of "the declaration of APEC in Kuala Lumpur [that] urged all members to cooperate and assist in the financial and commercial reconstruction, by speeding up the private capital flows, and strengthening the international financial systems."

In closing, President Lee remarked that he hoped with Taiwan's upcoming role in the Asia-Pacific region that the Republic of China would make an effort "to strengthen the financial development and stability in this region." He also added that he hoped that this conference would create a discussion which would benefit the Asia-Pacific economy.

As a student of President Lee from 1964 until December 1966, I was very lucky to have his continuous concern and instruction, which has helped me greatly in my academic research and career development. Since I took President Lee's class in 1964 until the end of his presidency, there had been improvements in the economy and in the politics in Taiwan. During President Lee's 12-year tenure (1988–2000), Taiwan showed its outstanding political and economic progress.

I remember back in August 1987, when I met the director of the

American Institute in Taiwan, David Dean, he told me that Taiwan was very lucky to have such talented people as Lee Teng-hui, who was expected to contribute greatly to the political and economic development of Taiwan. Now, President Lee's achievements on the economy and politics are just as Mr. David Dean predicted.

At last, I would like to mention that President Lee is an affectionate, righteous, and knowledgeable president. Having such a president is really an honor for Taiwan's people. As the election day of March 18, 2000 approached, I hoped all the Taiwanese people could elect a new president who would continue in line with President Lee's policies. That surely would be the real fortune to people in Taiwan. On May 20, President Lee turned over the presidency to President Chen Shui-bian, and I attended this important ceremony. Overall, I would like to thank my former professor, Lee Teng-hui, who had converted Taiwan from a dictatorship to a true democratic country. Small wonder that people call him Taiwan's "father of democracy."

Chapter

6

Relationship with Ex-Governor of the Central Bank Dr. Kuo-shu Liang

Prof. Kuo-shu Liang was another one of my teachers whom I was close with. In the summer of 1979, when I went back to Taiwan for the first time after studying overseas, I taught at Tatung Institute of Technology and Tamkang University. During this time, I called on two of my professors, Prof. Kuo-wei Chang and Prof. Kuo-shu Liang. Mr. Chun-nan Pai, the Deputy President of Chiaotung Bank, invited Prof. Chang and I over for dinner. We talked about academic research as well as the possibility of removing the ban on organizing new political parties.

Prof. Chang was also my advisor for my master's thesis when I studied at the Graduate Institute of Economics at NTU. He was very proud that I received the full professorship in the Department of Finance, UIUC, in just five years after getting my Ph.D.

Prof. Liang also invited me to join him for Japanese cuisine at Shou-Le Restaurant located at Chungshan North Road, Taipei. Prof. Chi-yuan Lin, from the University of South California, and Dr. Ho-sung Wang, from Asia Bank, also joined us for dinner. Prof. Lin and Dr. Wang were two years my senior in the Department of Commerce and Department of Economics, NTU. We told Prof. Liang what we had experienced overseas while Prof. Liang explained to us the current situation of domestic economic development and the expected outlook. He strongly encouraged us to visit Taiwan or to teach in Taiwan more frequently. He even suggested that we settle down in Taiwan. However, it took me seven years to return to Taiwan.

Since 1986, I have returned to Taiwan almost every year. In 1986, when I taught at Tamkang University, I called on Prof. Liang again. He invited me to dinner with Yung-san Lee and Fai-nan Perng. Since then, whenever I return to Taiwan, I have dinner with Prof. Liang, Fai-nan Perng, Jia-dong Shea, Pochih Chen, Yung-san Lee, or Chi Schive.

Prof. Liang was very familiar with President Lee because of their long-term friendship. He would tell stories about the good old days when he and President Lee were students or teachers. It was by way of Prof. Liang's arrangement that I was able to see President Lee. Because of Prof. Liang, I became friends with Yung-san Lee, Fai-nan Perng, Pochih Chen, Chi Schive, and Jia-dong Shea.

In August 1990, I returned to Taiwan for the 10th Convention of North America Taiwanese Professors' Association (NATPA). Prof. Liang invited Prof. Shu-tsung Liao and me to lunch. He mentioned that President Lee started to train Lien Chan as his successor. During the time, Premier Hau Pei-tsun visited the countryside quite often; so Prof. Liang suggested President Lee visit the country more too in order to strengthen his friendly image among the people. Prof. Liang mentioned that President Lee tried to invite him to serve as Minister of Finance, but failed due to the opposition of Premier Hau. But when Premier Hau appointed Wang as Minister of Finance, he accepted. When I gave a speech at the NAPTA Convention, I asked why Mr. Wang accepted the position: earlier he had resigned as vice minister of finance due to his lack of faith in Taiwan's government.

The following day, the *Independent Daily News* wrote that someone had put me up to ask those questions. This was not true. I acted on my own behalf because I was upset that Mr. Wang was appointed. I was upset because I believed Mr. Wang's qualifications were not suitable for the position.

In January 1992, Prof. Gili Yen invited me to come back to Taiwan to deliver a short course at the Management School of National Central University. When I returned, Prof. Liang called everyone for dinner. We discussed the feasibility of the Six-year National Development Plan proposed by the Council for Economic Planning and Development (CEPD); Executive Yuan finally came to the conclusion that the plan would have a very serious impact on Taiwan's finances. Prof. Liang hoped that I would do more research on the issue and expected me to give a speech at the Six-year National Development Plan symposium held by the China Economic Association (renamed the Taiwan Economic Association) in April of that year. I tried very hard to ignore his suggestion because I was afraid I would infuriate the chairman of CEPD, Prof. Shirley W.Y. Kuo, who was one of my professors at the Graduate Institute of Economics, NTU. However, Prof. Liang strongly encouraged me, and I could not help but accept this job. Pochih Chen, Jia-dong Shea, and Gili Yen all helped me a lot with the preparation.

Prof. Pochih Chen hosted the symposium in April 1992. In the opening ceremony, attendants included Prof. Chien-sheng Shih, Prof. Shirley W.Y. Kuo, Prof. Kuo-shu Liang, and his wife, Ms. Chin-ying Ho. The title of my speech at this symposium was "Financial Analysis of the Six-year National Development Plan and Its Impact on Financial Markets (refer to Appendix 6A for the details of this speech). During the symposium, I mentioned that the Six-year National Development Plan was too huge to complete. The government would require a massive financial loan in the future. Furthermore, the construction of a high-speed rail must be dealt with sincerity and more care. I expressed my similar opinions later regarding the building of the high-speed rail during the 7th Conference on PBFEA at Taipei on May 28 and 29, 1999. Now I will summarize the policy implications of this speech as follows:

1. The Six-year National Development Plan should be evaluated in accordance with investment policy, financial policy, and production policy. I used McDonnell Douglas and Boeing to show how investment policy should be evaluated in terms of rate of return.

2. I used investment, financial, and production policy to analyze the rate of return of the Six-year National Development Plan. I also evaluated two possible ways of collecting capital for the development plan as shown in Table 6A.1. It is necessary to issue public bonds for a total amount of about NTD 3.9 trillion in accordance with the first method while only NTD 1.1 trillion is to be issued in the second. Table 6A.2 shows the capital sources and applications in the Six-year National Development Plan.
3. In view of financial analysis, the analysis of capital sources is categorized in the financial policy while that of capital applications belongs to the investment policy. To a single company, its capitals mainly come from inner profit reserves, loans from financial institutions, or stocks and bonds issued by the company. The adequate division ratio among these three capital sources is the essence of the financial policy. If a company carries too much debt, the possibility of bankruptcy as well as the cost of capital increases. For example, let's review the case of McDonnell Douglas mentioned in the last section. The debt ratio of McDonnell Douglas reaches a very dangerous margin in recent years and that's why they invited Taiwan to invest USD 2 billion that may help to reduce their debt ratio. Similar to the ways of collecting money in a company, the capitals of the Six-year National Development Plan can be collected in the ways of "debt" and "non-debt."
4. I also analyzed the possible consequence of increasing income from tax collection or reducing the expenditure of ordinary income.
5. The Six-year National Development Plan is proposed for the welfare of all people in Taiwan. Its marvelous goals are supposed to be highly admired. However, in view of financial management, most professionals think the government should be more careful to promote such a huge plan. They worry especially about the unpractical slogan, "issuing public bonds, but not

> increasing taxes," which may mislead people. To reduce the negative effects, there are some main issues that the government should think over again, such as narrowing down the scope of the plan, re-evaluating the priorities, and estimating an adequate amount of tax increase. National developments are long-term plans that may bring about enduring impacts and big disasters for the society if we roughly make the decisions and carry them out in a hurry. Our conclusion is the same as President Lee's motto, "building up a prosperous country with diligence and thrift." We sincerely hope that administrators in charge of the National Development Plan will think through the whole plan once again.

This lecture marks the first time that Prof. Liang asked me to become directly involved in the discussion of financial and economic policies of Taiwan's government. Through this experience, I recognized that Prof. Liang was an economist with both theoretical and practical experience. Before this symposium, Prof. Liang and I both made keynote remarks at the Conference of Capital Market organized by Prof. Tsun-siou Lee of NTU in the spring of 1990. Prof. Liang addressed the future development of the high-tech industry in Taiwan while I talked about the future of the development of financial markets in Taiwan. At that time, Prof. Liang was Chairman of Chiao Tung Bank and made every effort to support the development of the high-tech industry in Taiwan. The prosperity and success of the present Hsinchu Science and Industrial Park was partly due to his great contribution.

In 1992, the Taiwanese government decided to build up Taipei as a financial market and business operation center in Asia, but there were two opposite opinions about liberalizing capital accounts. Between fall 1993 and spring 1994, I was invited to the Chinese University of Hong Kong as a Wilson Wong visiting chair professor for 10 months. During that time, I was invited to Taipei to give three lectures to the middle-to-high level officials of the CEPD, Ministry of Finance, and the Central Bank in the CEPD buildings by the invitation of Vice Chairman of the CEPD, Chi Schive. I made a series of analyses for the plan to build up Taipei as a financial operating center in Asia in these lectures.

In 1994, Prof. Liang accepted President Lee's appointment and succeeded Dr. Samuel C. Shieh to serve as Governor of the Central Bank of China, R.O.C. Prof. Liang then proposed to liberalize the capital accounts step by step. However, Vice Minister of Finance Linin Day, Prof. Nai-ping Tuan, Prof. Christina Y. Liu, and some other professionals advocated opening the capital accounts right away. When I finished my teaching in Hong Kong in May 1994, I went back to Taipei and directed the research on the plan to build up Taipei as a financial market and business operation center in Asia in the CEPD and the Central Bank. Prof. Liang also asked me to discuss with Deputy Governor of the Central Bank, Fai-nan Perng, the development of the plan. I agreed that capital accounts should be liberalized gradually for fear that it would have a huge impact on the development of the industry and upgrading of the technology. Thus, when Mr. Sen Yang from *Wealth Magazine* interviewed me in August, I proposed the idea of "industry is the root while finance is the leaf" on the development of the financial center (the original interview was published in the October 1994 issue of *Wealth Magazine*).

To further explore the policy of building up Taipei as a financial center, I decided to hold the 3rd PBFEA Conference at the National Library in Taipei, on August 8 and 9, 1995. At the end of August 1994, Prof. Liang promised me he would deliver the keynote speech at this conference. Unfortunately, he passed away in July 1995. Dr. Yuan-tung Hsu, the new governor of the Central Bank, was the keynote speaker instead. Before the conference I asked all the attendants to join in silence and pay their respect to Prof. Liang for a minute.

On August 8, during the opening ceremony I explained that both Prof. Liang and I myself believed in the development policy that "industry is the root while finance is the leaf."

Prof. Liang had gone through his life with extensive experience in academic societies, industries, businesses, and government offices. He chaired several major banks in Taiwan, such as Chang Hwa Bank, First Commercial Bank, and Chiao Tung Bank. In government offices, he served as vice chairman of the research, development, and evaluation commission, Executive Yuan; and deputy governor, and governor of the Central Bank. In his academic career, he was a teaching assistant, an instructor, an associate professor, and a full professor in the Department of Economics, NTU. Only President Lee had similar and comparable experience.

His suggestions to the government were summarized in the book entitled *Suggestions for Policies* published by Yuan-Liou Publishing Co. I still remember a conversation I had on the phone in March of 1995 with Prof. Liang; he told me he was very proud of the seven loans made to the high-tech industry in his term as chairman of Chiao Tung Bank. At that time, the market price of UMC's shares owned by the Chiao Tung Bank was four times that of its original investment.

With Prof. Liang's training and encouragement, I had the chance to participate in the policy research and give my advice regarding Taiwan's finance. President Lee and Prof. Liang's teaching and support were complementary and of great help to me. I was honored to have two opportunities to express my support of Prof. Liang's point of view in development policies. In June 1999, my classmate Dr. Sheng-cheng Hu, director of the Institute of Economics, Academia Sinica, and I edited a special issue (June 1999) for *Review of Pacific Basin Financial Markets and Policies* in memory of Prof. Kuo-shu Liang. Prof. Liang's wife, Mrs. Chin-ying Ho, wrote the first article in the issue, which was a review of Prof. Liang's professional career. The second article was Prof. Liang's entitled "Financial Reforms and Obligations of the Central Bank" published in Hong Kong in November 1994. Prof. Khee Giap Tan, NTU, Singapore, and I also published an article entitled "Policies and Suggestions to Capital Flows in Southeast Asian Countries." I would like to contribute this special issue with my most sincere appreciation and sympathy to Prof. Liang, who was well respected by all the academic institutes and scholars in Taiwan.

Appendix 6A

Financial Analysis of the Six-year National Development Plan and Its Impact on Financial Markets

This speech was given at the China Economic Association (currently the Taiwan Economic Association) in April 1992. In it I discussed how investment policy, financial policy, production policy, and the Six-year National Development Plan affect financial markets. My speech consisted of five parts and they were as follows: Section A was a brief introduction and overview, Section B detailed the relationship between the economy and financial management using the return rates of McDonnell Douglas and the Boeing Company as examples, and Section C discussed the sources and purposes of capitals for the Six-year National Development Plan. In Section D, I touched on some financial issues regarding the Six-year National Development Plan and Taiwan's financial markets, and for Section E, I concluded my speech by reviewing the national development plan.

The following was the main focus from the content of my speech:

A. Introduction

At the end of 1990, the Council for Economic Planning and Development (CEPD), Executive Yuan, proposed the draft of the Six-year National Development Plan which required a total investment amount of NTD 8.238 trillion that was 1.7163 times of the GNP in 1991. The sources of such a huge amount of expenditure and its impacts on future economic activities and financial markets are obviously concerned by academic institutes, industrials, and government officials. The main idea of this article is to analyze the financial aspects of this development plan and its possible impacts to the financial markets. First, I will discuss the relationship between economic and financial management and point out the importance of financial analysis with the example of comparing McDonnell Douglas to the Boeing Company. Next, I will integrate the financial analysis and macroeconomics analysis to explore the sources of capitals and whether their applications are adequate. Following up, I list some ways for capital collection, especially to issue public bonds, and their possible effects on financial markets. At last, I conclude with suggestions on Section E.

B. Relationship between economy and financial management

According to the textbook *Corporate Finance Theory, Method, and Applications*, coauthored by me and Joseph E. Finnerty, 1990, financial management is the comprehensive knowledge based on economic, accounting, and statistics information. In terms of policies, financial management includes: (1) investment policy, (2) financial policy, (3) dividend policy, and (4) production policy. Except the dividend policy, the analysis of the other three policies can directly or indirectly support the analysis of traditional macroeconomics to evaluate major governmental constructions.

The essence of the investment policy is to analyze the total return rate. In view of the changes of the return rates of McDonnell Douglas and the Boeing Company between 1971 and 1990, we obtain two conclusions: first, within the 20-year period, Boeing's return rates were higher than Douglas' in most cases. Second, from 1988 to 1990, McDonnell Douglas' return rates were far below the satisfied numbers. Financial policy reveals a company's capability on carrying debts. Adequately carrying debt will provide sufficient capitals for business operation and enhance the investors' return rate while inadequate debts may bring about financial crises and increase the possibilities of bankruptcy. From the related data, we find that most of the time

McDonnell Douglas carried much more debt than Boeing did, especially in the years between 1988 and 1990. That is probably why McDonnell Douglas expected Taiwan to invest USD 2 billion in the company.

Production policy focuses on the effects of quality improvement for products and its related cost on technology upgrading. In the following two sections, we will integrate the analyses of these three policies of financial management and the analysis of macroeconomics to further understand the return rates of the Six-year National Development Plan and its possible impacts on financial markets by issuing government bonds.

C. The sources and purposes of capitals for the Six-year National Development Plan

As stated by the CEPD, there are two possible ways of collecting capital for the Development Plan, as shown in Table 6A.1. It is necessary to issue public bonds for a total amount of about NTD 3.9 trillion in accordance with the first method while only NTD 1.1 trillion is to be issued in the second. Table 6A.2 shows the capital sources and applications in the Six-year National Development Plan.

In view of financial analysis, the analysis of capital sources is categorized in the financial policy while that of capital applications belongs to the investment policy. To a single company, its capitals mainly come from inner profit reserves, loans from financial institutions, or stocks and bonds issued by the company. The adequate division ratio among these three capital sources is the essence of the financial policy. If a company carries too much debt, the possibility of bankruptcy as well as the cost of capital increases. For example, let's review the case of McDonnell Douglas mentioned in the last section. The debt ratio of McDonnell Douglas reaches a very dangerous margin in recent years and that's why they invited Taiwan to invest USD 2 billion that may help to reduce their debt ratio. Similar to the ways of collecting money in a company, the capitals of the Six-year National Development Plan can be collected in the ways of "debt" and "non-debt."

In the first method stated by the CEPD, there is about NTD 6 trillion collected by issuing public bonds in the NTD 8.21 trillion required. On the other hand, 73 percent of the capitals of the Plan are coming from public bonds. If we analyzed the second method stated by the CEPD, there are only 13.4 percent of capitals from public bonds. Here, we must point out that the partial capitals collected by public enterprises, as shown in Table 6A.2 is NTD 2.1 trillion, which may also come from the sources of issuing bonds too.

If the first method proposed by the CEPD is workable, then by way of the analysis of financial policy, will Taiwan's government carry too much debt on completing the plan? Will it affect the economic growth? Will it boost capital cost in financial markets? Will it drop off investors' interest? And, will the industries fail with their efforts on technology upgrading? We will explore these questions in the next section.

As for the second method stated, we think it is quite unacceptable. The estimated NTD 2.5 trillion of surplus from ordinary accounts apparently is over-optimized. Over the past 20 years, the ordinary accounts of Taiwan's government have kept a huge surplus. However, in the near future the operation of the national health insurance program, personnel expense of government employees, and the boost of government employees' retirement expense will increase immensely in the expenditure in ordinary accounts without doubt. If we want to keep the huge surplus, the following consequences may happen once the economic growth rate is below seven percent or inflation becomes worse:

(1) Increase income from tax collection: Though it is not necessary to have a higher tax rate, it does make people suffer from higher tax expenses if the government strains tax collection to increase the actual income. There is no free lunch. Even though the government doesn't raise tax rates, to strain tax collection will make people's saving decrease and bring about the result of cash expelling. If, based upon real needs, the government does raise tax rates or add tax items to increase

the government's income and reduce the amount of issuing public bonds; the cash crowding-out effect will be the same.

(2) Reduce the expenditure in the ordinary accounts: For example, to reduce the educational expense in order to increase the surplus in ordinary accounts and to collect the capitals required for the Development Plan. However, the government will be criticized on placing wrong priority in doing so because there are many items far less important than education among the 775 items in the Development Plan.

In summary, if the second method is executed, the government must increase income from tax collection or reduce expenditure in ordinary accounts. If the government does not increase tax rates, according to my point of view, reducing the national defense expense may be a possible way to increase the surplus.

In view of corporate finance, the applications of capitals depend on the investment policy while the drafting of investment policy is mainly based on the return rates. For a governmental investment project, we need to pay attention to not only direct, but also indirect returns. Therefore, the priority of new development plans should be based on the industrial categories, the efficiency, and the return rates of the plans. Among the 775 plan items, the top three highest expenses are the national insurance program, two highway constructions in central and southern Taiwan and the high-speed railroad. To compare the advantages with its financial load, the construction of the high-speed rail was extremely criticized by many economists. Chung-hsin Yang (1990), Pochih Chen (1991), etc., have strongly suspected the efficiency of the high-speed rail. In early 1992, *Wealth Magazine* also reported the heavy load of interest payments on constructing the high-speed rail. I firmly believe that it is necessary to further analyze the financial issues related to the high-speed rail. In addition, some other major items in the Plan should also be re-evaluated and adjusted accordingly.

Table 6A.1. Capital sources of the Six-year National Development Plan.

Capital Sources	Method 1 (by CEPD)	Method 2 (by CEPD)
Surplus of ordinary accounts	0	2.5
Private sector	0	0.6
Public enterprises	2.1	2.1
Self-redeemed investment (paid off by issuing public bonds)	2.13	0
Accumulated surplus	0.08	0
Expenditures of ordinary accounts	0	1.9
Public bonds	3.9	1.1
Total	8.21	8.2

Table 6A.2. Capital applications of the Six-year National Development Plan.

Capital Sources	Method 1 (by CEPD)	Method 2 (by CEPD)
Expenditures of ordinary accounts		1.9
Purchase and compensate for land acquired		1.1
Fixed (public) investment	2.1	
Public enterprises investment	0.6	
Private sector	2.5	5.2
Government investment	2.5	8.2

Unit: NTD 1 trillion
Sources of data: K.M. Chen, S.W. Wang and K.N. Sun (1992)

D. Financial issues of the Six-year National Development Plan and Taiwan's financial markets

Financial markets usually include stock markets, bond markets, foreign exchange markets and markets of other new financial products (such as futures, options, and futures options). The extent of Taiwan's stock markets is comparably small with less than 300 stocks listed on markets while the bond market is still in early steps and the foreign exchange market exists only for current and forwards foreign exchanges. The markets for futures, options, and futures options are still under construction. In short, Taiwan's financial markets are incomplete and have limited globalization. Under such circumstances, to collect capital for the Development Plan by issuing great amounts of public bonds should be seriously evaluated again.

Collecting capital by issuing public bonds could effectively utilize people's savings to promote public constructions. However, public bonds will be redeemed by tax money. If tax income increases because of the Development Plan, it is not necessary to raise taxes to redeem the public bonds. On the contrary, if the Development Plan is not able to effectively increase tax income, raising taxes to redeem government bonds becomes necessary. According to the estimate of Pochih Chen (1991), the Taiwan government should limit its public bonds issuing under NTD 3 trillion for the following six years. This is because the government should limit its outstanding bonds to less than 40 percent of the GNP. (Before 1980 in Japan or before 1982 in the U.S., the total amounts of their outstanding governmental bonds were kept under 40 percent of the GNP. Not to mention the per capita income in Taiwan currently is lower than that of Japan or the U.S. in the period mentioned above.)

As per the estimate in the CEPD's draft, Taiwan's GNP can reach NTD 8.1485 trillion in 1996. Based on the GNP of that year, the outstanding amount of common public bonds accounts for only 25.6 percent of the national income. In fact, in Japan or the U.S., they include all kinds of public bonds in the ratio calculation of the outstanding amount of public bonds to national income. According to the first method stated by the CEPD, as shown in Table 6A.1, the total amount of bonds issued by different levels of government offices is about NTD 6 trillion. It means that in 1996 the outstanding amount of public bonds weighs 75 percent of GNP, which is much higher than the ratios in Japan or in the U.S. Furthermore, the financial markets in Taiwan are not as vigorous as America's or Japan's. Figuring out how to sell out such huge amounts of bonds without seriously affecting the financial markets should be very important. Thus, to complete the Development Plans successfully, Taiwan's government should definitely place "set up a sound and solid financial market" as an important item in the Six-year National Development Plan.

E. Conclusion

The Six-year National Development Plan is proposed for the welfare of all people in Taiwan. Its marvelous goals are supposed to be highly admired. However, in view of financial management, most professionals think the government should be more careful to promote such a huge plan. They worry especially about the unpractical slogan, "issuing public bonds, but not increasing taxes," which may mislead people. To reduce the negative effects, there are some main issues that the government should think it over again, such as narrowing down the scope of the plan, re-evaluating the priorities, and estimating an adequate amount of tax increase. National developments are long-term plans that may bring about enduring impacts and big disasters for the society if we roughly make the decisions and carry them out in a hurry. Our conclusion is same as President Lee's motto, "building up a prosperous country with diligence and thrift." We sincerely hope that administrators in charge of the National Development Plan will think through the whole plan once again.

Note. This article was revised from my keynote speech presented in the Symposium of the Six-year National Development Plan held in April 1992. I would like to extend my sincerest thanks to the symposium sponsors for their invitation. Furthermore, I would like to thank Prof. Gili Yen for his help on enriching this article.

References

1. Chen, K.M., Wang, S.W. and Sun, K.N., "Capital Collection Issues in the National Development Plan," *Proceedings of Symposium of Six-year National Development Plan*, China Economic Association (1992) 183–207.
2. Yang, S., "To Seriously Evaluate the Construction of High-speed Railroad — Daily Interest of NT$10,100,000,000 in the Completion of the Railroad," *Wealth Magazine* **121** (1992) 221–225.
3. Chen, P., "Some Macroeconomic Concerns for the Six-year National Development Plan," Taiwan Economic Forecasts and Policies 22, series 1 (1991) 107–119.
4. Yang, C.H., "Investment Priority of Six-year National Development Plan," *Proceedings of Symposium of Six-year National Development Plan*, Chinese Economics Association (1992) 69–106.
5. Yang, C.H., "Explore the Land Issues Related to Public Construction in the Six-year National Development Plan," *Proceedings of Symposium of Six-year National Development Plan*, China Economic Association (1992) 131–152.

Chapter

7

Teaching Method and Educational Philosophy

Based upon my undergraduate experience in Taiwan and my graduate experience in the U.S., my teaching career since 1973, and my experience with guiding my son John, daughter Alice, my grandson Michael Lee and granddaughter Michelle Lee, I have made some observations about education philosophy and methods.

John earned his B.S. in economics and accounting and his master's in accounting from the University of Illinois. Alice has earned her B.S. in electrical engineering from the University of Illinois and a Ph.D. in insurance and finance from Wharton School of Business. Currently, my grandson, Michael Lee, who graduated from Newark Academy, is a sophomore at Georgia Tech University and my granddaughter, Michelle Lee, is in the 11th grade at Newark Academy in New Jersey. My wife and I used a mixture of Eastern and Western parenting and educational upbringing. Both my son and daughter are well educated and perform well in their careers. In addition, both my grandson and granddaughter perform very well. Based on these observations, I have composed this chapter.

The Chinese education philosophy and method are essentially based upon Confucianism. It is well known that there are different ancient Chinese scholars who have explained that education is needed for the younger generations. They can be classified into three different schools of thought. First, Laozi regards human beings as being born with a good nature; therefore, the mission of education is to glorify this good human nature. Alternatively, Xunzi believes that humans were born with an evil nature; therefore, the mission of education is to remove the evil nature from humans. Confucius proposed a theory, which compromised the philosophy of the two previous concepts. To my best knowledge, the Confucian education philosophy has a huge impact on the education logic of China, Japan, Korea, Taiwan, Hong Kong, and Singapore.

Modern Western management theory can be classified into theories X, Y, and Z. I believe that theory X, which states that workers inherently dislike and avoid work and must be driven to it, is similar to the Xunzi theory. Theory Y, which states that work is natural and can be a source of satisfaction when aimed at higher-order human psychological needs, is similar to Laozi's. Theory Z, which was developed by Professors Ouchi and Maslow in the 1980s, focuses on increasing employee loyalty to the company by providing a job for life with a strong focus on the wellbeing of the employee, and is similar to Confucianism.[1] Therefore, it is worthwhile to use my 43 years of educational experience to compare alternative Chinese education philosophy with Western education method and management theory and propose a hybrid management theory to contrast Eastern and Western cultures.

Since I received my Ph.D. at SUNY-Buffalo, I have taught for 43 years at UGA (1973–1976), UIUC (1976–1988), and Rutgers (1988–present). In 1973, I received my Ph.D. in economics and finance from SUNY-Buffalo and I was offered a job as an assistant professor in the Department of Banking and Finance at the University of Georgia at Athens. Just a few days after my arrival, Department Chair Dr. Robert Dince had a long talk with me in his office. He mentioned that one of the main reasons they hired me was to attract more research and publications. The department also hired an American professor, Dr.

[1] http://en.wikipedia.org/wiki/Theory_Z

William Lloyd, who came from Indiana University. Dr. Dince suggested that I take on less of a teaching load in order to spend more time in research. I thanked him for his concern, but rejected his suggestion. I believed that teaching was just as important as doing research. I did not want to be looked down upon just because I was a foreigner and might struggle with English communication skills.

The following fall, Dr. Robert Dince spoke to me again in his office. He said, "Your teaching performance is much better than I expected; however, you have not published any papers so far. I am worried that if you don't publish any papers during the year, you may not be able to keep your job." I asked him to wait three months since I believed my papers would be accepted by some famous journals in the near future. In less than two months, I received acceptance letters for two of my papers from the *Journal of Finance and Quantitative Analysis*, which was ranked the second best financial journal in the United States during that time. Our chairman was so proud that he showed my acceptance letters to everyone and said, "Dr. Lee is not only good at research, but also excellent at teaching." Since then, I made up my mind to make more of an effort to teach my students and to produce more outstanding students.

During my three years at UGA, I devoted myself to teaching as well as research. I taught by combining Eastern and Western philosophies. Through my own experience and the participation in my kids' PTA activities, I realized that the Eastern education method puts an emphasis on memorization and the Western education method emphasizes the understanding of the subject and plays down the importance of memorization. I strongly believe that a mixture of these two methods is more suitable to educate the younger generations. In my experience, memorization and understanding can have some synergy effects. If students only memorize without understanding the subject, then he or she will lose interest in the subject and the knowledge they have learned cannot be retained. Alternatively, if students only understand the subject without remembering what he or she has learned, then the knowledge, which they have learned, cannot be easily applied in the real world. Sometimes memorization can help students make their learning process more effective and practical.

When I taught at UIUC, I frequently told my students to memorize the knowledge just like cattle and sheep eating grass in the field. The cattle eat the grass and immediately store it in one of the compartments in their stomachs, and because of this, they have the ability to regurgitate their cud to eat for later. Similarly, a student can remember what he or she learned from the class even if they did not entirely understand the subject. When they go home they can try and understand by themselves or they can ask their parents or friends for help.

Overall, I would like to propose a weighted average approach to educate the younger generations. In other words, students with high IQs can be educated with more of an emphasis on understanding the subject. If the student has an average IQ, he or she might find it more effective to be educated by memorization first, then by comprehending the subject matter after. A Western proverb says, "learning by doing." In other words, remember the subject first, then try to understand later when there is time to gradually digest it.

During the second week of my course "Essentials of Financial Management," in 1973, a student asked me what finance was. I asked him if he had been to a Chinese restaurant before. He said yes and that he liked Chinese chow mien. I responded to him that finance was the Chinese chow mien of knowledge. It was a comprehensive subject that was composed of accounting, economics, statistics, mathematics, and computer knowledge, the same way as noodles, pork, soy sauce, and salt are in chow mien. Students thought this metaphor was fun and interesting and I was enlightened for my future teaching and research from this way of thinking.

During my years teaching at UGA, I volunteered to teach adult financial management classes at Mekong Air Base too. One of my graduate students, John Martin, always went with me to the air base every week and we became good friends. Throughout our friendship, I realized that you have to teach wholeheartedly and that teachers and students can learn from one another.

In addition to teaching undergraduate students, I also advised some Ph.D. students. During my three years at UGA, I was on the oral defense committee for four Ph.D. students and was the advisor for two postdoctoral students. My first postdoctoral student was Son-nan Chen who had his Ph.D. in statistics from UGA. He had attended my investment classes and completed five academic papers with me. Three of these papers were derived from his research as a postdoctoral student. Son-nan Chen was a full professor of finance at the University of Maryland and he was the chairman of Department of Money and Banking, National Chengchi University.

My second postdoctoral student was Carl R. Chen. I was one of Carl Chen's Ph.D. committee members until I left UGA in 1976. Chen took my finance course and did research with me. Chen received his Ph.D. in economics and I helped him to obtain an assistant professor position in the Department of Finance at the University of Dayton. In 1992, he took the position as the editor of the journal *International Finance and Economics* with a strong recommendation from me. Chen is currently the distinguished William J. Hoben Professor of Finance at the University of Dayton.

From my experience advising these two excellent postdoctoral students, I found out that if I wanted to get the results I expected while teaching students how to do academic financial research, theories and methods had to be focused. However, it should be noted that it is essential to find out a student's previous background and relative strengths before teaching them either theory or methodology. In fact, it was quite rare at that time that, though an assistant professor, I was able to advise postdoctoral students. Overall, training postdoctoral students is very rewarding to me.

Because of my outstanding performance in both research and teaching, the University of Illinois at Urbana-Champaign offered me an associate professor position in 1976. After a thorough consideration, I accepted the offer and left UGA for the position at UIUC. UIUC was a well-known university and I was the first Chinese professor to teach in their business school. I might have been the first Chinese professor to teach finance at one of the top business schools in the world too. Two years later, I was promoted and became a full professor.

In the beginning, when I arrived at UIUC, the Department of

Finance expected me to re-organize the curriculum for the Ph.D. program. I had an opportunity to bring my experience of teaching Ph.D. and postdoctoral students at UGA into full play. First, I visited the professors who taught economics, statistics, and econometrics and asked them whether the Ph.D. students of the Finance Department had studied the appropriate courses. Most professors responded that the finance Ph.D. students were not required to have a Ph.D. level of economic theory and econometric method courses. In their opinions, the finance Ph.D. students should take the same courses as economics Ph.D. students. During the first year I changed the required courses for the finance Ph.D. students. I enforced the previously required courses and asked students to take microeconomics and macroeconomics as well as two semesters of econometrics. I also asked students to take at least one course in the statistics and management science departments. I believed that with a good understanding in theories and solid training in methods by taking these courses, students could learn how to better apply what they learned in the Department of Finance.

In the fall of 1976, I offered research courses for Ph.D. students. Before starting my classes, I told the chairman, Prof. N. Bedford, of the Department of Accounting that the courses would be helpful to Ph.D. students in accounting too. He immediately recommended my classes to two outstanding students. One of them was Mike Sandretto, who received an offer from Harvard University after graduation, and the other was David Smith, who worked at the University of Kansas and is currently the distinguished chair professor at University of Nebraska at Lincoln. From the Department of Finance, there were five students taking my courses and three of them asked me to advise their Ph.D. dissertations. D. Stock is currently the distinguished professor and Chairman of the Department of Finance, in Oklahoma University; Scott Harrington is the chair of the Health Care Management Department in Wharton; and D. Mohamed went back to teach in Tunisia. The great outcomes of my first Ph.D. research class established my reputation and secured my position at UIUC. Hence, my opinions about the department attracted more and more attention.

From 1976 to 1988, I taught Ph.D. research courses at UIUC.

From the very first class I asked students to write reports to enhance their writing and research skills. Due to the excellent result of the very first class, more and more students came to my classes. They included students from the Department of Accounting as well as those from the Department of Economics. The most famous class was my 1979 one in which there were nine students. Among them, V.L. Bernard, who had been the distinguished professor of accounting at the University of Michigan, was recognized as one the top 10 accounting professors in the world. Unfortunately, he passed away in 1995. R. Beatty is currently the Accounting Circle professor of accounting, USC, and T. Shafer is the distinguished professor and chairman of the Department of Accounting, University of Notre Dame in Indiana. In this class I also had Mike Alderson, who wrote his dissertation on pension funds. He began his career teaching at Texas A&M and he is currently a professor at the University of St. Louis. In the other classes, Stephen Baginski was the distinguished professor of accounting at Indiana University, and is currently the Herbert E. Miller chair professor of accounting at the University of Georgia.

I also instructed many Oriental students, four of them went back to teach in Korea. The students from Taiwan included Yun Lin, chairman of Department of Finance, NTU; Chunchi Wu, M&T Professor of Banking and Finance, University at Buffalo; John K. Wei, chair professor, Hong Kong University of Science and Technology; Quentin C. Chu, distinguished professor of finance, Memphis University; C.C. Yang, professor of finance, NTU; David Chen, professor of accounting, Fu Jen Catholic University; C.W. Chen, distinguished professor, Hong Kong University of Science and Technology; C.W. Hsin, chairman of Department of Finance, Yuan Ze University; and Ren-Raw Chen who was associate professor at Rutgers University and now a professor at Fordham University.

From revising curriculum for the Ph.D. program to teaching courses, I instructed many excellent students who obtained great achievements at many academic institutions. More than 15 of my previous students are now serving as distinguished professors or chair professors at well-known universities. It is such an honor to have the opportunity to teach the most talented students in the world and help them develop and succeed. In addition to American students, I also helped students from other countries by using different approaches to training them theoretical and empirical methods in accordance with their relative strengths and their academic backgrounds. These students came from countries such as China, Taiwan, Hong Kong, Canada, Korea, Bangladesh, and Tunisia.

After my promotion to a full professor, the Department of Banking and Finance assigned me the job of inviting outstanding professors and hosting weekly seminars. In order to complete this assignment, I contacted many well-known professors and enhanced my relationships with the scholars in the field. I tried my best to invite the most famous scholars, such as Prof. M. Miller of Chicago University, the Nobel Prize winner, Prof. R. Roll, the distinguished professor of the University of California, and Prof. Lawrence H. Summers, the distinguished professor of Harvard University, to speak at UIUC. Through these opportunities, I made a good amount of contacts with many professors. Along with my wonderful research results, my reputation and academic ranking advanced every day.

One of these people who I was able to get to agree to give a seminar was Dr. Summers. He scheduled his speech at UIUC together with that of Iowa University and planned to take a plane from Iowa City to Chicago, and then take a small plane from there to Champaign on the morning of the seminar. His lecture at UIUC was scheduled at 2 p.m. on that day. Unfortunately, the flight to Champaign was cancelled because of the lack of people to fill the flight. As soon as he knew of the situation, he called me right away and told me that he would take another flight to a nearby town and then take a taxi to Champaign. He arrived at my office just in time. Without having lunch, Dr. Summers delivered a wonderful two-hour speech. Afterwards, I drove him to the airport where he flew to Chicago and then back to Boston. His determination and reliability led me to believe that he would surely be able to handle great national affairs.

Following the seminar, my expectation came true and he became Secretary of the Treasury. His appointment was not only his own accomplishment, but also a blessing for the country. Overall, Larry did a good job for the United States of America in fiscal policy and other economic policy decisions.

After the weekly seminars, all of the finance faculty members took turns hosting parties for colleagues and the graduate students. I believe that you have to enhance the relationship between colleagues and students through social activities. My family also held these parties many times. In the spring of 1982, when Professor Miller came to UIUC to deliver a speech, he made a special request to have my wife and mother-in-law's cuisine. Since I took John and Alice with me most of the time, they were also acquainted with my students and colleagues. Often times we played bridge and baseball with my Ph.D. students. The famous time series statistician, Prof. P. Newbold, was my colleague and we trained Ph.D. students in both economics and finance together. Since I started a new journal entitled *Review of Quantitative Finance and Accounting* in 1991, I appointed him as one of the associate editors.

UIUC was the first college to provide a Ph.D. degree in accounting. In college rankings, the undergraduate and graduate programs of the Department of Accounting, UIUC, was ranked at the top. Even the Department of Finance ranked in the top five among colleges due in part to some of my contributions. Due to my background in economics, accounting, and statistics, I advocated that the undergraduate and graduate finance programs' curricula include more accounting and statistics materials. I insisted on improving students' analytical and writing skills by assigning projects. I pushed my students with my Oriental philosophy. All students, both American and foreign, were treated equally.

Once, a graduate student from Taiwan dropped by my office and told me that I was the only foreign teacher who dared to reprimand students, and she warned me to be careful. The following year, another one of my graduate students from Taiwan came to speak with me and said I was the only professor who dared to rebuke American students when they were wrong. In fact, American students usually were quite reasonable. If they were wrong, they would accept the teacher's instruction without arguing, but I would also say, "If I was wrong, I will apologize next time" and would not make them feel too embarrassed.

In order to have the best results, I believe that I must teach different students in different ways.

I had hoped to share my educational philosophy and instruction methods with other academic professionals, so I started writing books. In 1980, I edited *Readings in Investment Analysis* with J. Francis and D. Farrar. In 1983, I published *Financial Analysis and Planning: Theory and Application, A Book of Readings*. And then, the famous textbook *Financial Analysis and Planning: Theory and Application* was published in 1985. In 1986, I started to work with Prof. J. Finnerty on *Corporate Finance: Theory, Method, and Applications* and *Security Analysis and Portfolio Management*, two books which were later published in 1990 when I was at Rutgers University. I am certain that my publications benefit my academic reputation as well as the college's evaluation.

My 12 years of teaching at UIUC were very important in establishing my academic reputation. I worked on many things simultaneously — teaching, research, writing books, journal editing, etc. — to establish my reputation and academic ranking. I took on the responsibility as editor of *Financial Review* in 1985 and *Quarterly Review of Economics and Business* two years later. Those 12 years were the golden age of my career. I believe that there are not many scholars who have such magnificent achievements in their lives. I am lucky and also blessed by the good name my parents gave me — "Cheng-Few," which means "lots of luck" in Chinese.

When John and Alice graduated from UIUC in 1987, I hunted for other teaching jobs in bigger cities under the expectation of my wife, Schwinne. In spring 1988, I received several offers for distinguished professor from Rutgers University, State University of New York, Oklahoma University, and Memphis University. After discussing the offers with my wife, I decided to accept the position at Rutgers. There were three reasons for my decision. First, the reputation of Rutgers University was similar to UIUC's. Second, the location of Rutgers University was ideal. Rutgers is near New York City and a lot of Taiwanese live within the area. Lastly, there was an opportunity to chair the department. To be the chairman of the department would offer me a great opportunity to establish the finance department that I had envisioned. I looked forward to embracing the challenge.

Rutgers University is the seventh oldest university in the United States and was originally a private school. It was founded at the same time as Princeton University and Columbia University. The New Jersey state government took over it more than 60 years ago. Its management school was located in Newark and in 1987, the university set up a new management school in New Brunswick. I was hired to chair the Department of Finance and draft the undergraduate curriculum. I was also advising Ph.D. students for the Department of Economics at the New Brunswick campus and the departments of finance and accounting at the Newark campus.

When I arrived at Rutgers University in August 1988, my salary was the highest in the Management School and the Department of Economics; it ranked in the top 10 on campus. Moreover, since most financial and accounting professionals in the country confirmed Rutgers' determination on renovating its financial department, I carried many more responsibilities than I did in 1976 when I started working for UIUC. I planned to complete my goals from different directions by emphasizing teaching, research, and service. First, I continued to instruct Ph.D. students for the departments of finance, accounting, and economics in accordance with my experience from UIUC. Second, I designed the curriculum for undergraduate students with advanced methods in finance. Third, I continued to write textbooks as well as edit academic journals and annuals. Lastly, I organized two international conferences. My book writing, journal editing, and conference organization will be described in detail in Chapter 10.

At Rutgers University, I drafted the financial bachelor degree program in accordance with four principles:

1. Emphasize both theoretical and practical materials.
2. Emphasize the teaching methods of research projects and case studies.
3. Encourage students to take the practicum.
4. Offer more selective courses.

I spent seven years (1988–1995) building a curriculum for finance majors. As a result, students who graduated from the department were well trained and were offered job opportunities by large companies. In 1988, there were only about 30 students in the Department of Finance, while now there are more than 300 students each year. The Department of Finance used to be the second smallest department in the Business School, but has now grown to be the largest department. After seven years serving as a chairman, I was done holding administration positions.

Having been trained in economics, accounting, finance, and statistics and with my 12 years of teaching at UIUC, I found that finance and accounting complemented each other. Because of this I had always suggested that finance students take more accounting courses and vice versa. In 1989, I suggested to the chairman of the Department of Accounting, Prof. B. Jaggi, that he set up a department that interconnected the departments of accounting and finance. At that time, the members who participated in this plan included Prof. Y. Mensh and Prof. Oded Palmon. However, it didn't happen due to a lack of funding. Recently, because of the sharp drop of enrollment in the Accounting Department, Professors Jaggi, Mensh, and Goodman started to promote the project again. In other words, we allowed students to do double majors in finance and accounting. Over the past 25 years, college students have chosen to major in finance rather than accounting due to the vigorous stock markets in the United States. A similar situation happened in Taiwan and other countries in Asia as well. This phenomenon may not only be due to the vigorous stock markets, but also because of the out-of-date training for accounting students and it should be further analyzed and improved.

As I mentioned before, finance is comprehensive knowledge based on accounting, economics, statistics, mathematics, and computer science. It is more challenging to students while accounting tends to be slightly easier. Over the past 40 years, new financial products, (i.e., futures' options, foreign currency derivatives, etc.) have been widely applied in the banking systems, insurance companies, and other non-financial companies. On the contrary, accounting students generally do not take these courses. Thus, CPAs cannot accomplish their jobs in auditing. That's why I insist that accounting students take more financial courses. Besides, accounting students rarely utilize the calculus and statistics they learn and accounting becomes less challenging than finance. On the other hand, I advocate that financial students take more accounting courses in order to understand the basic financial structure and situation of a corporation. Therefore, whether or not it is necessary to separate the training for undergraduate accounting and financial students should be further discussed. Business or management school faculty and industry managers may think this over.

The management schools at American universities usually encourage their tenured faculty to take on consulting roles in enterprises. During my teaching at Rutgers University, I also spent some time in consulting. Being a consultant allows one to make extra money as well as receive practical experience that enhances one's teaching. When I was the department chairman, I never opposed other professors having consulting jobs. I believe that knowledge of finance is based on both theoretical and practical knowledge. While teaching at Rutgers, I found that some students who were working in the world's largest financial centers had more practical knowledge than some professors. Therefore, it was only logical that professors obtained practical experience so that they could incorporate their real life situations into their teaching and assist their students.

Management subject is a combination of both statistical methods and social science that should be integrated with theory and practice. When I started teaching at UIUC in 1976, I asked my undergraduate and graduate program students to do their financial analysis based on real company data and reports. I expected students to learn quantitative analyses, financial theoretical applications, improve their writing ability, and develop the ability to analyze real cases of a company's financial management. At the end of a semester, I would learn a lot about different companies' information from reading students' reports. In fact, I mentioned this teaching-and-learning method in my book, *Financial Analysis and Planning: Theory and Application* published in 1985. The third edition of this book was published in September 2016.

When I teach Ph.D. students, I ask them to read other scholars' papers first and then write a comprehensive report and evaluation of a specific topic. Later, I ask them to write a paper using their creativity, new theories, methods, and data. I encourage Ph.D. students to ponder on their dissertation title in the first year of their study so they can make progress both in taking courses and writing their dissertation. This way of learning challenges students more and most are able to shorten the time taken to receive their degree. Studying and writing dissertations simultaneously is the most effective way of learning. This is because students can effectively incorporate their knowledge from these courses into their dissertation. The next chapter will discuss my experience in training Ph.D students in finance and accounting.

From my experience teaching students, I recognize that talent may be important, but hard work definitely makes up for insufficiencies. If teachers can challenge students by allowing them to think, instead of listen, they can make students more intelligent. The Western philosophy of education emphasizes understanding, which is good for talented students, while the Eastern style focuses on memorizing, which is good for average students. From my teaching experience, I understand that if I can design my lectures in the ways of understanding and memorizing, I am able to cater to any kind of students.

In the Western behavioral science, there are three theories of learning: by force (theory X), by encouragement (theory Y), and by the middle way (theory Z). These theories are similar to the different schools of thinking in ancient China (i.e., people born evil, people born good, and the golden middle). According to my teaching experience, theory Y is more effective to gifted students while theories X and Z are best for the average students. However, the best teaching method must combine both Eastern and Western educational methods and philosophies.

During my time teaching at various universities, I have done research, chaired a department, edited journals, written books, organized conferences, and even taken consultant jobs for enterprises and government offices. In Chapter 12, I will share my experience on editing journals and writing books. Sometimes people ask me, how I can do so many things at one time. My answer is to work hard and efficiently. Of course, help from secretaries, assistants, and other people is necessary too. It is difficult to complete everything by oneself, but teamwork allows one to reach their goal. Overall, I try to combine theory, method, and application in my teaching methods. In Chapter 9, "Innovative and Active Approach to Teaching Finance," I discuss my teaching method and philosophy in further detail.

Chapter 8

Experience in Training Ph.D. Students in Finance and Accounting

In this chapter, I will expand on my education philosophy and method, which I have discussed in the previous chapter, and emphasize my experience in training Ph.D. students in finance and accounting. Finance is one of the most popular interdisciplinary areas in higher education; therefore, students from all different majors could consider working on a Ph.D. in finance. Since a number of majors can apply for the program, I suggest Ph.D. advisors to consider using my experience to guide Ph.D. students in finance or accounting concentrated in financial accounting.

These suggestions come from my personal experiences in training more than 100 Ph.D. students during the last 43 years. In addition, they come from my interdisciplinary training, my own experiences in research, editing journals, and organizing conferences. It's worthwhile to know that my method in the philosophy of teaching Ph.D. students is also inferred from my previous educational experience at National Taiwan University, West Virginia University, and SUNY-Buffalo.

In August 1970, I arrived at the Department of Economics at SUNY-Buffalo. One of my classmates from National Taiwan University, Winston Chang, was one of the professors of economics in that department. He introduced me to Professor Brown and told him that I may be one of the best students they ever accepted. Professor Brown immediately accepted me as one of his Ph.D. students. In November of that year and with the help of Professor Murray Brown, we decided my dissertation would be entitled "Errors-in-Variables Estimation Procedures: Theory and Application." After one and a half years, I almost finished my theoretical and methodological part of my dissertation. However, the empirical or the subject portion was still to be determined.

In the fall of 1971, I invited Professor Brown and his wife to my home for dinner. They brought a digital clock as a gift for my children. My children enjoyed this new toy very much. One week later I went to his office to discuss my dissertation. He asked me whether I was going home or staying in the U.S. I told him that I decided to find a job in the U.S. Then he told me that as an econometrics Ph.D. major from SUNY-Buffalo it would not be easy to find a good university to teach at. He suggested that I see Professor Frank C. Jen to discuss how I can use my "Errors in Variables" methodology to conduct finance- and accounting-related research. I made an appointment immediately to see Professor Jen to get his advice.

A couple of weeks later I met Professor Jen and asked him whether there was potential to use the "Errors in Variables" methodology in finance and accounting. Professor Jen immediately questioned my intention to use the methodology. Professor Jen told me that accounting data is carefully audited and stock price data is carefully recorded. So, he did not see how my methodology had any potential to apply to financial research unless I showed him some recent literature related to the research area.

After a lot of effort, I finally found two papers to support my intention to apply "Error in Variables" in financial research. These two papers were:

1. Roll, R., "Bias in Fitting the Shape Model to Time Series Data," *Journal of Financial and Quantitative Analysis* **4** (1969) 271–289.
2. Miller, M.H. and F. Modigliani, "Some estimates of the cost of

the capital to the utility industry, 1954–57," *American Economic Review* (June 1966) 333–391.

The first paper discussed the impact of measurement errors of market rates of return on beta coefficient estimation. The second paper discussed the impact of current earnings instead of permanent earnings on cost of capital estimation.

Finally, Professor Jen promised to be one of the members on my dissertation committee. I discussed my empirical portion of my dissertation with Professor Jen every two weeks.

The next step was to decide how many finance courses I should take. After a careful discussion and assessment, Professor Jen asked me to take a seminar first, then investment analysis, and finally, corporate finance. Since I was not a finance major, I did not have the knowledge of Markowitz's portfolio theory, Modigliani and Miller's propositions capital asset pricing theory, and option and future theory. I frequently received different reactions from finance Ph.D. students, E. Han Kim, Stanley Kong and Lemma Senbet. As an economics Ph.D. student, I could only show my strengths in economics theory and methodology in front of my classmates.

Since I discovered my classmates' training in economic theory and econometric methods was relatively weak, I suggested Professor Jen to ask my three classmates to take more courses in the Economics Department, which they did. After one year in my third Ph.D. seminar course, my classmates and I had a good understanding of both finance and economics. This kind of interdisciplinary knowledge helped all of us to do in-depth research in finance. These experiences gave me some indications on how to train my own Ph.D. students in the future.

Finally, all of us were hired by excellent schools to teach finance. Professor Frank C. Jen helped me get a job at the University of Georgia in 1973 and also helped me get recruited by the University of Illinois at Urbana-Champaign in 1976. E. Han Kim was hired by Ohio State University in 1974 and then moved to the University of Michigan. In 1975, the University of Wisconsin, Madison hired both Lemma Senbet and Stanley Kong.

Since we graduated, my classmates and I have published many research papers. The research productivity of our group has been rated as the top three most productive Ph.D. classes during the last 43 years. From these experiences I finally realized that financial research needs command in the depths of knowledge in finance, accounting, economics, and statistics.

During the last 43 years of advising Ph.D. students I have always suggested and recommended they have strong training in the areas of finance, accounting, economic theory, econometrics and statistics. Eventually I found that my Ph.D. students always benefited from this kind of in-depth education. I found that most students spend about 60 percent of their time taking courses and 40 percent of their time writing their dissertations.

Now I will discuss my own experiences in determining my Ph.D. dissertation topic. I have one master's degree in economics and another in statistics. In addition, I have five years of experience in banking. I was able to use this experience to help determine my dissertation topic. As I mentioned previously, I decided on my dissertation topic within three months after I started my Ph.D. program in 1970.

Since I realized what kind of knowledge I needed in order to complete my dissertation I decided to take more courses and seminars in statistics, finance, and economic theory during my two years and 10 months at SUNY-Buffalo. Besides taking the required courses I took a 16-credit statistics course, a four-credit time-series course, four credits of stochastic calculus and eight credits of multivariate statistics. In addition, I took a 12-credit finance Ph.D. seminar, a four-credit graduate investment analysis class, and a four-credit graduate corporate finance course. All of these extra courses helped me finish my degree in less than three years. From my dissertation I published four papers. I am planning to publish a fifth paper from my dissertation. The success of my thesis is partially due to my extra training in economics, finance, and statistics. This experience helps me advise my Ph.D. students to take extra courses if they have time.

When I taught seminar courses and advised Ph.D. students, I recommended my students read as many academic papers as possible and write review papers in accordance with his or her interests. From the first paper, students can develop his or her dissertation accordingly. While students are writing their dissertations I encourage them to use both theory and methodology as much as possible. In other words, I suggest they strike a balance among the data, theory, and methodology.

When I supervise my Ph.D. students' dissertations I use pressure, in addition to encouragement, to enhance the effectiveness of their writing. One of the hurdles for students writing a thesis is that many are hesitant when they first begin. However, I have found that they like to come to my office and present their ideas and empirical results. This kind of approach is neither useful nor effective. Therefore, I suggest to them that they write down their ideas and give them to me first. After I review their papers I can effectively discuss their dissertations and give the necessary comments.

I also tell them not to be hesitant with questions; however, I do not accept speculative thesis questions. I tell them that talk is cheap and that I am a scholar who comes from a background of both Chinese and American education. I believe that taking action is the best way to learn finance; therefore, writing a dissertation is one of the best ways to learn about finance or financial accounting.

After finishing his or her dissertation I allow students to go back to revise and improve their work within a limited time period. Most of my students finish their theses within four to five years. None have taken more than five years. I strongly believe their dissertation should not take a long time to finish. Since finance and financial accounting is not pure science training, they are not necessarily always going to have a definite answer. Therefore, students with sufficient training in the method and application are deserving of a Ph.D. degree.

Shortly after I started teaching at UGA, one of the Ph.D. students in the Statistics Department, Son-nan Chen, finished his Ph.D. in statistics and could not find a suitable job. I asked his advisor, Professor Backman, to give him a $7,000 stipend per year and I became his postdoctoral advisor. His postdoctoral dissertation was entitled "Statistical Distribution of Sharpe, Treynor and Jensen Measures." We wrote three papers from his dissertation. The first one was published in *Management Science* in 1981. The second paper was published in *Quarterly Review in Economics and Business* in 1985. Finally, the third paper was published in *Management Science* in 1986. From all of these publications, I helped him find a teaching job at Virginia Polytechnic Institute and State University. He then went on to teach at University of Maryland and National Cheng-Chi University, Taiwan.

From this experience, I found Ph.D. statistics could be used effectively in finance research. One year later, I had another Ph.D. student in economics, Carl R. Chen, also from the University of Georgia. After he wrote several good finance papers with me I found him a job at Dayton University where he is currently a chair professor. For his academic career, I helped him establish a journal entitled *International Review in Economics and Finance*. He is currently one of my associate editors for my journal, *Review of Quantitative Finance and Accounting.*

The University of Illinois at Urbana-Champaign hired me as an associate professor in 1976 and I stayed there until 1988 when Rutgers University hired me. My time at UIUC was the most exciting academic period where I could do my own research and train Ph.D. students.

The first four students I taught at UIUC were Duane Stock, David Smith, D. Mohamed, and M.J. Sandretto. All four of them had taken my first seminar at UIUC in the fall of 1976. Duane Stock wrote his dissertation on municipal bonds, David Smith had applied simultaneous equation technology in financial accounting research, and D. Mohamed wrote his dissertation on dividend policy by using mixed partial adjustment and adaptive expectation method to generalize a traditional dividend-forecasting model. After M.J. Sandretto graduated UIUC he taught at Harvard University.

My 1979 seminar class had one of the most successful groups of students I ever taught. Vic Bernard began his career at the University of Michigan; Randy Beatty and Vic Defeo began their careers at Wharton School of Business; Steve Sefcik began his career at the University of Washington, Seattle; Tom Shafer began his career at Florida State University; and Mike Alderson began his career at Texas A&M. Of them all, one of the most well-known was Vic Bernard. I had suggested that he consider a dissertation topic in the area of inflation. Later on, after he published a paper from his dissertation in the *Journal of Finance*, I recommended that he do research in the integrated field of finance and accounting. He later published several top journal articles in this field and became one of the most well-known professors in financial accounting before passing away in 1995. To memorialize Bernard's contributions to the field, his previous professors and classmates set up a scholarship at the University of Illinois in his name.

When I started my new journal entitled *Review of Quantitative Finance and Accounting* in 1991, I invited one of the most established accounting professors at the time, James Ohlson, to be one of my associate editors. At first he hesitated to accept my invitation; however, he ended up accepting my invitation after I told him one of my previous students, Vic Bernard, was going to be one of my associate editors as well. This story implies how good students can indirectly help his or her professor.

Another very memorable student from the 1979 seminar was Randy Beatty. Randy called me two years after starting his career at Wharton to ask me if I could help him find a job at either Northwestern University or the University of Chicago. I asked him why he was trying to change his job so quickly, and he responded by telling me his girlfriend worked at the University of Chicago and he wanted to be closer to her by working at one of the top universities in Chicago. I immediately called my friend, Professor Robert Hamada, who is the Dean of the Business School at the University of Chicago, and Bob offered Randy a visiting professor position at the university. Three years later, Purdue University attempted to hire Randy as an associate professor in accounting and he asked me whether or not he should accept the job. I told him that he should not leave the University of Chicago unless he was being offered a job as a full professor. A few years later, the University of Southern California wanted to hire him as an associate professor and he called me again to ask whether or not he should accept. I gave him the same answer as I had told him when Purdue called him. Randy listened to me patiently and waited, and he then was offered a chair position at Southern Methodist University, which he accepted. Because of my advice, Randy's career took off and both he and his wife appreciated my continued advice to him. This story taught me that a scholar should only change his job with some sort of long-term strategy and patience in mind.

I also had many successful experiences in training foreign Ph.D. students. My class of 1984 had many foreign students in particular. Among them were John K. Wei, Chen-Chin Chu, Dong Hang, David Chen, Kevin C.W. Chen, Seong Cheol Gweon, and Chunchi Wu. I recruited John Wei from Taiwan when I was there in 1980. The reason I wanted to bring him to Illinois was that I found his quantitative background to be outstanding, although his command of the English language was not great. I strongly believe that John's dissertation, which was related to asset pricing, was one of the top five dissertations I have been involved with in the last 43 years. He has published papers for *Management Science* with me and in the journal *Financial and Quantitative Analysis* (JFQA). Another coauthor of the JFQA paper was Chunchi Wu. Chunchi has written more than 10 papers with me, which included publications in JFQA, *The Accounting Review*, and the *Journal of Econometrics*. John Wei is currently a chair professor at Hong Kong Science and Technology University, and Chunchi is currently a chair professor at the State University of New York at Buffalo.

Overall my experience in training Ph.D. students in finance and accounting, can be summarized as follows:

1. Since finance is an interdisciplinary area, students should gain as much knowledge as possible in economics, accounting, econometrics, statistics, mathematics, computer science, and operations research.
2. Students should read as much academic literature as possible and write review and critique papers to improve their knowledge in the area of finance and accounting. Hopefully students can find a research topic for their own dissertation.
3. I would recommend that students' dissertations strike a balance between theory, methodology, and data analysis.

4. Students should realize that learning by doing is the best strategy to push forward their dissertation writing; therefore they should start to use updated methodology to analyze their data and integrate with sound theory.
5. After taking heed of the previous suggestions, students should carefully write their dissertation, and then most likely they will gain a rewarding progress. In case they encounter a hurdle, they should try to use all different kinds of approaches to overcome this obstacle.

A famous Chinese poem, written by a well-known scholar, Lu You of China's Southern Song Dynasty, says, "After endless mountains and rivers that leave doubt whether there is a path out, suddenly one encounters the shade of a willow, bright flowers and a lovely village." This poem implies that when you face a difficult moment in your life you should not give up and you should try, try, and try again and finally one day you will see the light and succeed. I believe that this poem applies to Ph.D. students in both finance and accounting and suggests that they should try hard for their research even if they face difficulties, and one day they will see the light and find success in their research. Even more so, this poem has similar implications for professors in both finance and accounting in their own research.

Chapter

9

Innovative and Active Approach to Teaching Finance

In Chapter 7, I discussed the teaching methods and educational philosophy and in Chapter 8, I explained how I trained Ph.D. students in finance and accounting. In this chapter, I will discuss and present my experiences using an innovative and active approach to teaching finance. This experience comes not only from my teaching in the classroom, but also from writing and editing textbooks, editing journals, consulting, and organizing conferences. I believe finance is based upon the knowledge of accounting, mathematics, economics, statistics, and computer technology. Therefore, I use this kind of view to teach not only undergraduate and master's students, but also to teach Ph.D. students in finance, accounting, and economics. The goals of training Ph.D. students in finance are to command the capacity and ability to do meaningful research, to learn how to effectively teach undergraduate, master's, and Ph.D. students, and to learn the knowledge that can make them capable and effective individuals in the finance industry.

If we review the history of business schools in the United States, the first Department of Finance was started at the University of Illinois at Urbana-Champaign in 1964. I was hired there in 1976 to improve the quality of research, teaching, and services. I was assigned to complete the following:

1. Move finance education from a qualitative approach to a quantitative approach.
2. Start a master's program in finance and improve the quality of the Ph.D. program.
3. Propose an interdisciplinary approach to the Ph.D. program (i.e. integrate finance with economics or accounting).

During my time at UIUC, I was able to achieve these goals, and I was later hired by Rutgers University at New Brunswick to set up a new Department of Finance to mimic the UIUC program.

In August 1988, I came to Rutgers University with the help of Professor Oded Palmon and others. We set up the Department of Finance based on three principles: a quantitative approach, a project approach, and an internship approach. Since Rutgers University is adjacent to the global center of finance, students have a higher chance of obtaining internships than at UIUC, which is located in a remote area. To my best knowledge, when UIUC set up their land-grant university, they tried to find a location at the center of the state, surrounded by farmland to allow students to focus and study.

Both the University of Georgia and UIUC are flagship universities. The students at these universities have an outstanding high school background, and their mathematical knowledge is better than the average high school students. Since the education level of New Jersey high schools is just as good as Illinois and Georgia, a state university like Rutgers University therefore has an advantage, as far as location is concerned. I believe we should fully utilize and glorify their quantitative background. A person's IQ is partially born with them; it also known that IQs can be improved by exposed training. I believe quantitative training can improve a student's IQ. Without analytical training, students cannot perform well in their jobs. In addition, applying computer programming to student projects can also enhance students' IQs and make them more marketable in the job market.

When I was in Illinois, I started to use a project approach to teach my undergraduate and MBA students. During that time, students used to go to the library, copy accounting and stock price data information from financial data publications, keypunch it into cards, and run statistical analyses on main frames. After they analyzed the data, they would write a term project and present it in class.

It is often said that the best way to learn is by doing. Understanding how textbook concepts and theories can be applied to real world situations is essential. Making this connection is what sets one job candidate apart from another. After students complete their projects, they are almost ready to understand the foundations of how companies work. I incorporated a project approach in all my courses, where students have to perform case scenarios of various financial topics to specific companies, and ultimately analyze components and statistics of the company.

During the last 43 years, I have taught the following courses: Investment Analysis, Futures and Options, Asset Pricing and Portfolio Analysis, and Corporate Finance. In each course, students are required to work on a term project comparing the various financial topics of either two or three companies. The following is a discussion on the investment analysis course based upon the syllabus in Appendix 9A.[1] This syllabus is divided into four parts: Part I states both required and reference textbooks used for the course, Part II reviews the grading policy, Part III goes over the topics which are covered in the course, and Part IV is the table of contents for the course project.

From the projects' tables of contents and the syllabi presented in this autobiography's website (http://www.worldscientific.com/worldscibooks/10.1142/10182), we can see how these three courses are interrelated. For example, there is a 30 percent overlap between Investment Analysis and Futures and Options and a 25 percent overlap

[1] In the website for this autobiography (http://www.worldscientific.com/worldscibooks/10.1142/10182), we will discuss not only investment analysis, but also futures and options, asset pricing and corporate finance courses.

between Investment Analysis and Asset Pricing and Portfolio Analysis. There is certainly a relative overlap between all three courses. I believe Futures and Options is the most important course for finance majors. This course teaches students new concepts, theories, and methodologies. The topics covered in Futures and Options applies to other financial courses. In other words, Futures and Options is just like soy sauce, which is used to cook many Chinese dishes.

In 2013, I published a book, *Security Analysis, Portfolio Management, and Financial Derivatives*, with my son, daughter, Professor Finnerty, and Professor Wort. This book was designed for three different courses — Investment Analysis, Portfolio Management, and Futures and Options with some supplemental materials.

In addition to the book mentioned above, I wrote some supplemental chapters to support our textbook. Books, such as the *Encyclopedia of Finance*, which I edited with my daughter, Alice C. Lee, and a statistics book, which I wrote with both my son and daughter, are also used to supplement the classes. This kind of innovative and active teaching approach is not only beneficial to students, but it also helps me improve my own knowledge about company analyses.

Using the required textbook and supplement materials, I lecture about the above-mentioned courses as follows.

1. Use extensive and complete PowerPoint presentations in lectures on the material.
2. Ask students to review the PowerPoint presentations and read the textbook.
3. Assign homework based on the textbook.
4. Bring students to computer labs and show them how to collect accounting and financial data, and to use Excel programs to do their projects.
5. Make students write the term project in accordance with the project outlines mentioned above and those presented in Appendix 9A.

Every semester I give two exams. Each exam includes a take home test, which is worth 25 percent and a class test, which is worth 75 percent. The take home test portion contains one or two essay questions and one derivation question, which asks students to apply calculus to derive some equations. The take home portion allows students to work with each other as well as my assistant and myself.

I also frequently teach Corporate Finance. I have written three books related to corporate finance; they are *Essentials of Financial Management*, *Corporate Finance*, and *Financial Analysis Planning and Forecasting: Theory and Application.*

In my experience, these four courses are interrelated. The Investment Analysis course is a prerequisite course for both Futures and Options and Asset Pricing and Portfolio Analysis. In the investment course, we need to teach students about the financial instruments and markets. Then we need to review students' accounting knowledge and their knowledge of finance theories and methods, which they learned from the financial management course. It is important to ask students to collect data on stock prices and the market index in order to calculate stock rates of returns. Then based upon their statistical knowledge and Excel program techniques, students need to calculate the average return, standard deviation, and skewness, and then they need to perform a risk return trade off analysis.

I use 12 chapters to cover all of the topics students need to know to have an understanding of investment analysis. A more detailed look at the content I cover in Investment Analysis can be found in Appendix 9A. In Chapter 1, we cover financial markets and financial instruments, which students are required to know. In Chapter 2, we review four financial statements for a company and show students how regression analysis can be applied to analyze this financial data. In Chapter 3, we use stock price and stock index to show how rate of return and market rate of return can be calculated. In addition, the growth rate of a company is also discussed. Finally, I show students how standard deviation can be calculated and show how risk return trade off can be demonstrated. In Chapter 4, we discuss alternative finance theories, such as classical theory, neoclassical theory, CAPM, APT, and options and futures. In Chapter 5, we first discuss alternative corporate bond, which has been issued by a company, then we use alternative methods to evaluate corporate bonds. In Chapter 6, we show students how alternative market indexes such as Dow Jones Index and the S&P 500 index can be compiled. In addition, we also show how these market indexes can be used to calculate market rate of return and be applied to financial analysis.

In Chapter 7, I discuss how sources of risk can be defined and analyzed. First, I classify the corporate risk into business risk and financial risk, and then I show how total risk can be also classified into systematic risk and nonsystematic risk. The application of these risk classifications will be explicitly used in the next chapter. In Chapter 8, we discuss the concept of risk-aversion, capital asset allocation, and the Markowitz model. We first discuss the definition of risk-aversion, and then we discuss how capital asset can be allocated in a portfolio. Finally, we show how the Markowitz model can be used to calculate an optimal portfolio. In Chapter 9, we discuss how capital asset pricing model can be derived and applied in financial analysis. In addition, we show how beta coefficient can be estimated and forecasted in terms of two alternative methods. In Chapter 10, the definition of option is carefully defined. In addition, we also show how seven alternative option strategies can be formulated. In Chapter 11, we discuss option pricing theory and how they can be used to determine firm valuation. In this chapter we explicitly show how Black–Scholes option pricing model can be derived, then we show how the option instrument can be evaluated in terms of Black–Scholes model. Finally, in Chapter 12, we show students how technical, fundamental, and contrarian method can be used to analyze the value of securities. Then we discuss alternative mutual funds and finally we show how mutual fund performance can be analyzed and determined.

In this class, we not only require students to do homework, we also require students to write a term paper. This term paper includes six sections. Section A is an introduction describing the company and project framework. Section B is an analysis of the company's financial statement and a ratio analysis. Section C discusses rate of return, market models, and CAPM. In Section D, students perform a portfolio analysis and evaluation of the company they chose. Section E is dedicated to option strategy and valuation, and Section F is a summary and includes any concluding remarks. Finally, students should have a reference section to describe the references they used for their term paper. In this term paper students should use Excel to do their empirical results related to Section C, Section D, and Section E.

From my experience and subjective opinion, students can start to learn some financial data analysis right from their beginning statistics course. Since I believe this to be true, I wrote a book entitled *Statistics for Business and Financial Economics*, which was published in 1993, 2002, and again in 2013. To my best knowledge, this business statistics book is the only book using finance, accounting, and economic data throughout the whole book. From the table of contents in this book, which is presented in Appendix II, I suggest a project approach to teaching a statistics course. Overall I use this type of approach to teach investment analysis, asset pricing and portfolio analysis, futures and options, and corporate finance. From my personal experience, it is best to use a project approach instead of Harvard's case approach to teach finance courses because the project approach is more innovative and active for training students.

In general, there are two alternative methods for teaching finance: traditional method and case method. By using traditional method, teachers only lecture on the material from the textbook and assign homework. In addition, they require students to take two or three exams. For the case method, teachers present different cases and let student discuss all of the cases with supplement text materials. It also requires students to take some tests. It is clear that in the traditional method students don't have a chance to relate to the real world. However, the case method guides students to understand real world issues. Unfortunately, materials used for the case method are generally out of date. The innovative and active approach I mentioned in this chapter try to strike a balance between the traditional method and case method.

Now we will go one step further and discuss the advantages of my innovative and active approach to teaching finance. As previously mentioned, I ask students to complete some homework. In addition, I also require students to do a project to analyze two companies' accounting information, stock price information, and option and futures information. This project involves a 30- to 50-page term paper and must be written by a team of two students.

For example, in one of my classes, two students used Delta Air Lines and American Airlines, two well-known airlines in the U.S., as the companies for their project.

Based on data from 2013, the students used these two companies to make a comparison for financial analysis. In Section B, they calculated the financial ratios for each of the two companies and made a comparison. For example, the current ratio is calculated as the current asset divided by current liabilities. Delta Air Lines has a current ratio of 0.62 and American Airlines has a current ratio of 0.58. The current ratio is one of the liquidity ratios that are calculated from the information on the balance sheet and measure the relative strength of a firm's financial position. That is the liquidity is higher for Delta Air Lines than for American Airlines. For the leverage ratio, which is defined as debt to equity ratio, Delta Air Lines is 21.9 and American Airlines is 0.57. That means Delta uses more debt financing and bears a higher financial risk. In Section C, they estimated the beta coefficient by regressing the past monthly returns for each of these two companies on the S&P 500 index. The beta estimated for Delta is 0.76 and for American, 2.02. Thus, the systematic risk for American Airlines is higher than that of Delta Air Lines. Then by using the estimated beta, risk-free rate and market risk premium, they estimated the expected return by using CAPM for these two companies. The expected return for Delta Air Lines was 0.0158 and American Airlines was 0.0253. In Section D, they did the portfolio analysis that consists of Delta Air Lines and American Airlines by minimum variance approach, Markowitz Approach, and Sharpe Performance Measure Approach. In Section E, they constructed seven option strategies and evaluated the call and put option values for each of the two companies. The seven option strategies include: long/short straddle, spread (Bullish and Bearish by using Call and Put options), protective put, cover call, and collar. They evaluated the call and put option values by using the Black–Scholes Option Pricing Model and put-call parity. The call option value for Delta was 9.4 and American was 8.9. The put option value for Delta was 8.65 and American was 1.78. The hedge ratio was calculated by using the estimated call and put option values. The hedge ratio for Delta was 0.49 and American Airlines was 1.0. By definition, the hedge ratio is the number of shares of stock needed to buy for each call option sold. For Delta, 0.43 shares of the stock should be bought for each call option sold and for American Airlines, one share of stock should be bought for each call option sold. In conclusion, they found that while Delta Air Lines is doing better than American Airlines in that it has less debt, it still lacks in the total asset utilization area.

From the project discussed above students can actively learn the following knowledge. First, students learn how to collect data needed to analyze the companies, which are related to the course lecture materials. Second, students learn how to apply accounting and market information, such as stocks price and options price. The byproduct of the project for students is that they learn how to use statistics and Microsoft Excel, a program that is necessary to understand in order for students to find a job in the industry, to analyze the data. Finally, students write a complete project, from which they learn how to write and present the report. In Chapter 12 entitled, "Editing Journal and Writing Books," I will discuss how and why I wrote textbooks and reference books to be used for innovative and active teaching in finance.

Appendix 9A

Syllabus for Investment Analysis

I. Textbooks:

A. Required books:

1. *Security Analysis, Portfolio Management, and Financial Derivatives*

   by Cheng-Few Lee, Joseph Finnerty, John C. Lee, Alice C. Lee, and Donald Wort

   World Scientific Publishing, 2013

2. Supplement Chapter 1 Financial Markets and Financial Instruments

3. Supplement Chapter 2 Raising Equity Capital and Security Trading

B. Reference textbooks:

1. *Statistics for Business and Financial Economics*

   by Cheng-Few Lee, John C. Lee, and Alice C. Lee

   Springer, Third Edition, 2013

2. *Encyclopedia of Finance*

   by Cheng-Few Lee and Alice C. Lee

   Springer, Second Edition, 2013

II. Grading Policy

1st Exam..20%
Term Project..30%
2nd Exam..30%
Class Performance 10%
Homework assignments...............................10%

III. Topics to be covered:

1. Introduction: Financial Markets and Financial Instruments
   Lee *et al.*, Chapter 1 and Supplement Chapter 1
   1.1. Introduction of the Course
   1.2. Financial Markets
   1.3. Financial Instruments
   1.4. Money Markets

2. Accounting Information and Regression Analysis
   Lee *et al.*, Chapter 2
   Encyclopedia of Finance, Chapter 72

3. Common Stock: Return, Growth, and Risk
   Lee *et al.*, Chapter 3 and Supplement Chapter 2
   Encyclopedia of Finance, Chapter 64
   3.1. Raising Equity Capital
   3.2. Security Trading
   3.3. Return
   3.4. Growth Rate
   3.5. Risk

4. Introduction to Valuation Theories
   Lee *et al.*, Chapter 4
   Encyclopedia of Finance, Appendix A (Derivation of Dividend Discount Model)

5. Bond Valuation and Analysis
   Lee *et al.*, Chapter 5 and Supplement Chapter 1

6. The Uses and Calculation of Market Indexes
   Lee *et al.*, Chapter 6 and Supplement Chapter 1

7. Sources of Risks and Their Determination
   Lee *et al.*, Chapter 7

   Encyclopedia of Finance, Appendix E (Derivation of Minimum-Variance Portfolio)

   Encyclopedia of Finance, Appendix F (Derivation of an Optimal Weight Portfolio Using the Sharpe Performance Measure)

8. Risk-Aversion, Capital Asset Allocation, and Markowitz Model
   Lee *et al.*, Chapter 8

9. Capital Asset Pricing Model and Beta Forecasting
   Lee *et al.*, Chapter 9

   Encyclopedia of Finance, Appendix I (Derivation of Capital Market Line (CML))

   Encyclopedia of Finance, Appendix J (Derivation of Security Market Line (SML))

10. Options and Option Strategies
    Lee *et al.*, Chapter 16

    Statistics for Business and Financial Economics, Chapters 7 and 13

11. Option Pricing Theory and Firm Valuation
    Lee *et al.*, Chapter 17

12. Security Analysis and Mutual Fund Performance
    Lee *et al.*, Chapter 21

IV. Table of Contents for Investment Analysis Project

Title: Investment Analysis for Companies A and B

Section A: Introduction

1. Company Description
2. Project Framework

Section B: Financial Statement Analysis and Ratio Analysis

1. Procedure for Comparing Cash Flow Statement
2. Ratio Analysis
3. Ratio Analysis Interpretation

Section C: Rate of Return, Market Models, and CAPM

Section D: Portfolio Analysis and Evaluation

1. Equal Weights Method
2. Optimal Weights by Minimal Variance Approach
3. Optimal Weights by Markowitz Model

Section E: Option Strategy and Valuation

Section F: Summary and Concluding Remarks

References

Chapter

10

World Records in Academic Achievements

Since I came to the U.S. in 1968, my career has been progressing smoothly. I had my doctoral dissertation topic ready before I started my Ph.D. program at SUNY-Buffalo. This helped me complete my Ph.D. degree in a little less than three years even while taking 16 extra credit hours in finance and statistics. Completing the doctorate degree in such a short period was a school record. My hard work and the thought-provoking advice I received from my professors made it possible.

In fact, this was similar to Prof. Lee Teng-hui's experience that he told me about before I went abroad. Prof. Lee had also prepared his dissertation topic before he started his Ph.D. program at Cornell University. Therefore, he was able to finish his degree in three years and even won an award in 1968 for the best national doctoral dissertation from the American Association for Agricultural Economics.

In 1976, three years after I began teaching at the University of Georgia, the University of Illinois at Urbana-Champaign offered me a position as an associate professor because of my outstanding research and teaching performance at UGA. I was promoted to full professorship at UIUC two years later. At the time it was very rare that a business school faculty member could be promoted to full professorship so quickly. On average, a Ph.D. takes six years to get an associate professor post. UIUC promoted me to full professorship in just two years, not only because of my record at UGA, but also for my excellent outcome on re-organizing the doctoral curriculum and inviting well-known scholars to lecture on campus. Furthermore, the *Journal of Financial and Quantitative Analysis*, the second best U.S. financial journal, invited me to be one of its associate editors in 1977. Four years later in 1982 I became a distinguished professor at UIUC and have been known worldwide as a famous financial professor since then.

Professor Sawa from the Department of Economics and Professor Al Roth from the Department of Business Administration were also promoted from associate professor to full professor within two years at UIUC. Before I moved to Rutgers University in 1988, Professor Sawa went back to Japan and Professor Roth transferred to the University of Pittsburgh. Since then, Professor Roth has earned the Nobel Prize in Economics in 2012 while he was a professor at Harvard University. He won the prize for his work on his matching theory, which was based on the research of Lloyd Shapely, who also won the Nobel Prize in Economics in 2012. Currently, Professor Roth is teaching in the Department of Economics at Stanford University. Both professors were my friends while we worked together at UIUC.

Once I received a full professor position, I started to write and edit books. I edited *Readings in Investment Analysis* in 1980 and *Financial Analysis and Planning: Theory and Application, A Book of Readings* in 1983. I also published *Financial Analysis and Planning: Theory and Application* in 1985, which was published by Edison-Wesley (World Scientific published the second edition of this book in 2009, which was coauthored with John Lee and Alice Lee). In 1986, with James B. Kau and C.F. Sirmans, I published *Urban Econometrics — Model Development and Empirical Results*, which became a required reading for studying urban econometrics.

In 1990, *Corporate Finance: Theory, Method, and Applications* was published with my UIUC colleague, Prof. Joseph E. Finnerty. This was a financial analysis textbook based on accounting. Its Russian version was published in 1999. In the same year, with Professors Joseph E.

Finnerty and Donald H. Wort, I also published *Security Analysis and Portfolio Management.* (The second edition of this book was published in 2013. The new title is *Security Analysis, Portfolio Management, and Financial Derivatives*. Both John Lee and Alice Lee coauthored this book as well.) Additionally, I cowrote *Foundations of Financial Management* with Joseph E. Finnerty and Edgar A. Norton in 1997. This book was translated into Chinese in 2004. Thanks to these publications, I gained a reputation in the field of financial textbook writing.

When I moved to Rutgers University in 1988, I began to write a business statistics book on the applications of finance, accounting, and economics. This textbook, *Statistics for Business and Financial Economics*, was published in 1993. My son, John, wrote the applicable computer materials for the book, while my daughter, Alice, compiled the multiple choice and true and false questions for the test bank. When the second edition was published, in August 1999, it was coauthored with my children. Writing a book together allowed us to learn from each other as well as form a closer bond.

Between 1973 and 2016, I published more than 225 academic papers that focus on both theoretical and empirical research in the journals of various fields, such as finance, accounting, economics, management science, and statistics. Before my papers were published, I presented most of them at U.S. or international conferences. Some of these were the annual conventions of American Finance Association, American Accounting Association, American Statistical Association, Econometrics Society, Financial Management Association, Western Finance Association, and European Financial Management Association. I did this so other scholars would recognize my research before it was published. This proved to be a very efficient way to advertise my research and also created opportunities to get acquainted with other professionals. I had written some of these papers by myself; however, most were written with my Ph.D. students, colleagues, or friends. The cooperation with other scholars made our research more enjoyable.

In my experience, a good business school scholar will research both theoretical and empirical topics, so his or her research will be well developed and balanced. In other words, theoretical research may be more challenging, while the research on real cases are more practical and helpful for consulting jobs.

In October 2008, I was invited to give a one-week lecture at University of Zaragoza, Zaragoza, Spain. The mission of this visit to teach Ph.D. students and faculty how to do research. My wife Schwine went with me to visit Zaragoza. We enjoyed visiting the city, especially a very famous church there.

In 2009 I was invited to present a paper at a conference in memory of Professor Han Levy's 70th birthday, which was held in Jerusalem, Israel. Professor Levy is the same age as me and is also one of the associate editors of *Review of Finance and Quantitative Accounting*. This was my first time visiting Israel. During the trip I had the chance to visit Tel Aviv and the Dead Sea.

In April 2013 I was invited to give a lecture at Stockholm University and I brought my wife along with me. This gave us the chance to travel around the beautiful city of Stockholm. We discovered that Sweden's economy was very well off and the people lived a peaceful life.

Since I was well trained in accounting, economics, finance, and statistics, most of my research was interdisciplinary. My textbooks and published papers all focused on several fields of study, which allowed them to expand the topic and findings on a greater level. Research that covers more than one area can enhance a researcher's knowledge and widen his or her point of view, allowing him or her to become better at teaching and research. I try my best to incorporate my interdisciplinary skills while teaching, writing papers and books, and organizing conferences.

In the United States, the American Finance Association and Financial Management Association are the two national financial associations. There are also five regional financial associations in the U.S. In 1985, Prof. Joseph E. Finnerty, my UIUC colleague, and I co-edited *The Financial Review*, the Eastern Finance Association's publication. To improve the publication's quality and reputation, we contacted our friends and other scholars to help us bring in the Mid-west Finance Association to support it as well. I also invited my teachers Frank C. Jen and Andrew H. Chen, my student Prof. Son-nan Chen, and my classmates Lemma W. Senbet and E. Han Kim as the associate editors to strengthen the editorial board. Other famous scholars included on the board were the Nobel Prize laureate Harry M. Markowitz and R. Kihlstrom of the Wharton School of the University of Pennsylvania. Having worked our hardest and with persistence for six years, the previously obscure journal had finally become a publication known around the world by the time we retired from the editorial board in 1991.

To keep up with practical needs and future development, I innovated the field of financial planning and analysis by publishing *Advances in Financial Planning and Forecasting* (AFPF) with JAI Press in 1986. I also edit these four annuals even until now: *Advances in Quantitative Analysis of Finance and Accounting* (AQAFA), *Advances in Investment Analysis and Portfolio Management* (AIAPM), and *Advances in Pacific Basin Business, Economics, and Finance* (APBBEF), which are all published by the same company. Although the editing jobs keep me busy, I enjoy being involved in them.

In 1987, UIUC invited Prof. R. Arnold and myself to edit and improve the quality of the traditional journal, *Quarterly Review of Economics and Business*. First I renamed the journal to *Quarterly Review of Economics and Finance*, and then I strengthened its editorial board and required a higher standard of quality for its publications. The reputation and quality of this journal had improved greatly when I transferred the editing job to Prof. Joseph E. Finnerty in 1989. That same year I finished my employment with UIUC. Although I left UIUC, my colleagues and the graduates appreciated my contributions to the school. They wondered how a first generation immigrant could present such excellent, comprehensive contributions to UIUC. They called it an academic miracle.

In 1988, Hong Kong University of Science and Technology (HKUST) invited me to serve as their first dean of the business school. However, I just moved from University of Illinois to Rutgers University, therefore, I couldn't take a leave to serve as dean for that school. If they asked me to consider this position when I was still teaching at the University of Illinois, then I could've taken a three-year leave to try out this new appointment. One of the main reasons HKUST was so eager to ask me to be their dean was because of my prestige and experience in the area of finance. In addition, during that period, there were very few senior Chinese professors teaching at the business school in the United States. However, my previous two Ph.D. students, Kevin Chen and Jung K.C. Wei, are their chair professors in accounting and finance, respectively.

In 1990, I signed a contract with Kluwer Academic Publishers, a publisher in Holland, to edit the *Review of Quantitative Finance and Accounting*. Since this new journal was set to debut in March 1991, I decided to stop editing *The Financial Review* that year. The editorial board for this journal was extended from the original team of *The Financial Review*. Eight more famous accounting professors were recruited for the board. Among them, Randolph P. Beatty and Chunchi Wu, who were my students; Lawrence H. Summers, the former U.S. Treasury Secretary, and other famous scholars from MIT, Columbia University, New York University, University of California at Berkeley, Northwest University, and the Wharton School of the University of Pennsylvania.

This journal accepted papers with useful theoretical and methodological results with support of interesting empirical applications on accounting, economics, and quantitative methods. The *Review of Quantitative Finance and Accounting* helped to set up a field of comprehensive knowledge combining finance, accounting, economics, and statistics. I believe that my academic reputation has been enhanced in conjunction with the publication of this journal. In recent years RQFA has been ranked one of the top 23 journals in the area of finance.

In 1997, when I lectured at Nanyang Technological University, Singapore, Dr. Kok Khoo Phua, Chairman and Editor-in-Chief of World Scientific Publishing Company, invited me to publish a book with them. I signed contracts to publish the second edition of *Statistics for Business and Financial Economics* and a quarterly journal. The new journal was named *Review of Pacific Basin Financial Markets and Policies*, and it debuted in March 1998.

The *Review of Pacific Basin Financial Markets and Policies* deals with interdisciplinary research on financial policies and financial markets. It covers many countries, such as the U.S., Taiwan, Japan, Korea, and

Mainland China. During 1998 and 1999, many papers regarding the Pacific Basin financial centers, Asian Financial Crisis, risk management in banking systems, and related to Taiwan's financial markets and policies were published in the journal.

Currently, I am the editor of two quarterly journals and four annual publications that cover the theories, empirical methods, and policies on finance, accounting, and economics. I spend at least 25 hours every week editing these journals. To edit these journals and annual publications I have assistants in both the U.S. and Taiwan helping me to expedite this process. Before the creation of email, the correspondence between the author and the editor relied upon airmail, which is costly. Email made it easier to communicate with both my assistants in the U.S. and Taiwan. It also made it easier for me to correspond with the author.

Since 1997, besides the business statistics book, I also published the second edition of *Financial Analysis and Planning: Theory and Application*. In addition, I published a book titled *Security Analysis, Portfolio Management and Financial Derivatives* with Joseph Finnerty, John Lee, Alice Lee, and Donald Wort in 2013. The third edition of *Financial Analysis, Planning & Forecasting: Theory and Application* was published in May 2016. In April 2016, Dr. Kok Khoo Phua invited me to edit a book series related to financial econometrics and statistics for his company. I am currently considering this opportunity. During our correspondence, he decided that my *Memoirs of a Finance Professor on Academia, Practice, and Policy* should be published, and he immediately assigned a senior editor to be in charge of this book.

In 1998, it was my second time visiting the School of Accountancy and Business as a Shaw Foundation professor. During both visits, I taught Ph.D. seminars and courses for master's students. In addition, I also did research with Professor Gillian Yeo, Sheng-Syan Chen, Keshab Shrestha, and others at the school. I was a Ph.D. committee member for the Ph.D. dissertations of Kim Wai Ho, Kim Wai Lee, and others. In addition, I also invited an external examiner for both master's and Ph.D. students.

In 1997 and 2002, I held my fifth and tenth Pacific Basin Finance, Economics, and Accounting conferences at Nanyang Technological University, respectively. During these two visits, Professor Gillian Yeo,

Khee Giap Tan, and Soon Beng Chew became my good friends. Gillian Yeo was head of the Division of Banking and Finance in 1997 and 1998. Currently, she is the associate dean of the Nanyang Technological University. Gillian Yeo was the associate editor of *Review of Pacific Basin Financial Markets and Policies* for more than 10 years and she attended my Pacific Basin Conferences frequently. I had a very close relationship with Soon Beng Chew when I visited Nanyang Technological University. Overall, I have a lot of contributions in the area of finance to the school of accountancy in Nanyang Technological University.

Professor Khee Giap Tan taught at Nanyang Technological University and is currently an associate professor at Lee Kuan Yew School of Public Policy, co-director of Asia Competitiveness Institute, and he is the chair at Singapore National Committee for Pacific Economic Cooperation. During the last 19 years, Professor Tan and I have developed a very close relationship in both our personal and academic lives. About 10 years ago, Tan brought me to visit Myanmar under the IMF project. In addition, he brought my wife and me to visit his parents in Malacca, Malaysia in 2014. Malacca is a beautiful city and has a lot of Chinese influence. Each time I traveled to the city I enjoyed my visit. Professor Tan is currently one of my associate editors for my journal *Review of Pacific Basin Financial Markets and Policies*. Recently, I attended his conferences on Chinese policy in 2015 and 2016.

Professor Tan is a famous macroeconomist and an expert on Chinese and ASEAN's economies. I have invited him to deliver a keynote speech at my NCTU international finance conferences in both 2015 and 2016. Currently, he is also an advisor for President Tsai Ing-wen's new southbound economic strategy.

Besides teaching, researching, writing books, and editing journals, I also organize three annual conferences. The first one is the conference for Society on Economics and Management in Pacific Basin Countries (SEMPB). SEMPB is a section member of the famous National Social Science Association that holds its convention in different U.S. cities at the beginning of every year. For example, one year the conference covered how to reform financial markets and improve the quality of the financial industry and prevent the hot money from interfering with the foreign exchange market. In addition, the convention also discussed how to upgrade the high tech industry.

Next, to enhance the interdisciplinary research of finance and accounting and also to meet the need of *Review of Quantitative Financial and Accounting*, I started the annual Conferences on Financial Economics and Accounting (FEA) in 1990 at Rutgers University. The goal of this conference was to bring together famous financial and accounting professionals to explore and discuss up-to-date research. There were many people who helped initialize this conference. The greatest contributors included: Prof. Frank C. Jen of SUNY-Buffalo, Profs. Martin Gruber and Kose John of New York University, Prof. Edwin Burmeister of Virginia University, Prof. Jack C. Francis of City University of New York, Prof. Stephen Ross of Yale University, Profs. Richard Kihlstrom and Robert E. Verrecchia of the Wharton School of the University of Pennsylvania, Profs. Victor Bernard and E. Han Kim of Michigan University, Prof. James C. Mckeown of Penn. State University, Prof. Vihang Errunza of McGill University, Dr. Todd Petzel of the Chicago Mercantile Exchange, and Profs. Bikki Jaggi, Ivan Brick, and Kenneth Lawrence of Rutgers University. Without their help, the conference would not have been possible.

Three days before the first FEA conference was held, the Nobel Prize Committee announced that the 1990 Nobel Prize in Economics winners were three financial professors, H. Markowitz, M. Miller, and W.F. Sharpe. Immediately, I decided to add a panel discussion during the luncheon on the first day to explore the significance of the Nobel Prize being awarded to financial scholars. Prof. Stephen Ross of Yale University hosted the discussion. The conclusion from this discussion and the written feedback from the attendants were all published in the *Review of Quantitative Finance and Accounting*, volume l, number 2 (June, 1991).

Since the conference was such a success, I managed to set up a conference executive committee, which was composed of six universities that took turns hosting the conference every year. From 1990 to 1996, the conferences have been held at Rutgers University, SUNY-Buffalo, New York University, Washington University in St. Louis, University of

Michigan, and University of Maryland. In 1997 and 1998, the seventh, eighth, and the ninth conferences were held at Rutgers University, SUNY-Buffalo, and NYU, respectively. In 1998 when the committee meeting was held at NYU, the executive committee agreed to include University of Texas-Austin into our consortium and to hold the 10th FEA conference in Austin on October 29–30, 1999. (A list of the host universities, program chairs, and the keynote speakers of the previous conferences on Financial Economics and Accounting (FEA) can be found at http://www.worldscientific.com/worldscibooks/10.1142/10182#t=suppl.)

Currently the FEA conference is a consortium of Rutgers University, NYU, University of Texas-Austin, USC, Indiana University, Maryland University, Georgia State University, University of Toronto, Temple University, and Tulane University.

Over the past 26 years, all of the research papers presented at this conference were excellent and all the keynote speakers were famous scholars in the fields of finance and accounting. Each year the conference brings together financial and accounting scholars from around the world to discuss the latest in finance and accounting. FEA is well admired and recognized as a distinctive conference with the highest quality of interdisciplinary research on finance and accounting. It is only with the help of my teachers, students, colleagues, and friends in these academic institutes that this conference has been such a great success.

In 1993, to enhance the financial, economic, and business research in the Pacific Basin countries, I initiated the first conference on Pacific Basin Finance, Economics, and Accounting (PBFEA) at Rutgers University. The makeup of the PBFEA conference papers is that about 60 percent are academic papers and 40 percent are empirical and policy papers. Since the first PBFEA conference was a success, I decided to hold the next conference in Asia. In 1993 and 1994, I served as the visiting distinguished professor at the Chinese University of Hong Kong, and they allowed me to hold the 2nd PBFEA conference in Hong Kong in May 1994. The conference's coordinator was Prof. Shao-ping Chiang and the keynote speaker was Dr. K.C. Leong, CEO of Hong Kong Exchange, who delivered the speech "Current Products of Futures Market in Hong Kong and the Future of Hong Kong Exchange," which was published in the annual *Advances in Pacific Basin Business, Economics, and Finance* (1996). The president of the Chinese University of Hong Kong, Dr. Kun Kao, also delivered his welcome remarks in the opening ceremony.

Professor Shao-ping Chiang, a professor at the Chinese University of Hong Kong, was my very good friend in both my academic and personal lives. Unfortunately, he passed away about 20 years ago. When I visited the Chinese University of Hong Kong, he and his wife helped me in many different aspects. During my visit, my main contribution to the Chinese University of Hong Kong was to teach finance courses and guide professors in doing research. In addition, I suggested the Department of Finance start a quantitative finance program; this program is the earliest quantitative finance program in Asia. To my knowledge, this program still does very well and is very profitable for the department.

Looking back to the past 43 years since 1973, with the help of the good timing, prime locations, and excellent personal relationships, I have completed many distinguished achievements in teaching, research, writing books, editing academic journals, and initiating and organizing conferences.

In addition to the previously mentioned conferences, in 1993, I started a Pacific Basin conference at Rutgers University. During the last 23 years, the conference has been held in Hong Kong, Singapore, Taiwan, Thailand, Australia, China, Vietnam, U.S., and Japan as indicated in the history of the conference below.

History of the Conference:

Year	Venue/Country	Host Organizer
1993	U.S.A.	Rutgers University, New Jersey
1994	Hong Kong	The Chinese University of Hong Kong, Hong Kong
1995	Taiwan	Taiwan Institute of Economic Research, Taipei
1996	U.S.A.	Rutgers University, New Jersey

Year	Venue/Country	Host Organizer
1997	Singapore	Nanyang Technological University, Singapore
1998	Hong Kong	Hong Kong Polytechnic University, Hong Kong
1999	Taiwan	National Taiwan University, Taipei
2000	Thailand	Chulalongkorn University, Bangkok
2001	U.S.A.	Rutgers University, New Jersey
2002	Singapore	Nanyang Technological University, Singapore
2003	Taiwan	National Chiao Tung University, Hsinchu
2004	Thailand	The Consortium of Thai Universities, Bangkok
2005	U.S.A.	Rutgers University, New Jersey
2006	Taiwan	Foundation of Pacific Basin Financial Research and Development

Year	Venue/Country	Host Organizer
2007	Vietnam	Ho Chi Minh City University of Technology, Ho Chi Minh City, Vietnam
2008	Australia	Queensland University of Technology, Brisbane, Queensland, Australia
2009	Thailand	University of the Thai Chamber of Commerce, Bangkok, Thailand
2010	China	Graduate University of Chinese Academy of Sciences, Beijing, China
2011	Taiwan	Foundation of Pacific Basin Financial Research and Development, Taiwan
2012	U.S.A.	Rutgers University, New Jersey
2013	Australia	Deakin University, Melbourne, Victoria, Australia
2014	Japan	Aichi University, Nagoya, Japan
2015	Vietnam	Saigon Technology University, Ho Chi Minh City
2016	Taiwan	National Chiao Tung University

Chapter

11

Traveling and Lecturing All Over the World

Since I received my Ph.D. in 1973, I have presented many research papers at conferences held in the United States and Canada. They include conferences for the American Finance Association, American Financial Management Association, American Economic Association, American Quantitative Economic Association, World Quantitative Association, American Accounting Association, American Statistical Association, and Western, Eastern, Central, Southern, Southwestern Finance Associations, as well as others. Presenting papers at conferences for these organizations has given me the opportunity to travel the world.

In the summer of 1980, on the way to the European Insurance Conference held in Geneva, Switzerland, Schwinne and I traveled to Germany and France as well. In the summer of 1982, we took a short trip to Europe for the European Finance Conference held in London. That same year, after joining the European Insurance Conference held in Rome, Italy, we traveled with Prof. Neil A. Doherty to attractions around the Vatican, Rome, and Florence. The following year, when I participated in the Chinese Enterprise Reform Meeting in Manchester, England, I took the chance to visit the University of Cambridge and the University of Oxford with Schwinne. After traveling in Europe,

I gained a better understanding of the origin of Western culture. I admired the beautiful sights and also envied the prevailing democratic politics in Europe. I hoped that Taiwan could enjoy the same freedom and democratic political systems someday.

In October 1982, I took my sabbatical and lectured on financial management at Wuhan University, China. My students were faculty of the university and managers of the Wuhan branches of China Commercial Bank. Whenever I mentioned the U.S. stock markets, my students would joke how there was no point in teaching about capital markets because they would never see stock markets in China. I could only reply by saying, "I hope you will have the opportunity to manage stock trading someday."

During my visit to Wuhan, I also conducted interviews for Min Tang's scholarship and recommended that he study at the University of Illinois. At the request of the Department of Economics, University of Illinois, Urbana-Champaign, I interviewed the applicant, Mr. Min Tang, to decide whether we should offer him a scholarship. After an extensive and careful interview, I found that Min Tang had a mathematics major. And his background is good enough to be granted a scholarship for him to study the Ph.D. program in economics. Therefore, I recommended the department to give him the scholarship. He came to the Department of Economics in 1984 and graduated in 1989. After he graduated from UIUC he was the senior economist of Asian Bank and currently he is an important economist for the Chinese Central Government. He is also one of the economic advisors to the Chinese Premier Li Keqiang. Min Tang's wife, Xiaolei Zuo, was also my student at UIUC. She is a famous economist in China and is currently doing economic research for the Chinese Government. In May 2014, both of them attended my policy conference that was held in Taipei. In this conference, Xiaolei Zuo delivered a keynote speech on financial markets in China.

Besides Min Tang, I have three other students who currently perform very well in China. They are Yi Gang, Yong Shi, and Guangping Zhang. Yi Gang, who is currently the Deputy Governor of the People's Bank of China, earned his Ph.D. in economics from Illinois. Yong Shi was my student at American Executive Training Center at Dalian in

1983. Since then I gave a lot of advice to his academic career regarding journal editing and conference organizing. He currently is Bai-Ren Distinguished Professor and Director of Key Laboratory of Big Data Mining and Knowledge Management, Chinese Academy of Sciences, China and Union Pacific Chair of Information Science and Technology, University of Nebraska at Omaha, U.S. In addition, he is currently one of the economics advisors for Premier Li Keqiang. Finally, Guangping Zhang was my postdoctoral student at Rutgers University in 1992. He is currently Deputy Director-General of CBRC (China Banking Regulatory Commission) in China.

Before I went to China, in October 1982, I decided to visit Hong Kong for two days. I took the chance to visit the Business School of the Chinese University of Hong Kong (CUHK) and spoke with Dean Jian-shu Min and some other professors. Later, I served on an external examination committee and also as an associate editor for its annual publication for CUHK.

When I left Hong Kong, I took the train to Guangzhou and then transferred to another train to Wuhan. I woke up one morning on the train and looked out of my window to find an amazing view of the rural area, south of the Yangtze River. It reminded me of Taiwan. During my stay in Wuhan, I lodged at the Donghu Hotel where Mao Zedong had visited many times before. Prof. Jun-Qian Hsu also invited me to try the famous delicacy of Yangtze River, Wuchang fish, which was said to be one of the most favored fish of Mao; he even wrote a poem about it. In my spare time, I visited many famous attractions and historic sites around the Wuhan area, such as Yueyang Tower, the site of the Wuchang Revolution, and many others.

At the end of my lectures, I flew directly to Beijing to go sightseeing. Mr. Yue-ning Zhu, whom I first met in 1981 when he visited UIUC, accompanied me to visit the Palace, Tiananmen Square, the Summer Palace, the Great Wall, the Thirteen Tombs of the Ming Dynasty, and other sites. He also took me to buy some beautiful jade decorations and silk products. It was a great pleasure to see so many unforgettable attractions and historic sites during my visit.

I also witnessed the slow economy and people's pessimistic attitude toward their jobs under the Communist Party of China. Prof. Hsu and Mr. Yue-ning Zhu told me how the Chinese government suppressed people and made their lives miserable during the Cultural Revolution. Prof. Hsu told me that he would try his best to help the country since he was lucky enough to have the opportunity to take part in Deng Xiaoping's reform. Mr. Yue-ning Zhu also mentioned that because he didn't want to lose the opportunity to get involved in the drafting of a document for economic reform, he postponed his ulcer operation and endured the pain. During our talks, I realized economic reform was possible and it was a must for China.

After my trip to Beijing, I visited Tokyo University to deliver lectures on theoretical and empirical issues of corporation dividend policies under the arrangement of Prof. K. Sato, one of my professors from SUNY-Buffalo. While in Tokyo, I visited the famous Tokyo Tower and Tokyo Imperial Palace. While there I bought a cultured pearl necklace for my wife. Since the exchange rate for the U.S. dollar to Japanese yen was 1:240, it was a good deal.

When I taught at Tokyo University, I became good friends with Prof. Yasuo Hoshino. He was very kind and picked me up at Tokyo International Airport and took me sightseeing around the Kyoto area. We even had an opportunity to call on one of my previous colleagues from UIUC, Prof. K. Morimune, who taught at Kyoto University. Whenever he visited UIUC or Rutgers University, he always stays at my house. Now, he is one of the associate editors of *Review of Pacific Basin Financial Markets and Policies*, of which I am the managing editor.

It was a wonderful experience visiting so many cities in China and Japan in just two months. At the same time, I was promoted to distinguished professor at UIUC. By then I was 43 and had lived in the United States for 14 years.

In July 1983, I taught a class in financial management at the Dalian Training Center for more than 100 managers. The Dalian Training Center was set up by the United States Department of Commerce and Dalian Institute of Technology, China after Deng Xiaoping visited the U.S. in 1979 and observed the productivity of American factories. He asked a representative at the factory he visited how to raise labor productivity.

The representative replied that their systems were only applicable in capitalist countries and not communist countries like China. In fall of the same year, the United States Department of Commerce sent a group of technical representatives to Beijing to discuss the technology support. The chief of the representatives clearly expressed that they were willing to help China train management experts. Although Chinese representatives worried that their staff might be affected by the capitalistic thinking after Western style training, they still reported the project to Deng Xiaoping. Surprisingly, the project was approved immediately.

During my time teaching at the Dalian Training Center there were two professors helping me organize my teaching materials. From these materials, one of the professors completed a financial management book in Chinese.

One day, I talked about the approaches of reform in class; I said that managerial staff should be open-minded and apply whatever they thought was good for economic development without caring about the origin of the thought whether it be from Marxism, Capitalism, or Chinese culture. My statement caused different reactions among students. Some open-minded students agreed with my view, while other conservative students opposed and suggested the school not have me teach them. Due to the insistence from the American dean, the school let me finish my teaching.

Dr. Yong Shi, a distinguished professor at University of Nebraska, was one of my students. His openness was quite obvious in the class. He asked me if fuzzy mathematics could be applied to the research of investment policies with uncertainty. Years later, we completed a paper together and presented at the 8th Conference of Fuzzy Mathematics held in August 1999 at the Grand Hotel, Taipei.

During my stay in Dalian, I was invited to the Beijing Automobile Factory to deliver a short course on the concepts of Western compound accounting and its applications in management for more than 100 accounting and economic staff. At that time, most Chinese companies used simple bookings or plus/minus accounting developed during the Cultural Revolution. No one used the Western compound journal entry. I told my students that although they might feel trivial about the job they were doing now, along with the economic growth, one day they would become more important. After 20 years of economic reformation, the accounting managers received well-paying jobs and high respects in China. Some famous universities, such as Tsinghua University, Shanghai University of Finance and Economics, and Xiamen University have set up accounting colleges to cultivate accountants and Ph.D.s in accounting.

Between 1985 and 1987, I taught in China three times. In 1985, I taught at the management colleges in Guangzhou and Lanzhou as the representative of World Bank. My daughter accompanied me to Lanzhou and we visited several famous landmarks. Later, I lectured for the general managers of enterprises and chairmen of provincial and municipal economic councils at the Dalian Training Center. President Chang of Wuhan Steel was one of my most famous students. Through this experience, I learned a lot about the management concepts of the Chinese enterprises from high-level financial managers. Once, the deputy chairman of Economic Council, Yen-lin Zhang, told me "We have taken huge risks in doing the reform. If the reform had failed, we would either be killed or put into jail. China has never succeeded in reformation since Shang Yang (390–338 BC) of Qin Dynasty.[1] We do hope that you and other overseas scholars can help us to succeed in this economic reform."

After speaking with him, I analyzed the deficiencies of the Chinese economic system and expressed the necessity of change in my lectures. Now every time I deliver short courses in China, I adjust the content and direction of my teaching in accordance with Mr. Zhang's saying.

In 1987, after finishing my courses at the Dalian Training Center, I accepted Prof. Ru-Xun Li's invitation to teach financial management for corporate managers and faculty at Shanghai University of Finance and

[1] Shang Yang was a minister to Emperor Qin (Qinshi Huangdi). He suggested a lot of reforms for Qin Dynasty and contributed a lot to its success. Unfortunately, he was killed by Emperor Qin: his body was torn apart by five horses. Since then until Qing Dynasty, most of the reformers of every dynasty were either put in jail or killed by the emperor. Therefore, Yen-lin Zhang was asking whether Chinese reform could be successful or not. Fortunately, since 1983 until now, Chinese economic reform has been very successful and the total GDP of China is now only second to that of the U.S. I am really happy to see this kind of success. I also feel very good that my efforts to help Chinese reform are not a waste.

Economics. The content of my teaching was based on my forthcoming book, *Corporate Finance: Theory, Method, and Applications*. Prof. Li asked three graduate students to translate the book into Chinese. In addition, I also helped advise some graduate students and even attended the wedding of Prof. Li's eldest son, Da-Qin Li. After completing my teaching, Prof. Li took me to see the famous Suzhou gardens, Lake Tai at Wuxi, and Shou Xi Hu (or Slender West Lake) in Yangzhou. I also tried the three famous fishes of the Yangtze River: Shi fish, turtle fish, and Wuchang fish. Additionally, I visited some small companies in villages and towns. I thought that small businesses would take on an important role in Chinese economic development. My view proved correct. The total production amount in the businesses of villages and small towns accounted for more than one third of the Chinese GDP.

In the summer of 1991, Schwinne and Alice accompanied me to the 30th Conference of World Management Science in Rio de Janeiro, Brazil. It was winter in Brazil when we arrived. Rio de Janeiro was a beautiful city, but it had poor public security. After three days of meetings, my family and I went to Iguazu Falls to go sightseeing. These falls are situated on the border of Brazil and Argentina and are part of the Iguazu River. Their longest drop is 269 feet and at nearly two miles wide, and they are the widest falls in the world. We also looked around the city and watched the Spanish dancing and equestrian shows in the suburban areas. We bought some handicrafts and Schwinne even bought an expensive fur coat. Alice had just finished her first year of her Ph.D. program at the Wharton School, so she took the opportunity to relax and enjoy the trip with us.

After staying a night at a nearby hotel, we took a bus to Buenos Aires, Argentina, by way of Uruguay and passed by beautiful scenery. The buildings in downtown Buenos Aires were magnificent. This city was one of the most prosperous cities in the world because of its successful beef business. However, due to the lack of industralization, Argentina's economy was developing more slowly compared to other countries.

In the spring of 1992, five of my Ph.D. students from UIUC invited me to South Korea to lecture. Prof. Ung Ki Lim of Yonsei University arranged my schedule. The very first day I arrived in Korea, my college classmate Shi-da Shih came to see me and showed me around Seoul. In addition to visiting the university, I also gave a speech about the management of mutual funds in Daewoo Group and received very exciting responses. After the lecture a senior manager told me that Daewoo applied the Value Line approach to rating South Korean stocks. Worsened by the Asian Financial Crisis of 1997, Daewoo Group was a very fragile company, which was impossible to imagine as it was prosperous at the time of my visit. That evening they brought my students and me to the best Chinese restaurant in Seoul to have dinner. Before my departure, my five students came to say good-bye and gave me a bottle of superior ginseng extract.

In July of the same year, with the invitation of Dr. Wu-lung Lin, I represented the United Nations and taught financial management for high-level financial officials in Hangzhou, Xi'an, and Beijing, China. Just a few days prior to my arrival, China removed the upper and lower limits in stock trading and began futures trading in metal. When I was in Hangzhou, I was also invited to the Municipal Hall to give a speech on the analysis of stock markets in front of hundreds of people. The big scene made me feel that the development of Chinese financial markets had come to a different level.

While I was in Hangzhou lecturing, I was also able to visit my uncle in Fuyang County, Zhejiang Province. My uncle was in good spirits and was pleased that he had the opportunity to see his nephew and grandniece in his hometown. It had been nine years since my first visit to Fuyang. I could see that there had been progress, which was the preliminary result of Deng's economic reform in the rural areas.

After my time in Hangzhou, I traveled to Xi'an. I spent a day lecturing on the methods of accounting analysis at Xi'an Yang-Sen Pharmaceutical. I learned from the deputy general manager that Americans and Chinese operated the company. The Americans received their initial investment of USD 50 million back in just five years. In addition to seeing Xi'an Museum, the Tomb of Concubine Yang, and Famen Temple, I saw the progress in Xi'an and was glad with what I witnessed after my first visit nine years earlier.

My last stop was Beijing. Before I reached the city, I visited Beidaihe, which was famous for summer vacations. Every year, many high-level government officials spent their summers there and the government held meetings there for critical decisions. This was my first time to Beijing after the Tiananmen Square protests. When I gave my speech at the Beijing Economic Development Council, many economic officials enthusiastically participated in the discussion and showed me models of their economic plans. In my speech, I told the audience that if China had opened the markets 20 years earlier, there would be no economic miracle in Asia's Four Little Dragons, namely, Taiwan, South Korea, Hong Kong, and Singapore. Everyone agreed with my view and regretted that China had been going in the wrong direction for economic development.

In November, I again represented World Bank in Beijing and participated in the International Conference on Chinese Corporation System Organization. In the conference, the execution of Chinese Corporation System Organization, the operation of European and American stock markets, and their relationship with microeconomic policies were thoroughly explored. I also delivered a speech entitled "Various Approaches of Fund Collection and the Operation of Stock Markets and Corporation." My conclusions from the speech were:

1. Apply the correct investment, financial, and dividend policies to improve the efficiency and profits of corporations.
2. Apply a good corporation financial report system to enhance and assure the investors' rights and benefits.
3. Utilize the effective government regulations and procedures to minimize or avoid the inside trading and speculative behaviors in stock markets.
4. Improve the efficiency and effectiveness of capital markets to complete the second stage of the Chinese economic reform.

The chairman of China Stock Exchange Council, Mr. Hueng-Wen Wang, also joined the conference and the discussion. This conference brought about an influential effect on the establishment of the primary plan for enterprises based on Chinese Corporation System Organization and also founded a solid base for the development of Chinese stock markets.

During my spare time at the conference, I called on Professors Da-Wu Yen and Sheng Fang from Renmin University of China. Prof. Fang mentioned that he had studied in the Department of Agricultural Economics, National Taiwan University, and was the classmate of President Lee Teng-hui. At that time, Prof. Fang wrote an article for *People's Daily*, which indicated the necessity for and the direction of the Chinese economic reform. He also gave me his book regarding the approaches of the second stage of Chinese economic reform. As I knew, his opinions greatly affected Deng's announcement, "The Second Stage of Chinese Economic Reform," which was presented later on when Deng toured southern China. Prof. Fang said that because he was in Japan and wasn't involved in the Tiananmen protests, he was able to present his opinions that were widely accepted. In May 1998, when the 6th Conference on Pacific Basin Finance, Economics, and Accounting (PBFEA) was held in Hong Kong, I made sure to invite Prof. Fang to address the cross-strait economic and trading relationship.

In May 1993, a conference discussing why Wuhan should set up a third stock exchange in China was held in Wuhan, China. I was one of the keynote speakers and explained why the third Chinese stock market should be in Wuhan. On the following day, the *Yangtze River Daily News* mentioned my speech in one of its headlines, "Professor Lee's Suggestion for Establishing a Third Stock Exchange is Coincidently Similar to Prof. Yi-Ning Li of Beijing University." In other words, both Prof. Li and I suggested Wuhan should set up a third stock exchange in the near future to help develop financial markets in Wuhan.

On the first day in Wuhan, Jun-Qian Hsu and his family took Schwinne and I to see Yueyang Tower and Lake Dong. The host of the conference also arranged for us to visit the Wuhan Stock Exchange, Wuhan Steel, Changfei, and other companies. Besides the Chinese scholars, the participants also included representatives from the U.S., Canada, Germany, Korea, Taiwan, and several other countries. The Chinese scholars who presented were the famous economists Zhi-wen An, Da-lin Tueng, Fu-qi Dueng, and Chueng-huai Li.

In June of the same year, Prof. Yasuo Hoshino invited me to Nagoya

City University in Japan, to teach financial management. During the week, I discussed some research topics with their faculty. The Japanese economy was still quite prosperous at that time. I also had the opportunity to tour Nagoya. I was most impressed with the automatic production lines at the Toyota Auto Company. The Japanese workers' high efficiency in production was just marvelous. As a kind gesture, Prof. Yasuo Hoshino invited me to his home for dinner and to meet his family; we enjoyed a wonderful evening together.

In the fall of 1993, CUHK offered me a one-year chair professorship. During the year, I taught courses on futures and options for undergraduate students, wrote research papers with several professors, and gave lectures on special topics for the faculty. In May of the following year, Prof. Shao-ping Chiang and I organized the 3rd Conference on PBFEA at CUHK. I invited Prof. Hsien-ping Lang and suggested that the school establish a master's program for quantitative finance.

During my term as chair professor, I frequently discussed research and communication with other professors at the College of Management at CUHK. In 1997, I even recruited Prof. Yang-Ru Wu for an associate professorship at Rutgers University. Looking back at my stay in Hong Kong of more than 10 months, I had visited most attractions in Hong Kong and was always treated warmly by my CUHK schoolmates. Hong Kong was very prosperous and the people who lived there were happy. However, since Hong Kong was returned to China in 1997, people have started to worry about their future.

In the summer of 1996, Singapore's Nanyang Technological University's (NTU, Singapore) business school invited me to teach as a distinguished professor for two months. During these two months, I cohosted with Professor T. H. McInish a two-day research symposium in which all the faculty and graduates from the country were invited. While at Nanyang Technological University I taught Ph.D. students for four weeks and helped advise Kim-hui Ho's dissertation. I also worked with Hsien-Ching Yang, Sheng-Syan Chen, and Kim-hui Ho on research projects, which were published in the American journal, *The Financial Review*, and the European journal, *Journal of Banking and Finance*.

Before I left, the Singapore–China Business Association invited me to give a speech entitled "The Review and the Outlook of the Development of Economy and Finance in Pacific Basin Countries." In this three-hour lecture, I explored the possible difficulties that might be encountered in the development process of the Pacific Basin economy and forecasted the problems that the Pacific Basin might face in its financial markets and policies. I also accepted Prof. Khee Giap Tan's invitation to participate in the second meeting of the Central Banks of Pacific Basin countries, which he organized. At that time, many people predicted that Thailand, Indonesia, or Malaysia might be the next country to have a financial crisis. Therefore, I spent more time studying the economic and financial conditions of these three countries. This gave me a deeper understanding of the Pacific Basin financial markets and policies.

During my stay in Singapore, I had dinners and exchanged views with Cheng-Nan Lin of the First Commercial Bank and Dien-hung Lu of Chiao Tung Bank, who were bank managers from Taiwan and were working for Singapore branches. Dien-hung Lu was my student when I taught at the Bank Research and Training Center in Taiwan in 1992. From our conversations, I learned more about the current situation of Taiwanese investment in Southeast Asia and the progress of the "Southward" policy of Taiwan's government. Moreover, I gained a lot of information about the business of foreign banks in Singapore and the process of how Singapore became a world financial center.

This was my first time in Singapore, so I spent every weekend visiting the local attractions, such as the Bird Park, Night Safari, S.E.A. Aquarium, and Sentosa, a popular island resort in Singapore. On Singapore's National Day, Prof. Tan took me to Malacca, his hometown, where I saw many relics left by Ho Cheng (1371– ca. 1433) when he sailed from China to Malacca 300 years ago. There I joined the Hungry Ghost Festival celebration held by the local Chinese. I felt very comfortable because the local Chinese spoke Min-Nan (Hokkien) dialect. He also showed me his uncle's palm tree plantation and palm oil factory. Palm tree, which is an excellent economic plant, can be extracted for balms and the stem can be utilized in many ways too.

In June and July 1997, I served as distinguished professor at NTU,

Singapore. My work focused on teaching Ph.D. students and conducting research with other faculty members. NTU, Singapore also asked me to be their external advisor for the master's program of the management school. Meanwhile, Kim-hui Ho passed his Ph.D. oral defense in July and I accepted another Ph.D. student, Ken-ping Hang, who graduated in 1999. I participated in the third meeting of the Central Banks of Pacific Basin countries organized by Khee Giap Tan. I again had dinner with the bank managers. This time they all told me it was difficult to continue to expand their business in Singapore. From my time there, I felt that Singapore was a great country. Although it is small, it is equipped with everything. Its construction was well planned, their population could speak Min-Nan (Hokkien) dialect, Mandarin, and English, which made it easy to communicate with most of the local people, and it was an internationalized country.

After the 5th PBFEA Conference, I flew to Kuala Lumpur, Malaysia, to present papers at the fourth meeting of Asian Finance. I took the opportunity to venture around the city and found the overall construction in Kuala Lumpur was quite thought out, although the traffic was somewhat chaotic due to the rapid development. At that time, the occupation of the famous Petronas Towers was less than 50 percent because of the impact of the Asian Financial Crisis. The number of occupants in the towers revealed the fact of a slow real estate market. From my visits I learned that Malaysia owned an abundant amount of natural resources and its economy was continuously developing. This is one of the countries that I recommended to Taiwan's businessmen in the government's "Southward" policy, which was suggested by President Lee Teng-hui.

In the first semester of 1998, I took my sabbatical from Rutgers University; this gave me the ability to travel and lecture more frequently in various Asian countries. Besides participating in meetings in Taiwan and teaching short courses, I took many trips to China, Hong Kong, and Singapore. It was the year after the Asian Financial Crisis and by traveling and lecturing in different countries in Asia I was able to see its impact.

In early February, I went to China to train some local financial and accounting managers for an important company in Chicago. I found out that the construction in China developed rapidly and the quality of

Chinese managers was much better than what I had seen in my earlier visits. However, I noticed that China was also slightly affected by the Asian Financial Crisis. The reform of state-owned enterprises faced bigger challenges and markets were slower than before. On the other hand, I also realized the operation of the local branches of American companies improved.

When I lectured in Shanghai, I met with Prof. Ru-xun Li. He took me to see the Huangpu River. I was surprised to discover that the area along the river was very clean. Prof. Li explained that was because the government distributed the cleaning job to private companies. Shanghai had changed a great deal since my first visit in 1983. When I was in Guangzhou, Mr. Kuang-ning Chang, who was the brother of my previous student, Kuang-ping Chang, invited me for dinner and took me to see Guangzhou at night.

In May, I accepted Prof. Kuo-liang Chang's invitation to lecture on the research approaches in finance and accounting to students and faculty of Hong Kong Polytechnic University (HKPU) and also to conduct a few research projects with HKPU's faculty. At the end of the month, the 6th Conference on PBFEA was held in Hong Kong and organized by HKPU and myself. In July, I visited Nanyang Technological University in Singapore again to investigate the business school's master's programs and to provide my suggestions for improvements. I was on the external examination committee for the Chinese master's programs until 2000.

I joined the fourth meeting of Central Banks of Pacific Basin countries organized by Prof. Khee Giap Tan and discussed the causes of the Asian Financial Crisis and its impacts on Asian countries. The Taiwanese representative for the meeting was Dr. Rong-yi Wu, president of Taiwan Institute of Economic Research, who addressed the role Taiwan had played in the Asian Financial Crisis. The other Taiwanese representative was Prof. Pochih Chen, who presented a paper about the impacts of the financial crisis on the import and export trading in Asian countries. Although this was my third time visiting Singapore, I still enjoyed my stay.

Indonesia was seriously wounded by the financial crisis and

took out a big loan from the International Monetary Fund (IMF). The government was forced to carry out the tightening policy with high product price and high interest rate and President Soeharto was forced to step down and the vice president, B.J. Habibie, succeeded. The life of the Chinese in Indonesia was severely affected. On the evening of July 19, when I had dinner with the Chairman of World Scientific Publishing, Dr. Kok Khoo Phua, one of the guests, an Indonesia merchant, complained to the president of UC Berkeley and me. He questioned why the U.S. didn't respond to the Indonesian government about the assaults suffered by the Indonesian Chinese. I felt very sorry and sad for the situation of the Indonesian Chinese.

At the end of January 1999, I participated in the Conference on Financial Crisis and Financial Policies in China held in Hainan Island and sponsored by the Chinese and German governments. I presented "The Past, the Present, and the Future of Financial Policies in Taiwan" at the conference and then took the chance to explore the city of Haikou, the capital of Hainan. The beautiful weather and abundant natural resources of Hainan impressed me. The trip to Hainan let me further understand China's financial markets and policies. Since the start of the new semester at Rutgers was approaching, I canceled my original plan to visit the famous attractions The Edge of the Sky and End of the Sea in Sanya.

In 1999, I was invited by Central Government of People's Republic of China to give a speech about the Asian Financial Crisis. Professor Yong Shi, P.L. Yu, and one other government officer brought me to visit Chengdu and Lhasa, Tibet. In Chengdu we visited the famous pandas at the zoo and we visited Buddhist and Taoist temples. In Tibet we observed the poor condition of the Tibetans. In Lhasa we visited several famous Buddhist temples.

In early June, Schwinne, President Hsin-fu Tsai, Prof. William Lin, and I arrived in Bangkok to discuss the related business of the 8th Conference on PBFEA, which would be held in 2000. Prof. K. Prasit, executive secretary of the Joint Doctoral Programs of three universities in Bangkok, was the host representative. He took us to call on the heads of the related organizations. We visited Dr. P. Maruey, ex-minister of finance; Prof. N. Watana, chairman of the Research Institute; Dean N. Virchs and Prof. K. Suchada, Chulalongkorn University; Prof. Prasit's elder brother and also the CEO of Thai branch of Japanese Mitsubishi Diesels, Mr. Chen-po Chang; and Mr. Huan-min Lin of Changfa Manufacturers Inc. On this trip, I also met with my schoolmate C. Som, who studied for his Ph.D. at SUNY-Buffalo too. Dr. Som had taken the positions as president of banks and minister of finance. During the two-day trip in Bangkok, we visited the Grand Palace and Summer Palace and enjoyed our time.

Between August 1 and 7, 1999, Prof. Po-lung Yu, Yong Shi, and I went to Beijing to deliver a five-day course at the Development Research Center of the State Council of People's Republic of China. I spent three days talking about "The Related Problems of Asian Financial Crisis and Taiwan's Financial Policies," while Prof. Yu spoke about "Habit Realm and Enterprises' Decisions," and Prof. Shi taught "The Future of Technological Development." China was extensively criticizing President Lee's statement of "Special Two Countries" and Hongzhi Li's Falungong Incident while we were teaching. These two events affected Chinese political climate; therefore, the atmosphere of our lecture was also affected to some degree. I told the attending researchers and officials that Zhu Rongji should slow down his steps in reform in order to keep the society stable.

Prof. Xiang Tao of Renmin University of China and Prof. Ying-xian Liu, director of Taiwan Research Center, Chinese Academy of Social Science, both joined our discussions. From the discussion with Prof. Tao, I realized how China collected funds for the construction of the Three Gorges Dam. In addition, since Prof. Liu's research center subscribed to all kinds of Taiwanese newspapers, he was quite familiar with my views of Taiwan's finance and markets. He said he had heard about me for a long time and it would be productive to share and discuss our views.

When I taught in Beijing, I met with some of my previous Rutgers students who worked in the Ministry of Communications. I also had breakfast with Dr. Kang Yi, who studied for his Ph.D. at UIUC and at the time was the Deputy Secretary of Policy Center of People's Bank. Dr. Yi is currently the Deputy Governor of People's Bank. Through our conversation, I learned more about the development of the Chinese financial markets. Dr. Yi mentioned that People's Bank was exploring the possibility of issuing bonds for real estate and planned to try it in Shanghai next year.

From August 9 to 11, I traveled with Professors Shi and Yu and a young official, Mr. Xian Yiang, to Lhasa, Tibet and Chengdu, Sichuan. I saw the magnificent Potala Palace and the glorious Brahmaputra River. This was my first time visiting the mountains and I was amazed at the beautiful sights. In Lhasa, half of the population was Han. Most Tibet residents could speak Mandarin and were deeply influenced by the Han civilization.

The following three days, we traveled to Chengdu, Sichuan and visited the Wuhou Memorial Temple, Dujiangyan, Emei Mountain, Mount Qingcheng, the Leshan Giant Buddha, the Panda Gardens, and other famous attractions. In the Wuhou Memorial Temple, we saw the historical characters of the Three Kingdoms period of the Han Dynasty. In Dujiangyan, we witnessed the great construction of water conservation by the father and the sons of Bing Li. At Emei Mountain we visited the Buddhist and Tao temples. Finally, at Mount Qingcheng, we visited temples, explored the origin of Taoism, and learned some basic concepts of Taoism. Over the three-day stay in Chengdu, we were impressed by the richness of this simple city and its abundance of relics and cultural property.

When I visited the Dujiangyan irrigation system and Mount Qingcheng with Prof. Yu, we reminisced about the times we had while we were studying at NTU. We also discussed the magnificent techniques used in building Dujiangyan. It was built around 300 B.C. and was the first multi-purpose water conservation system. Over the past 2,200 years, it has fully played its role in water conservation with its marvelous outlook, which was well described by Bing Li's poem: "Deeper the bays to make the weirs; straighten the turns and connect the corners to divert the mass."

We experienced the spectacular mountain views when we visited Mount Qingcheng, the origin of Taoism. Having humbly worshiped at some temples, we paid our respects to the Temple of Laozi. The trip from the bottom of the mountain to the top took about two and a half hours.

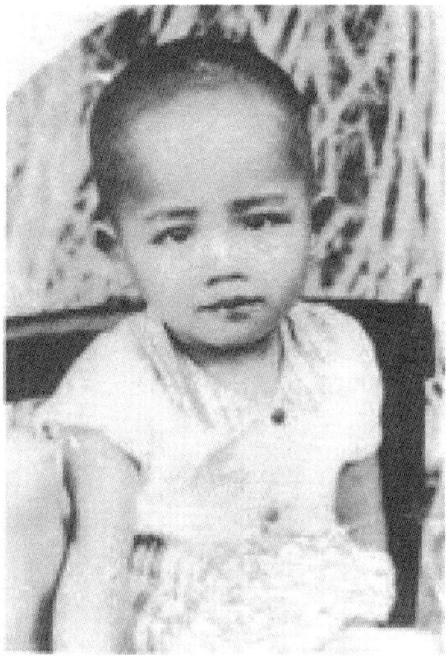

When I was a baby.

With my grandparents and high school classmates at Taoyuan, Taiwan in 1957.

My college graduation picture in 1962.

With my parents and grandmother at Taipei airport, 1968.

My wedding photo.

My son and daughter when they were young.

With my wife, son and daughter.

My son and daughter's graduation at
University of Illinois at Urbana-Champaign in 1987.

At Wuhan, East Lake, China with my wife Schwinne in 1993.

A party at Professor Junqian Hsu's house at Wuhan, China in 1993.

With Governor Fai-nan Perng (3rd from left) at my son's home in 1997.

With my wife and grandchildren in 2000.

With my son and grandson.

In Rome with Neil A. Doherty in 1982.

Group photo at the American Management Training Center, Dalian, 1983.

Celebrated U.S. Independence Day on July 4th, 1983
at Dalian American Training Center.

With Merton Miller (2nd from left) and Robert Litzenberger (4th from left) at National Taiwan's International Conference, Taipei in 1994.

With Professor Khee Giap Tan at Malacca, Malaysia in 1996.

Lhasa, Tibet in 1999.

With Professor Yong Shi (1st from left) and Professor P.L. Yu, Lhasa, Tibet in 1999.

Visited President Lee Teng-hui at Presidential Office Building, Taipei in 1999.

Group picture of FEA Conference at SUNY-Buffalo in 1999.

With Governor Fai-nan Perng (3rd from left), Yongmin Yang (2nd from left), Professor Da-song Huang and my wife Schwinne.

With Professor P.L. Yu at Qincheng Mountain, China, 1999.

With Professor William Lin (1st from right) and my wife Schwinne at Bangkok, Thailand in 1999.

Presented a gift to Mike Brennan at 7th PBFEAM Conference in Taipei, 1999.

PBFEAM Conference group picture with President Lee Teng-hui at Presidential Office Building in Taipei, 1999.

Group photo with President Chen Shui-bian at Presidential Office Building in Taipei, 2000.

With President Chen Shui-bian in Taipei, 2000.

Keynote speech at Economic and Financial Summit in Taipei, 2001.

Kuo-Ann Lyou (1st from left), Tang-Chieh Wu, Cheng-Few Lee, and Wayne Pai (1st from right) at Sun Moon Lake, Taiwan in 2004.

Cheng-Few Lee (1st from left), Franklin Allen (3rd) and Dar-yeh Hwang (5th) in Taipei, 2005.

With Professor Yahuda Kahane at Jerusalem, Israel in 2009.

Four classmates: E. Han Kim (2nd row, 1st from left), Stanley Kong (2nd row, 2nd from left) and Lemma Senbet (1st row, 1st from left) and Cheng-Few Lee at SUNY-Buffalo, 2010.

Keynote speech at ITQM, the First International Conference on Information Technology and Quantitative Management at Suzhou, China in 2013.

Received ITQM Conference Award at Suzhou, China in 2013.

At my 40-year Teaching Career Celebration Conference
with my previous students in 2014.

At NCTU conference in celebration of my 40 years of teaching,
with President Chang and my niece in 2014.

With Professor Jack C. Jen (my professor) and
Professor C.C. Wu (my previous student) in 2015.

26th FEA Conference group picture.

Received special recognition award from associate dean Yaw Mensah at 26th FEA Conference.

The 26th FEA Conference executive committee members.

At the 2015 Economics and Finance Policy Conference in Taipei, Taiwan.

Photo taken at my office at RBS, Rutgers University in 2015.

At the 23rd PBFEAM Conference at Ho Chi Minh City, 2015.

With Yaw Mensah and Bharat Sarath at
23rd PBFEAM Conference at Ho Chi Minh City, 2015.

At the reception of President Tsai's inauguration in Taipei, 2016.

With Chairman Paul Chiu (1st from left) and
Minister K.W. Ding (3rd from left) at the Policy Conference in Taipei, 2016.

With Yaqing Xiao and Yibing Chen (1st from left)
at Zhangjiajie, Hunan, China.

With Richard Kihlstrom at the national museum in Taipei, 2016.

Group photo at 24th PBFEAM Conference, NCTU, Taiwan on June 14 and 15, 2016.

At Rutgers Business School, 2016.

Special Recognition Award for establishing the FEA Conference in 1990, Rutgers.

Appointed as Member of the Board of Policy Advisor to Research Center on Fictitious Economy & Data Science, Chinese Academy of Sciences, Beijing, China.

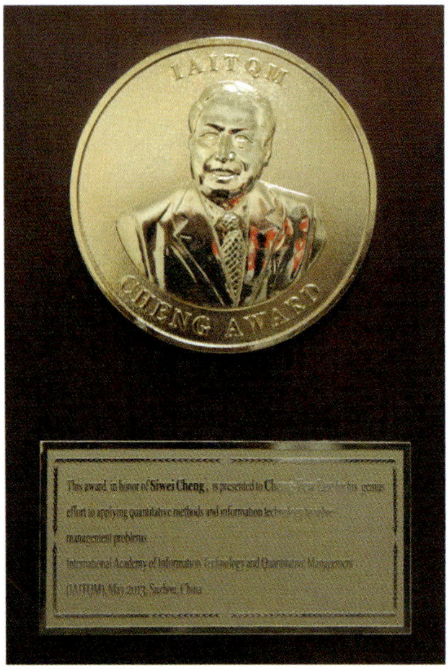

Siwei Cheng Award in Qualitative Management presented at Suzhou, China in 2013.

Dean's Meritorious Award for Lifetime Achievement in Research 2013–2014.

The view from the top of the mountain was so beautiful and calming that it could only be described by Du Fu's poem: "Shall not spit on thee, Mount Qingcheng my beloved. Ascending the red ladders, leading me to the tranquility of thee."

Between 1980 and 2000, I traveled and lectured in several countries. After 2000 I have continued to travel to many countries including Taiwan, Japan, Macau, Hong Kong, Spain, Israel, Sweden, and Thailand, which was detailed in the previous chapter. Traveling has helped me spread the seeds of academic knowledge around the world and has helped establish my reputation. It also provided me with a lot of opportunities to visit different countries, experience many cultures, and see the economic development in these areas. This opportunity of learning by traveling is rare in other professional careers. This is why I've never thought about retirement since I enjoy traveling and lecturing all over the world.

Chapter

12

Editing Journals and Writing Books

In addition to teaching, conducting research, and administrative responsibilities at University of Georgia, University of Illinois at Urbana-Champaign, and Rutgers University over the last 43 years of my academic career, I have also tried to contribute to the area of finance in five different ways. These areas are: editing journals, writing textbooks, organizing conferences, consulting for private companies, and suggesting policy recommendations to the government. This chapter will discuss my activities of editing journals and writing books. During the last 43 years, I was editor of *The Financial Review* from October 1985–December 1991 and *Quarterly Review of Economics and Finance* from 1987 to 1989. Currently, I edit the *Review of Quantitative Finance and Accounting* and the *Review of Pacific Basin Financial Markets and Policies.* I also edit four annuals, *Advances in Quantitative Analysis of Finance and Accounting, Advances in Investment Analysis and Portfolio Management, Advances in Financial Planning and Forecasting,* and *Advances in Pacific Basin Business, Economics, and Finance.*

Review of Quantitative Finance and Accounting deals with research involving the interaction of finance with accounting, economics and quantitative methods, focused on finance and accounting. The papers published present useful theoretical and methodological results with the support of interesting empirical applications. Purely theoretical and methodological research with the potential for important applications is also published. Besides the traditional high-quality, theoretical and empirical research in finance, the journal also publishes papers dealing with interdisciplinary topics including: Financial accounting which uses financial and economic theory and/or methodology; managerial accounting and auditing which use financial and economic theory and/or methodology to deal with internal accounting data and decision making; macro-economics which uses finance theory and/or methodology to analyze fiscal and/or monetary policies; and managerial economics which uses financial theory and/or methodology to analyze the decisions of a firm.

Review of Pacific Basin Financial Markets and Policies concentrates on global interdisciplinary research in finance, economics, accounting, and management. It particularly emphasizes the economic, financial, and management relationships among Pacific Rim countries. The major topics include:

1. Business, economic and financial relations among the Pacific Rim countries.
2. Financial markets and industries (banking and insurance of the United States and other Pacific Rim countries).
3. Options and futures markets of the United States and other Pacific Rim countries.
4. International accounting issues related to U.S. companies investing in Pacific Rim countries.
5. Marketing, management and business policy of the Pacific Rim countries.
6. International corporate finance of the Pacific Rim countries.
7. Global monetary and foreign exchange policy, and
8. Other high quality interdisciplinary research in global accounting, business, economics and finance.

Advances in Quantitative Analysis of Finance and Accounting is an annual publication designed to disseminate developments in the quantitative analysis of finance and accounting. The publication is a forum for statistical and quantitative analyses of issues in finance and accounting as well as applications of quantitative methods to problems in financial management, financial accounting, and business management. The objective is to promote interaction between academic research in finance and accounting and applied research in the financial community and the accounting profession.

Advances in Investment Analysis and Portfolio Management is an annual publication designed to disseminate developments in the area of investment analysis and portfolio management. The publication is a forum for statistical and quantitative analyses of issues in security analysis, portfolio management options, futures, and other related issues. The objective is to promote interaction between academic research in finance, economics, and accounting and applied research in the financial community.

Advances in Financial Planning and Forecasting is a publication, which includes articles that:

1. Present and develop finance theories that are innovative to financial analysis, planning, and forecasting.
2. Contribute substantially to the development of new financial planning and forecasting models.
3. Examine and illustrate, through empirical analysis, the application of important and useful statistical, econometric, mathematical, and computer techniques in financial planning and forecasting.
4. Present and analyze new and useful accounting, financial, and economic data for financial planning and forecasting in business policy decisions.

Advances in Pacific Basin Business, Economics, and Finance is an annual publication designed to concentrate on interdisciplinary research in finance, economics, and management. It particularly emphasizes the economic, financial, and management relationships among Pacific Rim countries. The topics in this publication include:

1. Business, economic, and financial relations among the Pacific Rim countries.
2. Financial markets and industries (banking and insurance of the United States and other Pacific Rim countries).
3. Options and futures markets of the United States and other Pacific Rim countries.
4. Marketing, management, and business policies of the Pacific Rim countries.
5. International corporate finance of the Pacific Rim countries.
6. Global monetary and foreign exchange policy.
7. Topics about different economic policies among the Pacific Rim countries.
8. Interrelationship between investment decision in terms of psychology and behavior signs.
9. The interdisciplinary between supply chain, finance, and marketing.

Based upon the previous discussion of the goals and scopes of these journals and annual publications, I have summarized how I have used quarterly journals and annual publications to promote finance research.

1. I have promoted financial theory, which includes classical theory, neo-classical theory, capital asset pricing model and arbitrage pricing theory, and options and futures theory.
2. I have promoted a policy aspect, which includes investment policy, financing policy, dividend policy, and production policy.
3. I have promoted interdisciplinary research among finance, accounting, economics, and management.

4. I have promoted research in financial econometrics and statistics.
5. I have promoted an application of finance policy and theory to real world application, which includes international research in finance, accounting, and management.

The following is a discussion of the important textbooks, which I wrote, and financial reference books, which I edited, and how I believe they have contributed to the area of finance. During the last 43 years I have published and edited:

1. *Readings in Investment Analysis* (with Jack C. Francis and D.E. Farrar), McGraw-Hill Book Company, 1980.
2. *Financial Analysis and Planning: Theory and Application, A Book of Readings*, Addison-Wesley Publishing Company, 1983.
3. *Foundations of Financial Management* (with Joseph E. Finnerty and Edgar A. Norton), West Publishing Company, 1997. [This book has been translated into Chinese and published in Taipei, Taiwan in 2002 (ISBN: 981-243-422-4)]
4. *Corporate Finance: Theory, Method, and Applications* (with Joseph E. Finnerty), Harcourt Brace Jovanovich, Publishers, 1990. [This book has been translated into Russian (ISBN: 5-16-000102-6 paperback, ISBN: 0-15-514085 hardcover)]
5. *Security Analysis, Portfolio Management, and Financial Derivatives* (with Joseph E. Finnerty, John Lee, Alice C. Lee, and Donald H. Wort), World Scientific Publishing Company, 2013. (ISBN: 978-981-4343-56-5)
6. *Statistics for Business and Financial Economics*, Third Edition (with John C. Lee and Alice C. Lee), Springer Academic Publishers, 2013. (ISBN: 978-1-4614-5896-8)
7. *Financial Analysis, Planning and Forecasting* (with John C. Lee), Third Edition, World Scientific Publishing Company, September 2016. (ISBN: 978-981-4723-84-8)

8. *Essentials of Microsoft Excel, Excel VBA, SAS and MINITAB for Statistical and Financial Analyses* (with John C. Lee, Jow-Ran Chang, and Tzu Tai), Springer Academic Publishers, December 2016.
9. *Financial Econometrics and Statistics* (with Hong-Yi Chen, Alice C. Lee, and John C. Lee), Springer Academic Publishers, forthcoming.
10. *Intermediate Futures and Options* (with John Lee), World Scientific Publishing Company, forthcoming.
11. *Encyclopedia of Finance*, Second Edition (with Alice C. Lee), Springer Academic Publishers, 2013. (ISBN: 978-1-4614-5359-8)
12. *Handbook of Quantitative Finance and Risk Management* (with Alice C. Lee and John C. Lee), Springer Academic Publishers, 2010. (ISBN: 978-0-387-77116-8)
13. *Handbook of Financial Econometrics and Statistics* (with John C. Lee), Springer Academic Publishers, 2015. (ISBN: 978-1-4614-7749-5)

Readings in Investment Analysis is designed for Ph.D. courses and *Financial Analysis and Planning: Theory and Application, A Book of Readings* is designed for upper-level MBA courses and Ph.D. students. It should be noted that both books need to be updated, however, both of them still have important papers in the area of finance.

Foundations of Financial Management is designed for commonly required courses for business school majors. This book is divided into six parts. Part I is the overview and background, Part II discusses valuation principles and applications, Part III covers capital budgeting and the risk/return tradeoff, Part IV goes into detail about the cost of capital, financing choices, and the dividend decision, Part V includes topics in short-term finance, and Part VI, is on special topics in financial management.

There are five chapters in Part I. Chapter 1 discusses financial management in the firm, Chapter 2 talks about organizational structure and taxes, Chapter 3 touches on domestic and global finance, Chapter 4 discusses accounting information and financial statement analysis, and Chapter 5 gives an overview on developing a long-term financial plan. In Part II, there are two chapters; Chapter 6 goes into detail about the time value of money and Chapter 7, valuation of stocks and bonds. Part III contains four chapters. Chapter 8 discusses project analysis and capital budgeting criteria, Chapter 9 talks about estimating project cash flows, Chapter 10 is about evaluating project NPV with uncertain cash flows, and Chapter 11 discusses total risk, systematic risk, and unsystematic risk.

Part IV consists of five chapters; Chapter 12 talks about the cost of capital, while Chapter 13 talks about the debt/equity mix. Chapter 14 discusses investment banking and raising equity capital, Chapter 15 is about debt financing choice, and Chapter 16 details dividend policy: theory and practice. The fifth section, Part V, has four chapters. Chapter 17 is about short-term financial planning and management, Chapter 18 talks about cash and marketable securities management, Chapter 19 details credit management, and Chapter 20 discusses short-term financing. The final section, Part VI has three chapters; Chapter 21 is on derivatives: options, futures, and swaps, Chapter 22 details business combinations and divestitures, and finally Chapter 23 discusses bankruptcy, workouts, and corporate reorganization.

In order for students to understand this book, they should have a background in economics, accounting, statistics, and some mathematics. Based upon accounting and stock price information we teach students to understand stock and bond valuation, which is called classical theory of finance. We also use mathematics and statistics to show students how to understand portfolio, theory, and Modigliani and Miller propositions. It is important that we teach students how to apply these to models. In the policy aspect, we teach students about investment decisions, financing decisions, and dividend decisions. All other applications of the above-mentioned theories and policies can be found in different parts of the book.

Corporate Finance: Theory, Method, and Applications is for one of the three courses required for finance majors. The two other required courses are Investment Analysis and Futures and Options. This book is divided into eight sections. Part I gives an overview, Part II discusses value and capital budgeting, Part III goes into detail about risk and capital budgeting, Part IV discusses capital structure and option pricing theory, Part V is about the cost of capital and alternative policy decisions, Part VI talks about long-term financing, Part VII goes into detail about financial planning and short-term financing, and lastly Part VIII is on special topics.

Part I contains two chapters; Chapter 1 is an overview of financial management and Chapter 2 talks about information and environment for financial management. Part II has three chapters; Chapter 3 talks about the concepts and methods of present values, Chapter 4 discusses present value of bonds, stocks, and preferred stocks, and Chapter 5 is about capital budgeting under certainty. Part III of the book has three chapters; Chapter 6 talks about risk estimation and diversification, Chapter 7 is about risk and return trade-off analysis, and Chapter 8 details capital budgeting under uncertainty. Part IV contains two chapters; Chapter 9, which talks about capital structure and valuation and Chapter 10, which is about option pricing theory and firm valuation.

The fifth section, Part V, has three chapters. Chapter 11 is about the cost of capital, Chapter 12 is about the dividend puzzle, and Chapter 13 details interactions of investment, dividend, and financing policies Chapter 14 is about long-term debt financing, Chapter 15 talks about common stock, preferred stock, and financing decisions, Chapter 16 details warrants and convertible securities, and Chapter 17 discusses the theory and practice of leasing. In Part VII, there are four chapters. Chapter 18 talks about short-term financial analysis and planning, Chapter 19 discusses credit management, Chapter 20 is about cash, marketable securities, and inventory management, and Chapter 21 touches on financial planning and strategy. The final section, Part VIII, contains three chapters. This section includes Chapter 22, which talks about the theory and evidence of mergers and divestitures, Chapter 23, which is on pension fund principles and policies, and finally Chapter 24, which discusses international financial management.

This book is a review and extension of the previous book entitled,

Foundations of Financial Management. In other words, after the financial management course, we need to review most of the topics that students learn from the previous course and we need to increase their understanding from both theoretical and methodological aspects. Certainly, we also teach them a few new topics that they did not learn from the basic financial management course. Overall, I believe for this course we need to spend 40 to 50 percent reviewing their previous knowledge in finance management and spend about 50 to 60 percent of the time to teach them new concepts, theory, methodology, and applications.

Security Analysis, Portfolio Management, and Financial Derivatives can be used for investment analysis, asset pricing and portfolio management, or derivatives courses with some supplements. How to use this book for these three courses has been discussed in detail in Chapter 9. This book is divided into five parts. Part I talks about information and security valuation, Part II discusses portfolio theory and asset pricing, Part III deals with futures and options, Part IV is about applied portfolio management, and Part V discusses some special topics.

We can summarize the special features of this book as follows. Part I discusses the information and the methodology needed to do security evaluation. In addition, the theory used to evaluate stock and bond is also discussed in some detail. Part II discusses portfolio theory and asset pricing model. Sources of risk and their determination are also analyzed in some detail. Three alternative models are used to obtain optimal portfolios. In addition, capital asset pricing model and market model are theoretically derived and the application of this stock model is empirically demonstrated. Three alternative efficient-market hypotheses are discussed and their implications to security valuation are demonstrated. Finally, arbitrage pricing theory and intertemporal capital asset pricing model are theoretically derived and their implication to security valuation is also explored.

Part III of this book discusses the topic of futures and options. The first two chapters of this part discusses futures valuation, hedging, and different types of financial and commodity futures. The next five chapters of Part III discuss option strategies, option valuation, and the comparative static analysis of option pricing models. From these five chapters, students can learn the basic concept of options, the theoretical derivation of alternative pricing option model, and the application of different option pricing models. Based upon the theory and methodology of Part II, Part IV discusses applied portfolio management. First, we discuss security valuation and mutual fund valuation and performance. Then we discuss how portfolio theory can apply to international portfolio management. Bond portfolio management and strategy are explored in some detail. Finally, based upon the theory and methods discussed in Part III, portfolio insurance and option strategy are discussed in detail. Part V of this book presents special topics. These special topics cover capturing equity risk premium, simultaneous-equation approach for security valuation, and Itô's calculus and the derivation of the Black–Scholes option pricing model.

Statistics for Business and Financial Economics is designed for business statistics courses for both undergraduate and MBA students in business schools. To my best knowledge, this is the only business statistics book that tries to use finance, accounting, and economics data throughout the whole book. In addition, we suggest a project approach to teach this course. This book is divided into five parts. Part I is an introduction and introduces descriptive statistics; Part II explores probability and important distributions; Part III goes into detail about statistical inferences based on samples; Part IV is about regression and correlation; and Part V is on selected topics in statistical analysis for business and economics. Further detailed information of this book can be found in Appendix II.

The first edition of *Financial Analysis, Planning and Forecasting* was published in 1985. The second edition of this book was published in 2009 and the third edition of this book was published in September 2016. The first edition of this book is the first finance book to use real world financial statements to demonstrate how finance theory and method can be used for financial analysis. In addition, this book tries to integrate finance, accounting, statistics, and computers into an action-taking type of learning approach. Based upon the third edition of this book, it is divided into six parts. Part I discusses information and methodology for financial analysis, Part II goes over alternative finance theories and their application, Part III is about capital budgeting and leasing decisions, Part IV goes into detail about corporate policies and their interrelationships, Part V is about short-term financial decision, and finally Part VI explains financial planning and forecasting. There are 26 chapters in this book. The detailed information of these chapters can be found in Appendix II.

The book entitled *Essentials of Microsoft Excel, Excel VBA, SAS and MINITAB for Statistical and Financial Analyses* is designed to show students how to use different types of computer programs to analyze statistics and financial data. This book is divided into three parts. Part A includes the first 21 chapters, which were proposed to supplement the textbook, *Statistics for Business and Financial Economics*. There are nine chapters in Part B, which explain how to do the advanced applications of Microsoft Excel programs. These nine chapters are: Chapter 22, an introduction to Excel programming, Chapter 23, an introduction to VBA programming, Chapter 24, professional techniques used in Excel and Excel VBA techniques, Chapter 25, binomial option pricing model decision tree approach, Chapter 26, using Microsoft Excel to estimate alternative option pricing models, Chapter 27, alternative methods to estimate the implied variance, Chapter 28, Greek letters and portfolio insurance, Chapter 29, portfolio analysis and option strategies, and Chapter 30, simulation and its application. There are two chapters in Part C on how to do the applications of SAS programs in financial analysis and research. These two chapters are Chapter 31, the methods and empirical results of simultaneous equations in finance research and Chapter 32, the theory and applications of hedge ratios. More information of these chapters can be found in Appendix II.

There are four possible applications of this book and they are as follows:

A. This book can be used to supplement a business statistics book, especially *Statistics for Business and Financial Economics*, Third Edition.

B. Chapters 1 to 21 can be used independently to teach statistics courses. Under this approach, the instructor can use data and computer programs to teach the course. In other words, this approach can be regarded as a data analysis approach to teach statistics.

C. This book can be used to learn how to apply Microsoft Excel, SAS, and MINITAB to financial data analysis.

D. This book can be used to supplement courses, such as, portfolio management and futures and options.

Financial Econometrics and Statistics is designed for master's students in quantitative finance or Ph.D. students in finance and accounting. From this book students can learn how econometrics and statistics can be used to analyze financial and accounting data. In addition, this book can show students how to use financial econometrics and statistics to improve the quality of their research. In Financial Econometrics and Statistics there are 24 chapters. Chapter 1 is the introduction; Chapter 2 discusses multiple linear regression; Chapter 3 goes over other topics in applied regression analysis; Chapter 4 talks about panel data analysis; Chapter 5 goes over time series analysis; Chapter 6 discusses hedge ratio and time series analysis; and Chapter 7 talks about spurious regression and data mining in conditional asset pricing models. Chapter 8 is on alternative methods to deal with measurement error; Chapter 9 deals with alternative asset pricing tests; Chapter 10 goes into detail about simultaneous equation models; and Chapter 11 is on the application of simultaneous equation in finance research.

Chapter 12 explains the binomial and multi-nomial distributions; Chapter 13 reviews the relationship between binomial distribution and option pricing; Chapter 14 is on the normal and lognormal distributions; Chapter 15 explores copula, correlated defaults, and credit VaR; Chapter 16 discusses multivariate analysis: discriminant analysis and factor analysis; Chapter 17 is on stochastic volatility option pricing models; Chapter 18 explains the alternative method to estimate implied variance; Chapter 19 talks about numerical valuation of Asian options with high moments in the underlying distribution; and Chapter 20 goes over Ito's calculus, a derivation of the Black–Scholes option pricing model. Chapter 21 explains alternative methods to derive option-pricing models; Chapter 22 is on the constant elasticity of variance option pricing model; Chapter 23 is about option pricing and hedging performance under stochastic volatility and stochastic interest rates; and Chapter 24 reviews and compares option bounds.

From the detailed table of contents in Appendix II of *Financial Econometrics and Statistics* we summarize the features of this book as follows. This book is divided into Part A "Financial Econometrics" and Part B "Financial Statistics". In Part A, we discuss the application of how single equation and simultaneous-equation can be used to analyze financial and accounting data. In the single equation portion we first discuss time-series analysis, which covers ARIMA, ARCH, GARCH, and fractional cointegration in detail. In the panel data analysis chapter we discuss the dummy variable technique and the error component model. In addition, the impact of firm effect and time effect on stock price valuation is also analyzed. In addition, we also discuss alternative methods to deal with measurement errors and alternative methods for asset pricing tests. Finally, superior correlation issue is also explored in this portion. In simultaneous-equation portion we discuss two-stage least and three-stage square method. We also apply simultaneous-equation technique to analyze investment, financing, and dividend policy.

In Part B we discuss how statistics technique can be used to do financial analysis. We first show binomial and multinomial distribution can be used to derive option-pricing model. Secondly, we show how normal, lognormal, and noncentral chi-square distribution can be used to derive. Then we generalize the Black and Scholes option-pricing model into Stochastic Volatility Option Pricing Models. Finally, alternative methods for estimated implied variance is also explored. Part C of this book discusses derivations of option pricing model and other topics. In this part we discuss other methods to derive option-pricing models. In addition, we review and compare alternative to derive option bond.

Intermediate Futures and Options is designed for both undergraduate and master's students to learn the topic of futures and options. This book uses a more statistical and computer based approach to teach students.

From the table of contents in Appendix II of *Intermediate Futures and Options* the special features of this book are as follows. In Part A, the introduction, we discuss financial market and financial instruments, which is the base to understand futures and options. Then in Chapter 3 we discuss the overview of futures, options, and swap. Finally, we discuss alternative finance theory, which is needed to understand futures and options. In Part B we first discuss commodity and finance future product in detail, then we discuss how a futures product can be used to hedge and risk. In addition, we have discussed how four alternative hedge ratios can be estimated. These four alternative hedge ratios are: naïve hedge ratio, minimize variance hedge ratio, sharp performance hedge ratio, and quadratic utility function hedge ratio.

In Part C option strategies, option pricing models and their applications are discussed. First, we theoretically discuss seven option strategies, and then we show how the Excel program can be used to analyze these seven option strategies. In Chapter 8 we discuss option valuation model and also show how option theory can be used to analyze the impact of the company value. Then we also show how option can be used to analyze warrants value. Finally, we show how earnings per share with warrant and convertible bonds can be calculated. In Chapter 10 we first discuss how normal and lognormal distribution can be used to derive option-pricing model. Then bivariate distribution argues to calculate American option. In Chapter 11 we show how index option, currency option, and interest rate option can be calculated. In Chapter 12 we show how comparative static analysis can be used to calculate Greek letters, Delta, Theta, Gamma, Vega, and Rho for option pricing model. Then we demonstrate how these Greek letters can be used to do hedging and risk management. In Chapter 13 we show how alternative methods can be used to estimate implied variance for option pricing model, then we compare implied distribution and lognormal distribution to determine the existent of volatility smiles. In Chapter 14 we first show how three alternative strategies can be used to do portfolio insurance, then we demonstrate how synthetic option can be formulated. Finally, we demonstrate how synthetic option can be effectively used to do portfolio insurance. In Chapter 15 we first show

how noncentral chi-square distribution can be used to derive constant elasticity of variance option pricing model. Then we demonstrate the constant elasticity of variance option pricing model can perform better than traditional Black and Scholes option pricing model.

In Chapter 16 we discuss alternative exotic options, such as nonstandard American options, forward start options, compound options, chooser options, barrier options, binary options, look back options, shout options, Asian options, basket options, etc. In Chapter 17 we show how option theory and technique can be used to determine capital budgeting under uncertainty. In Chapter 18 we show how Ito calculus used to derive Black and Scholes option pricing model.

In Part D of this book we discuss other related topics. These topics include: swap and bond portfolio, warrant and convertible bond valuation, credit risk and value at risk. Finally, in Chapter 22 of this book we use real world data to show how options strategy, option valuation, implied variance and hedging strategy could be used in real world analysis.

The first edition of the *Encyclopedia of Finance* was published in 2006 and the second edition of the *Encyclopedia of Finance* was published in 2013. This is one of the most popular encyclopedias of finance available on the market. This encyclopedia is divided into three parts. Part I includes more than 900 terms and essays, Part II includes 74 papers, and Part III includes 11 appendices. Part I and Part II are written for undergraduate, graduate, master's and Ph.D. students. Part III is designed for Ph.D. students and practitioners.

The *Handbook of Quantitative Finance and Risk Management* was published by Springer in 2010 (ISBN 978-0-387-77116-8), and this handbook includes 109 chapters, which are divided into five parts. This book is designed for Ph.D. students and researchers in the finance industry. Part I is "Overview of Quantitative Finance and Risk Management." Part II is "Portfolio Theory and Investment Analysis." Part III is "Options and Option Pricing Theory." Part IV is "Risk Management." Part V is "Theory, Methodology, and Applications."

The *Handbook of Financial Econometrics and Statistics* was published by Springer in 2015 (ISBN 978-1-4614-7749-5). This book is designed for Ph.D. students and quantitative researchers in the finance industry. This book includes 100 chapters and is divided into four volumes.

The 100 chapters of this handbook can be classified into 14 different topics. They are: financial accounting (Chapters 2, 9, 10, 61, and 97); mutual funds (Chapters 3, 24, 25, 68, and 88); microstructure (Chapters 4, 44, 96, and 99); corporate finance (Chapters 5, 21, 30, 38, 42, 60, 63, 75, 79, 81, and 95); asset pricing (Chapters 6, 15, 22, 28, 34, 36, 39, 45, 50, 85, 87, 93, and 100); options (Chapters 7, 32, 37, 55, 65, 84, 86, 90, and 98); portfolio analysis (Chapters 8, 26, 35, 53, 67, 73, 80, and 83); risk management (Chapters 11, 13, 16, 17, 23, 27, 41, 51, 54, 72, 91, and 92); international finance (Chapters 12, 40, 43, 59, and 69); event study (Chapter 14); methodology (Chapters 18, 19, 20, 29, 31, 33, 46, 47, 49, 52, 56, 57, 58, 62, 74, 76, 77, 78, 82, and 89); and banking management (Chapter 64).

In this chapter, we have discussed the textbooks in financial management, corporate finance, security analysis, portfolio management, and financial derivatives, financial planning and forecast, statistics for business and financial economics, and *Essentials of Microsoft Excel, Excel VBA, SAS and MINITAB for Statistical and Financial Analyses* and *Intermediate Futures and Options*. All these textbooks are written for innovative and active approach to teach finance, which has been discussed in Chapter 9. In addition, in this chapter, we also discuss *Handbook of Quantitative Finance and Risk Management, Encyclopedia of Finance* and *Handbook of Financial Econometrics and Statistics*. These books are designed for faculty, Ph.D. students, and practitioners, who are intend to do quantitative finance and risk management. Overall, I feel rewarding to have this opportunity to write finance textbooks for undergraduate students, graduate students, Ph.D. students and practitioners.

Chapter

13

Participation in Taiwanese Democratic Movements

Although I have lived in the United States for 48 years, I still actively participate in Taiwanese organizations and democratic movements. This chapter details the process and afterthoughts of my participation and also reviews what President Lee Teng-hui has contributed to the democracy of Taiwan.

I studied abroad in 1968 not only to pursue an advanced degree, but also to escape the intolerable political environment of Taiwan. I had hoped that I could contribute to promote a free and democratic Taiwan by studying in the United States. In July 1968, when I arrived at West Virginia University (WVU), to my surprise, I discovered that there were two Chinese student associations on campus. The Chinese Students Association (CSA) was supported by Nationalist Kuomintang (KMT) and was seen as a "legal" organization from most Chinese students' point of view, while the other, Taiwanese Students Association (TSA), was a partly nonconformist organization, since it promoted a democratic Taiwan. I decided to join the TSA, but since I still had some concerns at that time, I was only involved with the organization indirectly.

Prof. Bin-ming Chou at West Virginia University often had TSA students go over to his home to discuss Taiwan's political situation. I participated in these discussions quite frequently when I was at West Virginia University. My cousin, Yueh-jung Lee, and her husband, Dr. Chao-hsiun Chen, who was a medical professor at WVU, also supported TSA. On April 24, 1969, Chiang Ching-kuo, the president of Taiwan, was almost assassinated in New York City. TSA members held a series of discussions about this incident to express their concerns.

When I started my Ph.D. program at SUNY-Buffalo in 1970, I not only joined the TSA, but was also elected to chair the local section of the Taiwanese Association of America (TAA) after passing my Ph.D. qualifying exam in 1971. TAA-Buffalo was composed of students and local Taiwanese Americans. In my term as chairman, we played softball, went fishing, and discussed the future of Taiwan's politics. In the summer of 1972, we even drove to the University of Michigan to join the Midwest softball games. We also frequently participated in TAA-Rochester's activities.

In 1972, Taiwan was expelled from the United Nations. After this event, many students at SUNY-Buffalo held a special discussion focusing on the future of Taiwan and how we could help Taiwan secure its future. Over my three years in Buffalo, I invited many well-known people who were knowledgeable about Taiwan's democratic movement and who were enthusiastic enough about it to give speeches on campus.

After graduating from SUNY-Buffalo in 1973, I left to teach at UGA. There were only two Taiwanese professors, Chia-ming Chen and I, on the campus. So, without any hesitation, I participated in the TSA's activities and served as their advisor. In the winter of 1974, five mayors and county governors from Taiwan, including Mayor Cheng-hsing Chen of Keelung, visited Athens, GA. We welcomed them and discussed together the future and the possibilities of a real democratic Taiwan; however, most people were pessimistic.

Prof. Chia-ming Chen and I invited UGA students, including His-hunag Chen and Kuo-lung Huang, former professors of National Taiwan University; Son-nan Chen, former professor at National Chengchi University, Taiwan; Carl R. Chen, current William J. Hoben Professor of Finance at Dayton University, U.S. as well as others to our homes for dinner very often. We also joined TAA-Atlanta's activities.

At that time, the representative of the Taipei Economic and Cultural Representative Office (TECRO) in Atlanta was Mr. Stephen S.F. Chen, who in my opinion was an open-minded KMT member.

In 1976 after the Department of Finance at UIUC hired me, Schwinne and I invited many graduate students, including Tso-kwei Peng, Wu-hsiung Chen, Tse-han Lai, Yun Lin, Chao-cheng Yang, John K. Wei, David Chen, Chien-wen Chen, Chen-chin Chu, Ching-wen Hsin, and Wen-tzu Kao, from Taiwan to have dinner with us from time to time. All of these students have performed well in their careers. Even the president of Tamkang University, Clement C.P. Chang, visited us when he was studying at UIUC for his Ph.D. degree. Schwinne and I were impressed that most of these students became important officials or educators after they graduated.

During my time at UIUC, Schwinne and I participated in many TSA and TAA activities. I served as their consultant, played softball, went fishing with students, and invited famous democratic fighters to give speeches on campus. Some of these speakers included Chin-tse Chang, a village chief of Yiland County, Taiwan and David S. Hong and Ming-min Peng, who were leaders of the democracy movement. For the sake of saving money, some of our guest speakers would lodge at my home. In 1979, the KMT government arrested several important leaders of the democracy movement when people held demonstrations against the dictatorship in Kaohsiung, Taiwan. Linda Gail Arrigo, who is an American and has helped Taiwan's democracy movement, went all over the United States to speak of this incident and to search for supporters to rescue Ming-teh Shih. She came to UIUC for a lecture in December of that year. I introduced her and was in charge of her speech. Since I aided her, I was reported to the Taiwanese government as a "helper." Since then, my visa applications to Taiwan were handled as a special case, which greatly complicated traveling to Taiwan.

Every summer, I went to Chicago and Michigan to join the TAA-Midwest activities and analyze the stock markets for our Taiwanese friends. I invited Ming-min Peng, Hsin-liang Hsu, Shui-bian Chen, and others to deliver their speeches on the progress of Taiwan's democratic movements. I became acquainted with George T.H. Chang, Tain-tsair

Hsu, and Tan-sun Chen and was impressed by their dedication to the democratic movements.

In addition, to promote the Taiwan–U.S. relationship in economics and trading, Dr. Fu-tung Hsu and I held a conference on Taiwan's economy and trade on April 18, 1990 in Washington D.C. The attendants included scholars, executives of enterprises, and policy makers. The main topics of this conference were listed as follows:

1. The challenge and the future of the economic relationship between Taiwan and the U.S.
2. The up-to-date situation of financial markets in Taiwan
3. The current labor markets in Taiwan
4. Importing, exporting, and trading districts
5. Structures of Taiwan business
6. How to attract Taiwan enterprises to invest in the U.S.
7. Issues of the trading balance between Taiwan and the U.S.
8. Business opportunities of trading with Taiwan
9. Trading, saving, and property distribution in Taiwan

The attendants who came from Taiwan included the ex-governor of Taipei County, Ching You, Ding-nan Chen, Sheng-cheng Hu, Lien-fu Huang, Chao-huei Ou, Shen-tieh Hsiao, Liang-hsin Fan, Son-nan Chen, Kuo-lung Liang, Gili Yen, Chung-cheng Lin, and Chia-hung Kuo.

The U.S. representatives included George J. Donegan of Export-Import Bank of the U.S.; Ronald Cass, Deputy Secretary of International Trade Administration of U.S. Department of Commerce; Raymard Sancles, Chief of AIT Trade Center; and W.N. Morell, Chairman of Sino-U.S. Economics Association.

In 1980, Prof. Shu-tsung Liao and others organized the Association of Taiwanese Professors in Northern America (ATPNA) to strengthen academic research, communication, and to promote a democratic Taiwan. I have been a loyal member of ATPNA since the very beginning and have attended all of their annual meetings. I occasionally presented research papers at the meetings as well. In August 1990, I went back to Taiwan and addressed the hedging of new derivatives during the 10th annual ATPNA meeting. I suggested that Taiwan develop similar products as well. This lecture was supported by the presence of Ching You, Tzong-shian Yu, Rong-yi Wu, and Kao-chao Lee. At that time, Hau Pei-tsun had just served as premier of the Executive Yuan. He appointed Wang Chien-shien as minister of finance. I joked that Premier Hau and Minister Wang didn't really understand the economy and suggested the economists be their private tutors. As a result, the *Independent Daily News* reported on my speech with the headline "CF Lee fixed Pei-tsun Hau and Chien-shien Wang." Thankfully since martial law had been lifted, I did not get in trouble for my comments.

On the evening of August 14, 1988, Mr. Tien-tsai Hsu and I gave speeches at the Kaohsiung County government. I spoke about Taiwan's stock markets while Mr. Hsu spoke of labor issues in Taiwan. While at the Kaohsiung County government, I met the County Governor Yueh-ying Yu Chen, who later visited my home and sent her son, Cheng-tao, to study at Rutgers University. Cheng-tao was a member of the Taiwan Provincial Consultative Council and now is a member of the Legislative Yuan. I am proud of his achievements.

My most active year for participating in organization activities was 1992. I gave three keynote speeches that year. On February 1, 1992, I spoke at the University of Pennsylvania for the Intercollegiate Taiwanese American Students Association about the employment opportunities and the future of second generation Taiwanese Americans. I suggested that they go back and work in Taiwan. I told those students that with its rapid economic development, the future of employment opportunities in Taiwan would become greater. At the same time, Tan-sun Chen talked about the effects of economic development and American culture in Taiwan. On that occasion, I was glad to see so many excellent second generation Taiwanese Americans.

I went back to Taiwan in April and delivered a speech for the China Economic Association (now called the Taiwan Economic Association), on the financial analysis of the Six-year National Development Plan.

On July 9, by the invitation of Chairman David S. Hong, I delivered a speech, "The Past, the Present, and the Future of Taiwan's Economy," to a summer camp of Midwest Taiwanese Americans. (The outline of my speech can be found in Appendix 13A.) In the speech I discussed how the economic development in Taiwan had been upgraded to a promising level and would be more promising in the future, especially in the development of the communication industry. I also remarked on how the scope of the Six-year National Development Plan was too ambitious for the government as far as the finances were concerned; therefore, I suggested it was better not to carry out the plan in a hurry. And in order to develop Taiwan as a regional financial center a basic foundation with solid stock and foreign currency exchange markets must be established.

I also discussed how financial markets should be globalized and that capital accounts should not be opened completely. My speech detailed the risk, especially the political risk, in investing in Mainland China and I suggested that the government propose regulations for large companies investing in Mainland China. The last point in my speech was that after an effort led by President Lee Teng-hui the future of democratic politics was established and in order to promote democratic policies, Taiwan must welcome back all citizens who participated in the early overseas democratic movements.

Since the theme was to establish a democratic Taiwan, many famous democratic fighters, including Ming-teh Shih, Lung-chih Chen, Hung-hsi Lee, Fong-ming Chen, Yu-li Lee, and David S. Hong were present. At the camp I briefly explained my experience with participating in democratic movements in the U.S. over the past 24 years and how I was glad to see the current progress in Taiwan's democratic politics. The development in democracy not only enhanced people's welfare, but also became the solid foundation to receive support from the United States. I was proud that I had taken part in the democratic movements.

During September of 1994 to 2000, I actively participated the conference sponsored by Taiwanese Community in U.S. In September of 1994, Chao-huei Ou invited me to Washington D.C. to attend the Symposium for National Development. During this discussion, I promoted the principle "industry is the root while finance is the leaf" for developing Taiwan as a regional financial center. In addition, I also expressed my view about the political risks in investing in Mainland China and advocated that the government view the investment of Mainland China as part of an overseas investment. Deputy Chairman Kao agreed with my stance.

In September of 1995, I was invited to New York to participate in the Symposium for National Development to discuss the issue of developing Taiwan as a regional financial center. Ex-Governor Yuan-tung Shu, Chen Sun, and Susan S. Chang were also present at the symposium. I tried my best to promote my ideas, which were not to liberalize the capital accounts too quickly, to watch out for the political risks in investing in Mainland China, and to keep the conservative and steady financial policies. Governor Hsu and others also supported my ideas.

Several years later, Wu-lang Lee invited me to participate in the 10th North American Chinese Conference and address the financial policies of Taiwan after the Asian Financial Crisis. I mentioned that the policies should thoroughly consider the impact on the financial systems of building the high-speed railroad system in Taiwan.

The following are the topics discussed in our session.

Topic I: Exploring the financial problems of Taiwan's government and suggesting ways for improvement

Topic II: The liberalization and regulation on finance

Topic III: The legislation for financial markets

Topic IV: The risk assessment on investing overseas

To sum up, our session acknowledges that Taiwan's government has completed many achievements towards the execution and promotion of financial policies, although there are still many problems to be solved in the near future. The attending scholars and representatives of enterprises agree that the financial officials in Taiwan's government are with excellent quality and usually face the reality without making cosmetic speeches. Therefore, we believe that the officials will seriously think over the suggestions from academic institutions and industries to carry out the necessary financial policies to work further on the financial development in Taiwan.

Progress in Taiwan's politics and economy was due to the efforts of all residents as well as the successful execution of government policies. Most of the progress may be contributed to President Lee Teng-hui's efforts in promoting democratic politics and his determination for economic construction since his inauguration in January 1988. The goals I had been pursuing during the years I participated in the democratic movements in the United States were achieved during the 12-year term of President Lee. In May 1996, when Governor Fai-nan Perng and I took part in President Lee's inaugural ceremony, at Taoyuan International Baseball Stadium, I was moved by his magnificent speech. President Lee revealed his view on the cross-strait relationship and proposed the "special two countries policy" on July 9, 1999. His point identified the true relationship between Taiwan and Mainland China, which I completely agreed with.

In January 2000, I published my Chinese autobiography and had a big celebration in Taipei. A lot of my friends participated in this celebration. During that time Taiwan held its presidential election and Mr. Chen Shui-bian was elected as the new president. This was the first time that the KMT lost its presidency and Democratic Progressive Party (DPP) took over the government from the KMT. On May 20, 2000, Chen Shui-bian became the new president of Taiwan. This was a big achievement for the Taiwanese democratic movement. In 2008, DPP lost to KMT. In January 2016, DPP won the election again. Dr. Tsai Ing-wen became the new president on May 20, 2016. Overall, the Taiwanese democratic movement made Taiwan one of the most democratic countries in Asia.

After having lived in the United States for 48 years, I have just finished my 43rd year of teaching in the United States. During these 43 years, I have taught three years at UGA (1973–1976), 12 years at University of Illinois at Urbana-Champaign (1976–1988), and 28 years at Rutgers University (1988–present). I not only participated in different academic activities, but I also participated in various organizations' activities and democratic movements both directly and indirectly.

Appendix 13A

Outline of the Speech Entitled "The Past, the Present, and the Future of Taiwan's Economy"

I. Introduction

II. Economic Development in Taiwan
   1. Agricultural products
   2. Light industrial products
   3. High tech products
   4. Export-leading economy
   5. Contributions of small and medium businesses

III. Changes of Economic Structures in Taiwan
   1. Relationship between the rise of New Taiwan Dollars and the upgrade of industries
   2. Losing control to the foreign currency exchanges
   3. Up-to-date situation of investing in Mainland China
   4. Development of financial markets

IV. Economic Future in Taiwan
   1. Six-year National Development Plan
   2. Internationalized enterprises in Taiwan
   3. Opportunities and risks in investing in Mainland China (risks in politics and in currency exchange rates)

4. Internationalized condition in Taiwan financial markets
5. Relationship between the democratic politics and the economic development in Taiwan

V. Conclusion

The major conclusions of this speech are summarized as follows:

1. The economic development in Taiwan has upgraded to a promising level and will be promising in the future, especially in the development of the communication industry.
2. The scope of the Six-year National Development Plan is too ambitious for the financial load of the government; therefore, it is better not to carry out the plan in a hurry.
3. The basic foundation must have solid stock and foreign currency exchange markets in order to develop Taiwan as a regional financial center.
4. Financial markets should be globalized step by step and capital accounts should not be completely released.
5. Risks exist in the investment of Mainland China, especially the political risks. The government should propose the regulations for big companies to invest in Mainland China.
6. Being led by President Lee Teng-hui, the future of democratic politics in Taiwan is established. In order to promote democratic policies, Taiwan must welcome back all citizens, who participated in the early overseas democratic movements.

Chapter

14

My Relationships with Important People in Academic Institutes, the Industry, and Taiwan Government

In this chapter, I will explain my relationships with some important individuals within the industry, the academic circles, and the Taiwanese government, such as ex-ministers of finance, Robert Chun Chien, Shirley W.Y. Kuo, Chen-kuo Lin, and Paul C.H. Chiu, governors and deputy governors of Central Bank, the vice chairman of Council of Economic Planning and Development (CEPD), the chairman of International Commercial Bank of China (ICBC), the chairmen of Chiao Tung Bank and the Farmers Bank of China.

Ex-Minister Robert Chun Chien graduated from the Department of Economics, NTU. He was also one of my coworkers during my last year (1967–1968) at Bank of China (renamed ICBC). My main responsibility was to help him edit the English version of *The Economy Bimonthly*. When I went back to Taiwan I visited his office at the Ministry of Finance twice, and each time I came, we discussed the economic and financial policies regarding the country.

Ex-Minister Shirley W.Y. Kuo was one of my professors at the Graduate Institute of Economics, NTU. I learned a lot in her research on policies class. She served as a professor in the Department of Economics at NTU, deputy governor of the Central Bank, chairman of CEPD, minister without portfolio, the Executive Yuan, and made many great contributions to Taiwan's financial and banking systems. When the 3rd Conference on PBFEA was held in Taipei on August 7, 1995, I invited her to be the keynote speaker at the dinner banquet. There she delivered a speech on the necessity of establishing futures markets in Taiwan.

Ex-Minister Chen-kuo Lin graduated two years before I did from the Department of Economics, NTU. He was also the teaching assistant in Prof. Kuo-wei Chang's class, Advanced Statistics. He, Prof. Chih-ming Cheng, and I also worked together in Prof. Chang's statistical research office in 1961. Minister Lin had served as director of Bureau of Finance, Taipei City Government; director of Bureau of Finance, Taiwan Provincial Government; and chairman of the China External Trade Development Council.

Ex-Minister Paul C.H. Chiu also graduated two years after I did from the Department of Economics, NTU. I became acquainted with him when we studied at NTU and met up with him again in Columbus, Ohio, when he studied in the U.S. Paul returned to Taiwan after he received his Ph.D. from Ohio State University. He served as an economics professor at NTU, deputy governor of the Central Bank, and chairman of the Chinese Financial Association, which I initially helped organize. In the summer of 1994, when I went back to Taiwan for the conference "Develop Taipei to an Asian Financial Operation Center," he and Mr. Fai-nan Perng were both appointed as deputy governors of the Central Bank under the supervision of Governor Kuo-shu Liang. At the conference we discussed the topics related to the Chinese Financial Association and establishing Taipei as an Asian financial center.

When Dr. Chiu served as minister of finance in 1996, I had more opportunities to discuss the government's financial policies with him. Minister Chiu helped me organize academic activities in Taiwan, including the opening of the 7th Conference on PBFEA held in Taipei on May 28 and 29, 1999. He supported the conference with all of his resources and delivered the keynote speech "The Approaches of R.O.C. in Coping the Asian Financial Crisis and Financial Reform" at the luncheon on the second day of the conference. From July 3 to 5, 1999,

Minister Chiu extended this topic and delivered another keynote speech at the Conference of North American Chinese Association. These two presentations were published in the "Collection Papers of Pacific Basin Financial Markets and Policies" edited by Prof. Hong-chang Chang and myself.

Minister Chiu contributed greatly to Taiwan's stock markets and financial policies. When he served as deputy governor of the Central Bank, he proposed a comprehensive plan for Taiwan's monetary policy. His efforts were remarkable on the promotion of "Unifying Two Taxes" (to avoid double taxation), dealing with banks' bad loans (loans cannot be recovered any longer), the management of local financial crisis, and other financial reforms. Minister Chiu also proposed several alternative strategies to stabilize the fluctuating stock markets. Since 1998, I was honored to have the opportunities to provide my suggestions to the policies on stock markets and the deduction of business taxes. After the biggest earthquake of the 20th century happened in Taiwan on September 21, 1999, the government had to carry out a plan with a heavy financial responsibility to recover from the damage caused by this natural disaster. However, with his experience and excellent ability in dealing with financial issues, I had faith that Minister Chiu would successfully complete this demanding job.

I know most of the previous governors of the Central Bank. I have already explained in detail my relationship with Governor Kuo-shu Liang in Chapter 6. Herein, I will describe my relationship with Governors Samuel C. Shieh, Jia-dong Hsu, and Fai-nan Perng.

In 1964, when I was in President Lee Teng-hui's class, "Agricultural Policies in Taiwan" at the Graduate Institute of Economics, NTU, I read articles written by Governor Shieh and President Lee. I admired Governor Shieh because he was a knowledgeable scholar. In 1987, I returned to Taiwan to teach a few short courses. The deputy chairman of the Bank, Mr. Chun-nan Pai, first introduced us when I delivered a speech at Chiao Tung Bank regarding the bank's financial management. Later, when I visited the chair of China Trust, Jeffrey L.S. Koo, I met Mr. Chun-nan Pai again. At the time he was the senior consultant of China Trust. In addition to exchanging our views on Taiwan and international finance, he also gave me a set of hardcover books, *The Collection of Governor Shieh's Speeches*, as a gift. From reading this collection, I learned more about Governor Shieh and the process of Taiwan's economic and financial development.

Through the introduction of Governor Liang, I became acquainted with Director Fai-nan Perng of the Department of Foreign Exchange some years earlier. To better prepare the professional skills of the employees of Department of Foreign Exchange, Director Perng sent Cho-kun Hsu, Yu-min Chen, and Chi Ouyang to my classes at Rutgers University in 1991. He even invited me to deliver a 10-day short course, Financial Management and Analysis for Banks, at the Training Center for Financial and Banking Employees in August 1992.

Governor Perng and I have a close relationship that is based on our shared points of view of economic policies, which have strengthened over time. Governor Perng served as director of the Department of Economics Research for the Central Bank, director of Department of Foreign Exchange, deputy governor of the Central Bank, chair of the Central Trust, and chair of ICBC. With such abundant experience, he was appointed as governor of the Central Bank. During his two years serving as governor, his excellent performance fulfilled the expectation of President Lee.

From August 1993 to October 1994, when I served as the distinguished professor at the Chinese University of Hong Kong, Governor Perng asked me to conduct research in Pacific Basin financial markets and policies. During the summer of 1994, I did my research on how to develop Taipei as a financial center in CEPD and the Central Bank. I also completed a report of more than 200 pages with Governor Perng, Director A-ting Chou, and several others. The outline of this report was published in the *Quarterly Review of the Central Bank*, in March 1995.

Vice Chairman Chi Schive was another one of my classmates at the Department of Economics, NTU. He strongly supported the academic activities I organized. In March 1994, he invited me to CEPD to speak about the Pacific Basin financial markets and policies for the mid-to-high level officials in the Ministry of Finance, CEPD, and the Central Bank. We also discussed the related issues of developing Taipei as a regional financial center.

When I conducted research on the development of Taipei as a regional financial center with Governor Perng at the Central Bank in August of the same year, I asked Deputy Governor Hsu for more information and any issues regarding Taiwan's financial markets. I gained a lot of practical business knowledge about the Central Bank during my discussion with Deputy Governor Hsu.

In July, Vice Chairman Chi Schive invited me again to CEPD to supervise a research project on futures options and the internalization of finance in the Taiwan area. When the Conference on PBFEA was held at Rutgers University in April 1996, Vice Chairman Schive was invited to deliver the keynote speech. His speech was entitled "Toward 21st Century: Liberating Economy in Taiwan and the Development of Operating Center." When the 7th Conference on PBFEA was held at the Grand Hotel, Taipei, on May 28 and 29, 1998, Vice Chairman Schive contributed again with great efforts helping to open the conference. He also served as the keynote speaker at the dinner banquet on May 28 and joined the discussion panel on Pacific Basin financial markets and policies. In addition, he chaired the discussion panel on privatization of public constructions. Previously Vice Chairman Schive chaired the Department of Economics, NTU and led Taiwanese representatives to the negotiation of Taiwan's participation in the WTO. He was very experienced and contributed greatly in the promotion of developing Taiwan as a financial operation center in Pacific Basin areas.

Vice Chairman Kao-chao Lee also contributed to domestic economic construction and development. In July 1994, when we worked on developing Taipei as a regional financial center at CEPD, Vice Chairman Lee provided an exceptional analysis to the future of economic development in Taiwan. On June 9, 1998, Vice Chairman Lee invited me to CEPD to deliver a speech on the financial competence of the U.S. I spoke about the necessity and reasons for forbidding domestic corporate to trade on NDF. On August 16, 1998, Director Ching-chi Lai invited me to CEPD to speak about exploring Pacific financial markets and policies after a financial crisis. On May 28 and 29 of the following year, Vice Chairman Lee was invited to join the discussion panel, "Taiwan's Financial Markets and Policies," at the 7th Conference on PBFEA held in Taipei.

With his own professional style, Governor Yon-dong Hsu was a practical and experienced banker. Since he was appointed as the governor of the Central Bank in 1995, we had met many times. On August 8 and 9, 1995, at the 3rd Conference of PBFEA held in Taipei, he was one of the two keynote speakers. He gave a speech entitled "How to Develop Taipei as a Regional Financial Center," which was published in the *Review of Pacific Basin Financial Markets and Policies* (March, 1998) of which I am the editor. On the afternoon of August 8, I accompanied some foreign scholars to see President Lee Teng-hui at the president's office. President Lee expressed his high regards for Governor Hsu's approaches in dealing with the financial crisis. In October 1995, Governor Hsu and I participated in the National Development Symposium held in New York City to explore the issues of Taiwan's financial markets and policies.

In May 1996, I returned to Taiwan for President Lee Teng-hui's inaugural ceremony. At the party held by the Minister of Foreign Affairs, Governor Hsu suggested that I spend more time promoting the set-up of the financial college, which I had mentioned two years earlier. It happened that some reporters asked him about the development of financial centers and Governor Hsu deliberately gave me the opportunity to express my views on how to develop Taipei as a regional financial center. I appreciated Governor Hsu's support and encouragement about this matter.

In September 1997, when the Asian Financial Crisis seemed to affect more and more of Taiwan's finances, I was worried and called Chairman Perng of ICBC from the U.S. I asked him if I should call Governor Hsu to ask about closing or narrowing the NDF (non-deliverable forward) trading. He told me that he'd mentioned this to Governor Hsu already. Later, when Perng served as governor, I mentioned my thoughts on NDF. In May 1998, Governor Perng expressed that he might consider forbidding domestic corporations to trade on NDF. He also showed me some research reports about how NDF affected the foreign exchange trading. I completely agreed with his decision.

On May 21, the Central Bank announced that domestic corporations would not be allowed to trade NDF. However, the opposition from the domestic corporations was much larger than we expected. In the *Economic Daily News* on May 21, I expressed my support for the new policy of the Central Bank. I also joined a luncheon about this policy held by Deputy Governor Shea where I communicated with some liberal scholars.

Because of the depreciation of the Japanese Yen, the exchange rate of the U.S. Dollar to Japanese Yen reached 1:146.75 in early June. The New Taiwan Dollar depreciated following this trend, while Taiwanese stock markets fell sharply. As a result, many people blamed the ban of NDF trading. To correct this, I let the *China Times* print my bold forecast, "CF Lee: Foreign Cash to Flow Back to Taiwan Within Two Months," on June 16 and explained that the downturn of Taiwanese stocks was just one of many manipulating approaches of foreign investors. At the end of June, when I analyzed Taiwan's stock markets in the one-day course held at the Training Center for Financial and Banking Employees, I advocated that it was not necessary to completely open capital accounts. I believed it was necessary to execute different policies to stabilize the New Taiwan Dollar.

On February 26, 1998, my speech, "It is Not Necessary to Totally Remove the Restrictions for Capital Accounts" was printed in *Commercial Times*. A few days later, in an international meeting organized by the Department of Finance of National Taiwan University, Prof. M. Scholes, the 1997 Nobel Prize in Economics winner, and a few other domestic professors publicly expressed their opposing opinions. Governor Shieh called Governor Perng right away and asked him to tell me that Governor Perng completely support my views. Governor Shieh had served as secretary-general at JCRR, professor of National Taiwan University, deputy chairman of CEDP, director of Asian Bank, and chairman of Chiao Tung Bank, and therefore had an abundance of experience in dealing with economic and financial issues. From *The Collection of Governor Shieh's Speeches*, I found that Governor Shieh's view of policy drafting was very practical and applicable. For example, he took into account the economic and political conditions Taiwan was in and advocated to promote policies for internationalization and liberalization.

In April 1998, Chung-Hua Institution for Economic Research (CHIER) sponsored the conference "How to Promote the Stability of Southeastern Finance and the Regional Economic Development through the Cooperation of Taiwan and Mainland China." Governor Shieh and Dr. Chao-cheng Mai, the president of CHIER, invited me to lead a discussion. In the opening ceremony, Mr. Pin-kung Chiang, chairman of CEDP, was the guest speaker while Ms. Pei-chen Chang gave the introduction. Besides myself, the other discussants included Prof. Chen-min, Vice Chairman Chi Schive, Vice Chairman Chi-shang Kao, Director Don-cheng Fu, Director He-sung Wang, Chairman Casey K. Chuang, and Director Chien-hsun Chen. In June of the same year, I delivered a lecture entitled "How to Cope with the Current Financial Problems in Taiwan" at CHIER again. From these two contacts with Governor Shieh, I further recognized that he was a knowledgeable and friendly gentleman.

In early February 1998, I taught financial and accounting courses for Chinese managers in Mainland China for the United Group, Chicago. Deputy Governor Jia-dong Shea invited me to give a talk to the Central Bank of R.O.C. in the afternoon of February 28. However, in the morning of February 17, I received a message that Governor Hsu, Chi-ming Chien, Huang Chen, and two other Central Bank colleagues died in a China Airlines accident that happened near Taiwan Taoyuan International Airport. On February 26, I went to the Central Bank and expressed my sympathy to Governor Hsu in person. The scene was very depressing and made me feel the same way that I felt when I went to Governor Liang's home on May 5, 1995 to pay tribute to him after his death.

On August 26, 1998, I visited President Lee in his office and told him that it was a smart idea to appoint Mr. Fai-nan Perng as the governor of the Central Bank. President Lee cheerfully agreed. He said, "Governor Perng had followed Governor Liang for a long time. He is not only knowledgeable, but also very diligent. I believe he will be a wonderful governor." I was very glad to participate in Governor

Perng's inauguration held in the auditorium of the Central Bank on February 28, 1998.

Among the other important economic and financial officials, I also kept a strong relationship with Deputy Governors Jia-dong Shea and Yi-hsiung Hsu, the Central Bank of China, and Vice Chairmen Chi Schive and Kao-chao Lee, CEPD. Deputy Governor Jia-dong Shea was one of my classmates in the Department of Economics, NTU. He served as an economics professor at NTU and director of the Institute of Economics, Academia Sinica. Ex-Governor Yuan-tung Hsu appointed him as deputy governor in 1995. He helped me a lot in preparing for my speech, "The Financial Analysis of the Six-year National Development Plan and Its Impacts on Financial Markets," which I gave at the symposium sponsored by the China Economic Association in April 1992. On February 28, 1998, he also invited me to deliver a speech titled "Review and Prospective after the Asian Financial Crisis" at the Central Bank. In June of the same year, Deputy Governor Shea hosted a luncheon discussing the ban on domestic corporations to trade NDF; he invited me as one of the main guests to express my views on this matter. Through my experience with him, I consider Deputy Governor Shea an excellent government official with both theoretical knowledge and practical experience in economics and finance.

I also had close relationships with Chairman Yung-san Lee, ICBC; Chairman Patrick C.J. Liang, Chiao Tung Bank; and Chairman Mu-tsai Chen, the Farmers Bank of China. Chairman Yung-san Lee graduated a few years before me from the Department of Economics, NTU. He had served as director of the Department of Economics Research, the Central Bank; director of the Institute of Economics, Academia Sinica; general-manager of Chiao Tung Bank; and chairman of the Farmers Bank of China. Chairman Lee, Dean Gili Yen, and I organized the Chinese Financial Association together. He also served the first term as chairman for the association. He helped me a great deal with organizing the 7th Conference on PBFEA held in Taipei in May 1999. In July 1999, Chairman Lee and I joined the Northern American Chinese Conference held in Washington D.C. We discussed the financial problems faced by Taiwan at that time. He is no doubt a financial expert with an abundance of practical experience.

The chairman of Chiao Tung Bank, Patrick Chen Jin Liang, served as vice chairman of CEPD and deputy governor of the Central Bank before. During my summer vacation in 1994, I learned a lot of valuable financial knowledge from Chairman Liang when I participated in the special research project "Developing Taipei as a Regional Financial Center" at CEPD. When he was appointed to deputy governor of the Central Bank, I met with him frequently. He always supported my academic activities held in Taiwan and always encouraged me to express my views regarding financial policies. He is indeed one of the most remarkable and experienced financial experts who have served in the banking industry in Taiwan.

Mr. Mu-tsai Chen, chairman of the Farmers Bank of China, was also one of my classmates at the Graduate Institute of Economics, NTU. He served as director general of the Bureau of Monetary Affairs and vice minister of the Ministry of Finance. When I worked on the research project "Developing Taipei as a Regional Financial Center," I found out that Chairman Chen was familiar with every move of the Taiwanese stock markets and the problems that Taiwanese banks faced. He always supported my academic activities and was also one of the best financial banking experts in Taiwan.

I also became acquainted with Director Susan S. Chang, Chairman Tzong-yeong Lin, and Director Sheng-yen Lee. Ms. Chang served as director general of Bureau of Monetary Affairs and director of the Department of National Treasury, Ministry of Finance. We discussed issues related to the Taiwanese financial stock markets at the Symposium of Chinese in New York held in October 1995 and at the North American Chinese Conference held in July 1999. Mr. Tzong-yeong Lin was chairman of the Securities and Futures Commission (SFC), Ministry of Finance. He served as deputy chairman of SFC and general manager in a brokerage company before. Since Minister Chiu appointed him as chairman of SFC, he had handled several stock market crises effectively. Director Sheng-yen Lee was an economics professor teaching in Japan. Governor Kuo-shu Liang invited him to serve as director general of the Economic Research Department, the

Central Bank. Previously, he was the director general of the Banking Department, the Central Bank. In July 1999, he and I both joined the North American Chinese Conference and discussed the liberalization and regulation over Taiwanese stock markets.

Dr. Kuang-sheng Liao has been a good friend since we studied at NTU together. He is also an alumnus of Chien Kuo High School. He has worked as chair and professor of the Department of Government and Public Administration, the Chinese University of Hong Kong. Afterwards, he was elected as an Oversea Member of the Legislative Yuan, R.O.C. In 1995, when he completed his term as an Oversea Member, he and his wife resigned from their teaching jobs in Hong Kong and returned to Taiwan. President Lee Teng-hui soon appointed him to the Consultant Committee of the Council of National Security. In March 1999, when I held the Conference on Pacific Basin Stock Markets and Policies in New York, he and his wife both attended. Dr. Kuang-sheng Liao also helped me with organizing the 7th Conference on PBFEA held on May 28 and 29, 1999, in Taipei. He is an expert on the political and economic development of Mainland China.

In the field of banking and stock investment, I am familiar with Mr. Shu-sheng Wang, general manager of ICBC; Mr. Chieh-chien Chao, general manager of Chiao Tung Bank; Mr. Chi-tang Lo, chairman of Taiwan Bank; Mr. Tien-lin Huang, chairman of the First Commercial Bank; Mr. Shih-sung Cheng, chairman of International Security Investment Trust Corporation; Mr. Peter T. Yang, chairman of First Bank Investment Advising Inc.; Mr. Ching-hsiung Chou, manager general of the Shanghai Commercial and Savings Bank; Mr. Jong-shong Lin, chairman of E. Sun Bank; Mr. Chung-ying Lee, chairman of Taiwan Stock Exchange Corporation; Mr. Kuo-hwa Wang, manager general of the United World Chinese Commercial Bank; Mr. Te-tsai Teng, manager general of Taipei Foreign Exchange Trading Corporation; Ms. Ching-ing Hou, chairman of Taiwan Academy of Banking and Finance; Mr. Ching-yi Wang, chairman of Taiwan Arthur Anderson Accounting; and Mr. A-ting Chou, director general of the Foreign Exchange Department of the Central Bank. They are all very supportive of my academic activities organized in Taiwan and the Asia-Pacific area.

In the financial industry, my friends include Mr. Yu-hao Chen, chairman of Tuntex Group; Mr. Jen-shyong Ho, chairman of Tung Ho Steel Enterprise Corp.; Dr. Tai-ying Liu, chairman and CEO of China Development Industrial Bank; Dr. Vincent P. C. Lin, chairman of Vertex/Vertech Group; Mr. Jervis Cheng-hsing Chen, chairman of Maifung Co. Ltd.; Mr. Chien-chih Chen, chairman of Syntex Semiconductor Co.; and Mr. Tai-chi Lee, chairman of Tidehold Development Co. These friends have supported me in organizing international academic activities in Taiwan and abroad.

As for the academic circles, I am friends with Dr. Rong-yi Wu, president of Taiwan Institute of Economic Research; Dr. Chao-cheng Mai, president of Chung-Hua Institution for Economic Research; Dr. Sheng-cheng Hu, director of the Institute of Economics, Academia Sinica; Dr. Wei-Jao Chen, president of National Taiwan University; Dr. Ting-wong Cheng, president of National Chengchi University; Dr. Clement C.P. Chang, president of Tamkang University; Dr. Hong-chang Chang, president of See-Hai Technical and Business College; Dr. Zau-nan Chen, academician of Academia Sinica; Dr. Tzong-shian Yu, academician of Academia Sinica; Dr. Pochih Chen, professor of Department of Economics, NTU; Dr. Gili Yen, dean of College of Management Science, Chaoyang University of Technology; Dr. Yu-tsung Lin, professor of Department of Finance, NTU; Prof. Ta-hou Lin, vice president of Taiwan Research Institute; Dr. David S. Hong, vice president of Taiwan Institute of Economic Research; Dr. Mao-wei Hung, professor of the Department of International Business, NTU; Dr. Shu-hsing Li, professor of the Department of Accounting, NTU; Dr. Li-lun Chu, currently member of Legislative Yuan. All of my friends are also very supportive of the domestic and international academic meetings and conferences I have organized in Taiwan and abroad.

To fulfill the needs for organizing conferences on PBFEA and the incorporated journal, *Review of Pacific Basin Financial Markets and Policies*, the Foundation of Pacific Basin Financial Research and Development (FPBFRD) was established in March 1999 with the support and help from my friends in different fields. I served as the chairman; the other board members of the foundation included:

1.	C.C. Lee	Chairman of Maywufa Company, Ltd., Representative of the National Assembly
2.	Vincent P.C. Lin	Chairman of Vertex/Vertech Group
3.	Shau-dai Lin	Chairman of Taiwan Futures Exchange
4.	Paul C.H. Chiu	Minister of Finance
5.	Chi-huei Yao	President of Republic of China Business Association
6.	Jervis C.H. Chen	Chairman of Maifung Co., Ltd.
7.	Peter C. Chen	Chairman of Syntek Semiconductor Co. and the Fortuner Co.
8.	Yi-ping Chen	Manager General of the Shanghai Commercial & Savings Bank
9.	Chin-tsai Chen	Chairman of Nam Chow Chemical Ind. Co., Ltd.
10.	Fai-nan Perng	Governor of the Central Bank of China, R.O. C.
11.	Min-jun Huang	Manager General of Gei-Tai Stock Exchange
12.	Cheng-tien Chan	Chairman of Yi Jinn Industrial Co., Ltd.
13.	Chih-ming Liao	President of Enlight Corporation
14.	Kuan-ya Chi Liao	Honorary Professor of the Hong Kong Polytechnic University

The organizational objectives and accomplishments are as follows:

I. Objectives:

The FPBFRD is committed to extend and promote the related financial activities for international academic researches and opinion exchanges. In accordance with the laws and regulations, it deals with the following businesses:

1. To promote the research related to the financial development in Pacific Basin countries.
2. To enhance the operation of the international Conferences on

Pacific Basin Finance, Economics, and Accounting and the journal *Review of Pacific Basin Financial Markets and Policies.*

3. To hold international conferences in Taiwan and other Pacific Basin countries.
4. To use this activity to promote international diplomacy for Taiwan's government and universities.
5. To promote the research related to the financial development in Pacific Basin countries and provide information and references for the governmental and private investments in the Pacific Basin areas.
6. To assist in the cultivation of financial related personnel for enterprises.

II. Accomplishments:

1. Published *Review of Pacific Basin Financial Markets and Policies*, a quarterly journal that is issued in March, June, September, and December each year, which prints the practicum and the academic research papers related to the financial policies, stocks, and other new financial products in the Pacific Basin countries.
2. Sponsored the Conference on Pacific Basin Financial Markets and Policies, which was held on March 25 and 26, 1999 in New York. The theme for this conference was the discussion of financial markets and policies of the Pacific Basin countries and the coping proposals for financial crises. The discussion and conclusions were collected and published.
3. Held the 7th Conference on PBFEA at the Grand Hotel, Taipei, on May 28 and 29, 1999. This conference brought together many famous and important economic and financial scholars, enterprisers, and government officials, including Dr. Lee Teng-hui, ex-president of R.O.C.; Mr. Fai-nan Perng, governor of the Central Bank of China, R.O.C.; Dr. Paul C.H. Chiu, ex-minister of Finance, R.O.C.; Dr. Pin-kung Chiang, ex-chairman of the

Council of Economic Planning and Development, R.O.C.; Dr. Michael Brennan, Distinguished Professor of University of California; and Mr. Khun Tanya Serivedhin, governor of the Central Bank of Thailand. It assembled constructive suggestions from domestic and overseas scholars to the development direction for Taiwan's economy and spread out the Taiwanese experience to the world stage and achieved a successful academic diplomacy for Taiwan.

In the afternoon of June 8, 1999, FPBFRD held its opening party. I reported the process of setting up the foundation and Minister Paul C.H. Chiu delivered the welcome speech. Governor Perng was also present to deliver his congratulatory speech. Herein, I would like to sincerely thank all the guests who joined the party and those who sent flower baskets as congratulations. Since 1999, the Foundation of Pacific Basin Financial Research and Development has been sponsoring the PBFEAM conference activities (refer to Chapter 10). In addition, this foundation also sponsors the publication of the *Review of Pacific Basin Financial Markets and Policies* as depicted in Chapter 12.

With the help from all my friends in different organizations and fields, I was able to contribute to the management of education in Taiwan and provide my suggestions to the government for Taiwan's financial and economic policies. The activities and contributions during the last 20 years (1996–2016) to Taiwan's economic policy and management of education will be explained in the following two chapters.

Chapter

15

Contributions to Taiwan's Economic and Financial Policies

In this chapter, I will discuss my contributions to Taiwan's economic and financial policies during the last three decades. I will describe how I helped develop Taipei into a regional financial center, proposed stock market policy decisions, and lastly I will discuss the policies on the construction of the high-speed railway.

The most important financial centers in the world are New York City, London, Tokyo, Hong Kong, and Singapore, along with a few others. Since early 1990, every Asian-Pacific country has desired to take a more important role in the world of finance. Seoul, Shanghai, Bangkok, Kuala Lumpur, Jakarta, Sydney, Manila, and Taipei are all proposed to become a regional financial center. In the meantime, Taiwan's government has also devoted itself to the plan of developing Taipei into a regional financial center. By relaxing the restrictions for setting up securities business and private banks, Taiwan put forward a plan that would help it step towards a more liberalized financial market.

Before 1991, there were only 25 banks in Taiwan. The banks were all under government protection, and it was almost impossible to set up a new bank. Then, with the implementation of new bank laws, this difficulty no longer existed. Seventeen new banks were launched and by 1996 there were a total of 42 banks in Taiwan. However, some officials, scholars, and enterprisers didn't understand the pre-requisites in developing a financial center and the risks that a country's economic activities could bring in. They simply advocated promoting the plan without counting the costs. As a result, two groups in Taiwan were formed, the moderates and the conservatives. At this moment I would like to illustrate the advantages and disadvantages of developing Taipei into a financial center.

A successful case of developing a financial center will bring about high value-added economic activities to the country. It can develop rapidly without investing in costly factories and equipment and usually won't cause any pollution problems as manufacturing sites would. A good example of a world financial center in the United Kingdom is London. About seven percent of the United Kingdom's GNP comes from finance-related activities. The financial centers employ about one million people and take up an area of about one square kilometer of the city.

However, there is no free lunch. The development of a financial center may pay a higher price as follows:

I. The business of a financial center is a series of fragile activities, which have no solid foundation. Any unexpected problem that happens in this kind of activity may bring big trouble to the business. For example, the impact is apparent when a large amount of capital flows out of a country.

II. When a large amount of capital flows out of a country, all of the other economic activities in the country are greatly affected. A small country, therefore, may lose control over its economic activities and be controlled by other countries.

III. The business in a financial center usually invests less on fixed assets and relies heavily on human resources. The human resources are easily acquired and dismissed. Throughout history, there have been many cities and countries that have prospered from becoming a financial center, but have only been able to keep that position for a short time.

IV. Without a regulator to supervise financial brokerage activities, many corrupt and illegal actitivies can easily arise.

V. The activities of a financial center are easily affected by the change of economic policies.

VI. The telecommunication and traffic infrastructure of an international financial center should be continuously updated. Therefore, their scale somehow affects the economic activities of the center. Thus, there are not many countries or cities qualified to become international financial centers.

Most people agree that the main cause of the Asian Financial Crisis of July 1997 was that the Central Bank of Thailand allowed banks to overshoot their business in trading foreign currency. At that time, most financial activities of Thai banks, both domestic and overseas, focused on borrowing Japanese Yen or USD at lower interest rates without hedging. After exchanging the foreign currency into Thai Bahts, the banks lent out the money at higher interest rates and made a profit from the differential in interest rates. The Thai banks' loans, lent from its domestic foreign banks, quickly jumped from USD 8 billion in 1993 to USD 50 billion at the end of 1998. Sixty percent of the money (about USD 30 billion) was lent to its domestic enterprises and only 20 billion was lent out overseas. With such a huge non-hedged amount of capital flowing in and out, the Thai Central Bank could not keep its promise to maintain a fixed exchange rate system. Thus, a huge amount of capital flew out of the country and the Thai Bahts depreciated sharply. With such a large amount of capital flowing in and out of the country within such a short period, the fluctuation of domestic capital flow was enlarged and other economic activities were affected negatively.

The Central Bank of Thailand had to sell large amounts of foreign reserves to try to stabilize the fixed exchange rate, which meant it lost its foreign reserves quickly and the domestic enterprises owed a great amount of foreign debts. With this double hit, the country had no choice but to ask for the assistance of the International Monetary Fund. As a result, it lost its sovereignty in drafting its own economic policies, which worsened the crisis. This is an example of the failure in developing a financial center.

In 1993, the CEPD of Taiwan's government entrusted McKinsey & Company with the feasibility study on developing Taiwan into an Asian-Pacific financial operation center. The report from McKinsey & Company was completed with an unfavorable view of the plan in early 1994. However, the Taiwanese government wanted to have a third party's opinion. Deputy Chairman of the CEPD, Dr. Chi Schive, invited me to Taiwan in March 1994 to give three speeches to the officials of the CEPD, the Ministry of Finance, and the Central Bank. During these speeches some important government officials, including Deputy Chairman Schive, Deputy Chairman Kao-chao Lee, Deputy Chairman Patrick C.J. Liang, Vice Minister Mu-tsai Chen, Deputy Governor Yi-hsiung Hsu, and Deputy Director-General Susan S. Chang, were present and discussed strategies with me.

In my speech, I analyzed the world financial activities at that time and discussed the pros and cons of developing Taipei into a regional financial operation center. I concluded that it was necessary to develop Taipei into a regional financial center because finance activity is very important to promote Taiwan into a developed country. However, it must be done with careful planning because Taiwan would pay a high price if the plan failed. As the world's economic activities became more and more globalized, it was tempting to speed up the financial activities, in order to step into the level of developed countries. However, we should not be in a hurry because it will take time, and with patience, Taipei will be able to become a global financial center.

At the time I pointed out that when I left Taiwan in August 1968, the GNP was about USD 300 per capita and there were little foreign reserves. However, in 1994 the foreign reserves grew to more than USD 100 billion and the GNP was more than USD 12,000 per capita. Because of the positive contributions from officials in finance during those 26 years, I believed Taipei was capable of becoming a regional financial center.

At the end of June 1994, I returned to Taiwan from Hong Kong and spent one month doing research at the CEPD and the Central Bank.

I also provided my opinions and suggestions for the plan to develop Taipei into a regional financial center. During my stay at the CEPD, my research mainly focused on the development of the futures and options in the New Taiwan Dollar. I attended many financial reform meetings and learned a lot about Taiwan's economic development policies and the problems faced by the financial systems. At that time, I witnessed dedication shown by our finance officials to financial reforms and believed that the future of Taiwan's finance industry was full of hope.

One day, during my conversation with Deputy Chairman Patrick C.J. Liang, I learned that most finance scholars in Taiwan were quite young and lack experience. Furthermore, there were many leaders who were unwilling to listen to other opinions. Deputy Chairman Liang believed that an older scholar with more experience was needed to integrate everyone's opinions. He suggested that I take this role. That was when I decided to express my views regarding financial policies more in the newspapers and start editing the quarterly journal *Review of Pacific Basin Financial Markets and Policies*, which debuted in March 1998.

In August, I continued my financial research in the Central Bank. At the time, ex-Governor Kuo-shu Liang asked Deputy Governor Perng to assign a private office to me and asked Mr. A-ting Chou, Ms. Ming-chih Chang, Mr. Chung-hua Lei, Mr. Tao-ming Su, and Mr. Pang-hai Liu to assist me in collecting data and recording research results. Every two or three days, our research team would report to Deputy Governor Perng who would then give his opinions and suggestions on the report. Deputy Governor Perng and I detailed our progress to ex-Governor Liang every week.

In addition, to further understand McKinsey's report about developing Taipei into a regional financial operation center, we invited a consultant from McKinsey & Company to the Central Bank to exchange views. From the discussion, we found there was nothing special in McKinsey's research approaches. They were just some common methods widely used in academic institutions and the industries. Furthermore, we found the author did not fully understand the situations in Taiwan either. We decided that McKinsey's opinions of the plan were not worth referring to and that we should take other more practical approaches in conducting our research.

I suggested we compare Taipei to other international examples for our research. We collected the strategies and policies taken by Hong Kong and Singapore for promoting financial activities and then compared Taipei with these two in their conditions in developing a financial center. Our comparison was divided into three major areas: the general requirements, financial management, and financial markets.

From our analysis, we found that many improvements were needed if we wanted to develop Taipei into a regional financial center. We could not completely copy Hong Kong or Singapore's experience; instead, we needed to come up with a development model that is suitable for Taipei. Since Taiwan's manufacturing industry was much more developed than Hong Kong or Singapore, the effect on it would be much worse than Hong Kong and Singapore if we implemented inappropriate financial policies. Besides, Taiwan was not a member of IMF, so there was concern that Taiwan would not be able to receive financial support. The last concern was the uncertainty of the cross-strait relations. Thus, we suggested a more conservative economic and financial policy, which might not have jeopardized the country or cause any financial crisis.

After more than a month under the collaboration of ex-Governor Liang, Deputy Governor Perng, and other team members, we finally completed a report with more than 200 pages. We published the report in the *Central Bank Quarterly*. Herein, I have listed our suggestions, which included the general suggestions and those specific to the improvement of financial markets:

General Suggestions:

1. To set up a work team in promoting financial business:
   The government should appoint officials of the Central Bank and the Ministry of Finance to organize a work team to promote financial business. The work team should invite the related organizations to discuss and conduct research on specific problems and follow up with the results.

2. To relax the restrictions for international financial organizations to set up branches in Taiwan; and to process their applications more efficiently.

3. To modify tax regulations by following the international common practice and to conclude taxing and rental agreements with other countries.

4. To aggressively cultivate more financial professionals.

   (1). To train financial professionals:
   To extend the organization of the Banking and Finance Institute and set up a financial college to cultivate more financial professionals.

   (2). To bring in foreign financial experts:
      A. To simplify the exit-and-entry procedures and increase the allowed percentage of foreign employers can hire (the current limit is 10 percent of employees).
      B. To allow foreign attorneys and accountants to practice in Taiwan.

5. To attract famous foreign colleges to set up overseas campuses in Taiwan.

6. To organize a preparatory committee for constructing an international financial building and to complete the building as soon as possible.

7. To extend telecommunication facilities, connect public networks with special international lines and charge the service according to standard international rates, and improve the quality of telecommunications products.

8. To loosen the restrictions on the location choices for financial organizations and other related regulations.

9. To modify related regulations to meet the international common practice.

Suggestions for the Improvement of Financial Markets:

10. To speed up the process of transforming public banks to private institutions in order to improve the efficiency of debt markets.

11. Monetary market:

    (1). To simplify the procedures of issuing IPO and establish a credit evaluation system.

    (2). To set up monetary brokers to process the New Taiwan Dollar brokerage business.

12. Bond market:

    (1). To set up credit rating agencies
        A. To attract well-known international rating agencies to set up business in Taiwan.
        B. To develop domestic rating agencies.

    (2). To waive the transaction tax and stamp tax for corporate debt and financial bonds.

    (3). To permit commercial banks to issue financial bonds for collecting long-term capital.

13. Stock market:

    (1). To draft regulations for trading foreign listed stocks in Taiwan stock markets.

    (2). To encourage domestic blue-chip stocks to issue IPO, improve the surpervision on the financial status of listed companies, and strictly execute the supervisory regulations to maintain the market discipline.

14. Foreign currency markets:

    (1). To support banks in trading foreign currency, withdraw some national foreign reserves from overseas and manage them in Taipei.

(2). To increase the operation efficiency of foreign currency brokers.

15. Overseas financial markets:

    (1). To loosen the requirements for setting up overseas financial centers to allow more participation.

    (2). To extend the scale of foreign currency loaning and exchange markets and securities business in overseas financial centers, thus achieving the functions as payment centers.

16. Insurance markets:
    To draft regulations for Captive Insurance Company, to encourage domestic and international companies to found Captive Insurance Company by reducing capital requirements and dishing out preferential tax rates; and to attract enterprises to set up their risk management and operation centers in Taiwan.

17. Gold markets:

    (1). To allow healthy and solid financial institutions to issue certificates for gold deposits and promote the night trading in gold.

    (2). To establish accredited gold identification organizations and melting factories.

18. Financial derivatives markets:

    (1). To promote new financial derivatives among foreign currencies and enhance risk management.

    (2). To require higher percentage of bank equity to ensure the healthy operation of banks.

19. To set up Taipei International Monetary Exchange (TIMEX).

In August 1994, Mr. Sen Yang, senior reporter of *Wealth Magazine*, interviewed me at Central Bank and asked about the major policies of financial reform. This interview was published in the October 1994 issue of *Wealth Magazine* with the title "Industry is the Root, While Finance the Leaf." Here, I will explain some main ideas from this interview.

There were four sub-titles under this article:

1. Foreign hot money flows in and out of Taiwan's markets; the foreign reserves of USD 90 billion might be gone with the wind.
2. If Mainland China had opened its market 20 years earlier, there would have been no economic miracles in Taiwan and South Korea.
3. The future of Taiwan depends on the upgrading of the industry.
4. It is worth to learn from Singapore's "firewall model".

To the first point, since foreign capital flows in and out of Taiwan markets too quickly and leads the domestic investors' trading, foreign investors win the game most of the time. It is clear that short-term foreign capital flow might be helpful to the short-term economic activities for a country, but it might hurt the long-term economic interests, such as in Thailand during the Asian Financial Crisis. When the Asian Financial Crisis spread out, a similar situation was repeated in South Korea, though South Korea owned more than USD 70 billion foreign reserves. If a similar financial crisis happened in Taiwan, where could Taiwan find the help?

On July 10 and 11, 1997, when I held the 5th PBFEA Conference in Singapore, a reporter from the *Lianhe Zaobao* interviewed me regarding my opinions on the Asian Financial Crisis. The headline of the newspaper on July 11 appeared as "NTU (Nanyang Technological University) Distinguished Professor of Shaw Foundation, Dr. CF Lee: If monetary crisis happens again in Asia, it will be impossible for Singapore to handle all by itself." In the interview, I again explained my thoughts in regards to the principle "industry is the root, while finance the leaf," which was published in *Wealth Magazine*, October 1994. I emphasized that economic foundation was based on the solid development of various industries and commercial and service businesses. Later, this interview was reproduced in Mr. Lo-lee Li's book, *Financial Crisis: Overview of the Southern Asian Financial Crisis*, which was published in October

1997, by China's Guizhou People's Publishing Press.

When the Asian Financial Crisis worsened, Mr. Ying-hou Cheng wrote four reports regarding Taiwan's finance for the *Lianhe Zaobao* in Singapore. In his fourth report headlined "When the Weather Changes — Shaking in Taiwanese Finance", he indicated the following four reasons why Taiwan was affected by the financial crisis, but did not fall as the other four Southeast Asian countries and South Korea did:

1. Taiwan's finance is founded on the solid development of manufacturing.
2. Taiwan holds a large amount of foreign reserves.
3. There is almost zero foreign debt in Taiwan and no problem of over-expended credits in financial markets.
4. Taiwan's financial market is not totally open and therefore, the regulators can exert better and stricter supervision than other countries.

The last three paragraphs of his article admired the accuracy and efficiency of the development principle of "industry is the root, while finance the leaf." The following is an excerpt:

> In August [should be July] of this year, Prof. CF Lee of Rutgers University, U.S., was interviewed and pointed out that Taiwan should stick to the principle of "industry is the root, while finance the leaf" in developing a financial center and build up its financial business on the solid basis of manufacturing. In addition, the development procedures should not be carried out in haste. Instead, the market should be liberalized gradually in a moderate pace lest Taiwan follows the failing steps of Southeast Asia and bring in risks by misplacing priorities.
>
> To sum up the difficulties faced by some Pacific-Asian countries during the financial crisis, his saying proved true.

> Between Taiwan's manufacturing and financial industries, the former is more promising and more important.
>
> Simple messages are the most important messages. If the root is planted well, the days with comfortable shadow of green leaves shall come one day.

As expected, at the end of the 20th century, Taiwan's electronics industry had already occupied an important position in the world, which was fully reflected in the shock to the international electronics stock markets immediately after the big earthquake happened in Taiwan on September 21, 1991. This example shows that Taiwan has a strong industry base to support the financial sector.

In reference to the second point, it is the conclusion I came upon from the study of China's financial reforms completed between 1982 and 1994. In 1992, when I gave a speech to the Economic Reformation Committee in Beijing, I gave similar opinions to the participants. This was a warning to Asia's Four Little Dragons (Taiwan, Hong Kong, South Korea, and Singapore) and other countries that China played a very important role in the Asian financial markets.

The third point is the conclusion of my experience from years of lecturing in Mainland China and attending policy discussions. Labor-intensive industries were no longer able to survive in Taiwan, which were encouraged to move to Mainland China or Southeast Asian countries where they could still have lower labor costs. To avoid moving them wholesale from Taiwan, we had to upgrade our industry to be able to keep the "root" in Taiwan. In fact, the policies of developing information technology were quite successful in Taiwan back then. If we adopted rash policies for financial development, we might get the short-term gain but lose the benefits from the upgraded technology.

The fourth point indicates the difference in economic development between Taiwan and Hong Kong. During my teaching at the Chinese University of Hong Kong between August 1993 and June 1994, I found out that "stores in front and factories behind" had become the development policy in Hong Kong. That meant most industrial productions that were previously run in Hong Kong were relocated to Shenzhen or other cities in Mainland China. Therefore, the liberalization of financial activities in Hong Kong would not cause a large impact to its manufacturing.

The situation in Singapore was another story. Its scale of manufacturing was between Taiwan and Hong Kong, thus, they implemented the "internal control, external freedom" ("firewall") model in which onshore and offshore financial businesses were separated to prevent the domestic financial market from being impacted by external financial shocks. However, the Singapore model was not easy to adapt to Taiwan's case since the situations were quite different. I advocated that Taiwan should adopt its own approach. Furthermore, this approach should be more similar to Singapore's and different from Hong Kong's.

When the Central Bank publicized our policy suggestions on November 2, Taiwan's *Commercial Times* also published detailed reports and discussion. The title in the *Commercial Times* was "Central Bank Suggests an Inter-Department Work Team to Promote the Development of the Financial Center". Within the report, there were two major subtitles:

1. Proposed solid plans for the first time to develop Taipei into a regional financial center.
2. Advocated to modify related laws and regulations and to reform financial and taxing systems to meet the international common laws.

The report concluded with "Cheng-Few Lee in charge, and Central Bank expresses determination" to explain Deputy Governor Perng's and my serious, but optimistic views in developing Taipei into a financial center.

Upon learning the result of our report, the liberals refused to accept our views. The liberals and the moderates decided to hold a debate in December of that year at the Central Bank. The attendants included Vice-Minster Li-ning Dai, Director General Po-hsin Chang, Member of Academia Sinica Zau-nan Chen, Director Jia-dong Shea, Prof. Ya-huei Yang, Prof. Son-nan Chen, and Prof. Christina Y. Liu.

Among them, I recommended Prof. Son-nan Chen to Deputy Governor Perng. At last, the radical liberals lost the debate and Taiwan didn't completely open its capital accounts. It decreased the impact of the Asian Financial Crisis in Taiwan and as a result Taiwan suffered much less than South Korea.

Since early 1998, I joked that I must have been one of the few people who had benefited from the Asian Financial Crisis. Because of my suggestion to develop Taiwan into a regional financial center, the Asian Financial Crisis caused much less of an impact to Taiwan's economy, unlike its effect on South Korea. In early February 1998, when I met the deputy representative of the World Bank, Mr. Chang-tao Hu, in Beijing, he described to me the terrible situation faced by South Korea due to the Asian Financial Crisis. I am very glad that I had the opportunity to make a contribution to my home country after spending over three decades away. If Prof. Lee Teng-hui hadn't encouraged me in economic policy research, I might not have been able to come up with the economic development policy of "industry is the root, while finance is the leaf" for Taiwan.

Stock Markets and Economic Policies

In a modern corporation, most companies' working capitals come from investors or loans. Stocks represent the investors' shares of ownership to a company. Company stocks offered publicly are usually put in the markets or over-the-counter. In the United States, stock purchasing is one of the most popular ways of investment. According to finance scholars' research, the long-term return of stock investment is more than double that of bonds.

There are four common approaches in stock investment analysis: fundamental analysis, technical analysis, contrarian analysis, and dynamic asset allocation. The first three methods are used for individual or institution investors while the last usually applies to the cases of institutional investment.

The focus of fundamental analysis is the profit-earning ability of the stock-issuing company. The basic data comes from the accounting statements provided by the company. Besides the analysis of a company's financial status, fundamental analysis also takes into account the prospective performance of related industries and economy.

To let investors understand a company's financial status, the U.S. Stock Exchange Commission requires all listed companies to publicize their annual and quarterly financial reports. In Taiwan, the Securities and Futures Commission also requires all listed companies to publicize their financial statements. These requirements ask listed companies to make investment information transparent and protect investors' rights. Therefore, investors should keep their eyes open on the information shown on these financial statements.

Technical analysis concentrates on the short-term trend of individual stocks. The Moving Average Analysis is one of the most commonly used approaches. It locates certain time points to sell or buy a stock from the analysis of its moving average price and trend. In general, 50-day and 200-day averages are two of the most common methods to indicate when to buy or sell a stock. Technical analysts set up many other indicators or characteristics to decide the selling or buying point. Some think technical analysis is only used as a gambling tool, but I believe that the fundamental and technical analyses complement each other as stock analytic measures.

Contrarian analysis applies psychology and other investment analytical tools to decide whether to buy or sell certain stocks. People who employ contrarian analysis usually purchase unpopular stocks, thus this analytical technique somehow manipulates stock investment in the opposite direction of the general population. For example, if stock prices fall due to non-economic factors, contrarian analysts will purchase those under-valued stocks, which usually have relatively low P/E ratios.

Mutual fund managers usually adopt dynamic asset allocation analysis. They classify their portfolio assets into fixed income, bonds, and stocks. Along with the change of markets and economic conditions, fund managers will invest by allocating different percentages into these three kinds of assets. They apply certain numerical models to decide the allocation percentages for the portfolios.

No matter which kinds of analytical techniques are adopted, investors usually pay a great deal of attention to the directions of governmental economic policies. The macroeconomic policies of a country can be classified as fiscal policies and monetary policies. By adequately applying these two kinds of policies, a country can regulate its economic activities. Monetary policies are directed by a country's central bank while fiscal policies by the Ministry of Finance.

Fiscal policies dominate a country's income and expenditure. A country's income includes income tax, business tax, and other tax income. Its expenditures may include expenses in defense, diplomacy, education, and other public constructions. The issuing of government bonds and the management of stocks, futures and options, and financial institutions are all under the supervision of the Ministry of Finance.

Changes in fiscal policies from the Ministry of Finance will directly affect a company's income and expenditure and further influence its profits and thus change the fundamentals of its stocks. For example, it may lead to prosperous business in construction and boost the stock prices of construction companies if the Ministry increases the expense on public construction. In addition, tax deductions may also increase a company's net profit and improve its fundamental financial position and as a result stop the downturn of its stock. For instance, at the end of 1998, two domestic financial crises happened which caused a sharp fall in Taiwan's stock market. Taiwan's stock index fell below 7,000. At that time, I presented two suggestions to President Lee:

I. Reponses needed to deal with current economic problems in Taiwan (December 16, 1998)

For Taiwan, the primary economic problem is to improve on the fundamental economic issues. Before the export business can be improved, it is essential to meet domestic needs. Since the high-speed rail cannot be constructed quickly, it is necessary to come up with other ways to expand the construction projects, as well as to stimulate investment and increase consumption through fiscal means.

As for the monetary policies, since the exchange rates of foreign currency have been stable and inflation rates are low, the Central Bank could lower the deposit reserve rate and interest rate. However, in my opinion, the liquidity trap seems to have happened in Taiwan. Therefore, it is not effective enough to only apply the fiscal policies, but Taiwan needs to further cut tax and interest rates. In May and June 1998, when I was in Hong Kong and Singapore, I suggested taking both banking and financial approaches to solve the current economic problems.

We must strengthen investors' confidence in the stock market. Avoiding sharp falls in the stock market by investing with public funds to lower transaction fees (e.g. 0.1 percent cut) can also have an immediate effect. In the long run, cutting down on a company's business taxes and encouraging a company's investment with tax deductions can also bring in an upward trend in the stock market.

I believe that the world's electronics industry has been recovering. Asian and European markets are booming as well. If the Taiwanese government can take effective approaches to sweep away the lack of confidence in the stock market, the outlook after the first quarter of next year should be bright.

II. The proposal of applying fiscal policies to promote economy and stabilize as well as solidify banking systems (December 29, 1998)

The world financial markets have been stabilized. The American and European stock markets have reached record highs while Asian markets are also almost back to normal along with the economic rebound of Asian countries. Unfortunately, at this moment our financial markets are encountering some problems. Both our stock index and trading volumes have decreased. If we do not do anything, it will cause severe impacts to our financial markets. Investing public funds into the market will not stop stocks from falling or solve the fundamental problems of the stock market. It will only bring other negative side effects to our financial markets. We must improve the economic fundamentals.

Improving the fundamentals is a long-term goal. This is in accordance with what I mentioned before, "industry is the root, while finance the leaf." If companies can earn higher profits, then investors' confidence will automatically return to their previous state while the stock index will be boosted. Currently, our inflation rate is low and the foreign exchange market is stable. Thus, it is applicable to stimulate needs and increase profits by adopting moderate deficit fiscal policies. Therefore, I suggested that the President cut tax rates to solidify companies' financial structures and increase personal spending. My suggestions were as follows:

1. Speed up the depreciation of a company's facilities to encourage more investments and to reduce a company's business taxes in order to gain more profits. With higher profits, the P/E ratios are lowered and stock prices will rise. As a result, the financial structures of the financial institutions, which invest in these stocks, will improve. In addition, since the company's finances have improved, banks will be more willing to provide low-interest-rate loans to companies. As a result, a virtuous cycle and interaction forms.

2. Taiwan should lower personal income tax and business tax to stimulate personal consumption and real estate investments, the latter of which can be done with low-interest-rate loans. Consequently, the real estate market will rebound and individuals will be capable of paying their mortgages. It further prevents the possible damages caused by the real estate bubbles that may destroy the whole financial system.

Of course, in addition to using the fiscal policies mentioned above, monetary policies must be persistently adopted too. For example, the Central Bank has to support a loose monetary policy and stabilize the foreign exchange market. In January 1999, the Ministry of Finance cut banks' business tax rate from five percent to two percent and the stock market rebounded shortly after.

Having suffered from the impact of the Asian Financial Crisis, Taiwan's economy has encountered the so-called "domestic gloom and export boom" problem. To compensate for the insufficiency of domestic demand, the government should more aggressively accelerate public construction plans. For example, the government should concentrate on the building of the high-speed rail, which is highly anticipated by construction, steel, and other manufacturing companies. However, it was postponed due to a financing problem.

Unfortunately, a massive earthquake, which would become known as the "921 Earthquake," hit Taiwan in 1999. The Taiwanese government spent a large amount on reconstruction due to the catastrophe. According to the reconstruction blueprint, the expenses would reach a total of between NTD 140 billion and NTD 160 billion in the first year. Many traditional industrial stocks, such as the steel and cement industry, benefitted from the promotion of these projects. Therefore, it was expected that many traditional industrial stocks would rebound from the current prices, which were far below their face value.

The Ministry of Finance can also affect the stock market using other approaches. For example, the Securities and Futures Commission of the Ministry of Finance can lift the financing percentage to enlarge the transaction volume in stock market to further improve the overall stock performance. In addition, it can encourage foreign capital to invest more in Taiwan's stocks if we allow foreign institutions to own a higher rate of a domestic company's shares. However, to avoid upheavals in the stock market, the amount of a domestic company's shares owned by foreign institutions should still be limited to a certain amount.

The Central Bank controls the monetary policies. In the U.S., the Federal Reserve System (FRB) is able to increase or decrease the money supply by adjusting the required reserves rate or discount rate. The FRB can also change the money supply by open market operations. The U.S. Reserve Banks mostly adjust discount rates to influence economic activities or the financial markets, and, therefore, the stock markets. The monetary policies of the United States not only affect their stock markets, but also stock markets all over the world. Therefore, people regard the chairman of the Board of Governors of the U.S. Federal Reserve System (the incumbent is Janet Yellen) as the most powerful person in the world economy, next to the U.S. president. The following examples will verify this point.

When President Clinton was inaugurated in 1993, the U.S. economy gradually recovered. Stock markets were into the bull run, which meant the stock prices were expected to go up. In early 1994 when the U.S. faced higher pressures on the inflation problem, the Federal Reserve Banks decided to take action and raised the interest rate. Since then, the Federal Reserve Banks raised interest rates seven times until mid-1995. In the beginning, when the Federal Reserve Banks started to raise the interest rate, the Dow Jones Index was about 3,600 while Hong Kong Hang Seng Index was about 12,000 and Taiwan Stock Index 7,100.

Although the U.S. stock markets were affected as expected, other countries had endured much more than the U.S. For example, the Hong Kong Hang Seng Index fell below 8,000 and the Taiwan Stock Index fell to 5,100. Meanwhile, the fall of the Dow Jones Index never exceeded 10 percent during this period. We can see the fluctuation of stock indices in larger countries is less than those in smaller countries.

Table 15.1 shows the fluctuations of the stock indices between 1987 and 1999 in Taiwan, New York, Tokyo, Korea, Hong Kong, Thailand, and Singapore.

Table 15.1. Comparison of stock index changes in New York and some Asian countries between 1987 and 1999.

	Taiwan	New York	Japan	Korea	Hong Kong	Thailand	Singapore
Year	Stock Index	Dow Jones Index	Nikkei 225 Stock Index	Stock Index	Hang Seng Stock Index	SET Stock Index	Straits Times Stock Index
1987	2,339.86	1,938.83	21,564.00	525.11	2,320.75	284.94	828.21
88	5,119.11	2,168.57	30,159.00	907.20	2,687.44	386.73	1,038.62
89	9,624.18	2,753.20	38,915.87	909.72	2,836.57	879.19	1,481.33
90	4,530.16	2,633.66	23,848.71	696.11	3,243.40	612.86	1,154.48
91	4,600.67	3,169.95	22.983.77	610.92	4,297.33	711.36	1,490.70
92	3,377.06	3,301.11	16,924.95	678.44	5,512.39	893.42	1,512.46
93	6,070.56	3,754.09	17,417.24	866.18	11,886.39	1,565.12	2,425.68
94	7,124.66	3,834.44	19,723.06	1,027.37	8,191.04	1,360.09	2,239.56
95	5,173.73	5,117.12	19,868.15	882.94	10,073.39	1,280.81	2,266.54
96	6,933.94	6,448.27	19,361.35	651.22	13,451.54	831.57	2,216.79
97	8,187.24	7,908.25	15,258.17	376.31	10,722.76	372.69	1,529.84
98	6,418.43	9,181.43	13,842.74	562.64	10,048.58	355.81	1,392.73
99	8,448.84	11,497.12	18,934.34	1,028.07	16,962.10	481.92	2,479.58

From Table 15.1, we can see that:

1. The historical fluctuation of stock markets in Asian countries is much bigger than in the U.S.
2. The stock markets of Thailand and Korea suffered the most in the 1997 Asian Financial Crisis.

On September 23, 1998, after mistakenly gambling on a convergence in interest rates of government and corporate bonds the U.S. flagship hedge fund, Long Term Capital Management (LTCM), suffered a tremendous loss. This almost jeopardized the U.S. financial system. Federal Reserve Bank of New York President William McDonough convinced 15 banks to rescue LTCM from bankruptcy. In the meantime, the Federal Reserve Bank had continuously lowered discount rate three times to prevent U.S. stocks from falling and further stimulate the other stock markets around the world to rebound.

Upon an unexpected financial problem, governments usually adopt special monetary policies to help stock markets. For example, in late July of 1995, the crises of "Fourth Credit Co-Operative" and "International Bills Finance Corporation (IBFC)" occurred in Taiwan. I suggested that the Taiwanese government solve its problem by:

1. Gradually opening markets to foreign capital
2. Increasing money supply
3. Cutting deposit reserve rate
4. Re-constructing the supervisory system for financial organizations

At the end of 1995 and in the beginning of 1996, Taiwan's stocks fell sharply because Mainland China threatened to attack Taiwan with missiles. At that time, the Taiwanese government did a good job by investing public funds in stocks to stabilize the market. To prevent the whole economic system from the effects of non-economic issues, Taiwan's government started to raise a National Security Fund in May

1999 with a total amount of NTD 500 billion. I fully supported this investment because Taiwan's stock market had long been suffering from unexpected variables due to the military threat from Mainland China. From the four measures of analysis mentioned above, the operation of the National Security Fund can keep the stock market stable by using fundamental analysis or contrarian analysis to decide whether to get involved in stock trading.

To sum up, a country's economic policies dominate its economic activities and as a result affect its stock market. An investor's decision on trading stocks should not only be based on the research of a company's financial structure, but also the trend of macroeconomic policies in the country. Similarly, a policy maker, such as a governor of the Central Bank or Minister of Finance, should fully understand the influence that economic policies have on stock markets. They should also know the effect that foreign exchange markets have on drafting policies, since stock markets in turn also affect the overall performance of a country's economy.

Suggestions on the Participation of Private Enterprises in Public Construction

To solve the problems of insufficient public finance, ineffective public administration, and overflowing private capital, many developed and developing countries have tried to attract private funds, technologies, and experiences to promote public construction. To help accelerate development, the Taiwanese government invited private enterprises to participate in public construction. This section explains the related concepts and details the benefits and costs of private funds in public construction with the building of a high-speed railway as an example. It further explains the importance of thinking about the side effects caused by government-guaranteed loans and the possible impacts brought about by such a huge construction project on the whole financial system.

In general, there are three models with which private funds are applied in public construction:

1. Build-Transfer-Operate (BTO): The private enterprise completes the building assignment and then transfers it to the government. The government itself or its delegated organizations take charge of the management afterwards.
2. Build-Own-Operate (BOO): The private enterprise completes the building assignment, keeps the ownership, and operates by itself.
3. Build-Operate-Transfer (BOT): The private enterprise completes the building assignment and operates by itself within a certain time period, licensed by the government. When the license expires, the private enterprise transfers the ownership and management to the government.

Taiwan's government took the BOT approach to promote the Twenty-two Major Public Construction projects, including the second highway in northern Taiwan, the high-speed rail, incinerators, and other construction projects. The building of the high-speed rail required the most investment and will be discussed here.

The contract for building the high-speed rail was bid on by China High Speed Rail Consortium (CHSRC) and the Taiwan High Speed Rail Consortium (THSRC) in September 1997. THSRC won the contract. The total investment required for the high-speed rail was over NTD 480 billion (USD 15 billion) at the time of operation. At that time, it was one of the world's largest privately funded rail construction projects. Previously, I mentioned that the government might be willing, but unable to complete such a large investment project by making loans in 1992. Three-quarters of the project's funding in the construction phase came in the form of syndicated loans from banks.

Once the THSRC won the bid, many people analyzed the investment with the NPV method. They found that the project had failed to meet its original intents because THSRC's estimate of ticket income was higher and too many stations were planned to be built. In May 1998, I also spoke about the issues of Taiwan's high-speed rail when I lectured on the Asian Financial Crisis at China Development Industrial Bank (CDIB). Chairman Tai-ying Liu, President Benny T. Wu as well as other senior managers attended the meeting. They mentioned that the THSRC's quote was incorrect and the proposal was impractical. Having analyzed all the information, I came to the conclusion that the China High Speed Rail Consortium might have been the lucky one because they didn't win the bid.

I agreed with the viewpoints of CDIB's senior managers at the time and believed that the expected net cash income had been over-quoted by the THSRC. Later, when I met with Deputy Chairman Kao-chao Lee of the Council for Economic Planning and Development (CEPD) and my classmate, Chairman Jen-shyong Ho of Tung Ho Steel Enterprise Corp, I had the opportunity to find out why they believed in the necessity and applicability of building the high-speed rail. Chairman Ho used the example of Japan to explain that the major income of the high-speed rail would not rely on the sale of tickets, but on the associated income from land and station development. Deputy Chairman Lee also emphasized the external economic benefits brought about by the building of the high-speed rail, including developing new townships and stimulating domestic demand. These ideas should be added to the expanded NPV method when evaluating the whole project. It was possible that CHSRC did not count the yields of options on capital budgeting. The THSRC might have evaluated their case with Formula I, and as a result they came to the conclusion that this case was applicable. However, they still needed to face two important issues — financing and timing.

Expanded Net Present Value (NPV) = Standard Net Present Value (NPV) + Option Premium (Formula I)

The most criticized point of the financing project provided by THSRC was that the company did not put in enough self-owned capital. THSRC would only invest NTD 121.9 billion out of the total amount of over NTD 400 billion. The five major companies of the consortium would only invest NTD 50 billion in the project. The rest of the amount would be borrowed from banks. With the help of CEPD, NTD 210 billion was refinanced from the mid- and long-term postal savings. The lending banks were unwilling to make such loans: by lending such a large amount under this unbalanced risk-profit condition, these banks' international ratings would be immediately downgraded. Therefore, there were only two ways for the THSRC to borrow money: to increase its self-owned capital or to ask for government guarantee (they added one more percentage point in interest rate in their conditions of lending to the THSRC). Since the THSRC was not capable of increasing its own capital, it could only do the latter to satisfy the banks' requirements. So, if anything went wrong in the construction of the high-speed rail, the people would take the risk. This is why I suggested delaying the project. My suggestions were reported on TV that day and in the newspapers for the following two days.

As early as 1992, I had researched the financial problems of building a high-speed rail. At that time, the late Governor Liang and many scholars advocated that if the government had to take on debt, it was not a good time for construction. Although Taiwan's economy had been rapidly growing, some other new expenses also increased the government's financial burdens, such as the implementation of the National Health Insurance Program. What was worse was that the government also inherited the Provincial Governmental debts totaling NTD 800 billion. Thus, it would have been impossible for the government to build the high-speed rail by taking on even more debt. The BOT approach became the only applicable consideration. However, since the government had to provide guarantee for a total of NTD 300 billion in loans, it had to take on debt indirectly. In practice, it worsened the government's finances and was unfair to all the people on the island. As the THSRC's own invested capital was low, the possibility of quitting the project mid-way was greatly increased and the structures of the banking systems were also greatly impacted. As a result, it might have caused local financial crisis and hurt the development of the local economy.

Since it was necessary to build the high-speed rail, the financing had to be completed in other ways. There were several ways in which this could be done. For instance, the five major companies of the THSRC could have done the following: invest NTD 100 billion, issue transferable corporate bonds in another NTD 100 billion to domestic or overseas investors, borrow from domestic or overseas banks for yet another NTD 100 billion, and then refinance an additional NTD 100 billion from the governmental mid- and long-term funds. Lastly, they could have issued preferred stocks for the last portion of NTD 70 billion to the building-material suppliers. Thus, the financial structure of the THSRC would significantly improve and there would be no need for government guarantee. If a company cannot collect 20 percent of the required investment itself, it is doubtful that the company is qualified for participation in the public construction via the BOT approach. If THSRC undertakes the project of building the high-speed rail with an unreasonable financing plan, it will cause other BOT projects to be executed with unhealthy financing. If the government makes too many guarantees on unhealthy loans, then the country will end up getting hurt from private BOT projects. The damages may be even more severe than complete liberalization of the capital account. Hence, the "Slow Trading" policy is not only applicable to investment in Mainland China, but also to the building of the high-speed rail in Taiwan.

Just when the financial plan of building the high-speed railroad was almost solved, an earthquake measuring 7.3 on the Richter scale struck Taiwan on September 21, 1999. The cost of reconstruction for damages caused by this major quake and its constant aftershocks was expected to reach NTD 300 billion. The Central Bank provided over NTD 100 billion of postal savings for low-interest-rate loans to the affected victims. This earthquake also made a great impact on the banking system and insurance industries and banks had become reluctant to lend to the high-speed rail project. As a result, delaying the building of the high-speed rail seemed necessary after this unexpected natural disaster.

My foundation has helped 12 policy conferences during the last 12 years. The twelfth policy conference was held on May 28, 2016. I invited two distinguished speakers, Paul Chiou and Kung-wha Ding. Paul Chiou was the wise minister during Lee Teng-hui's administration and currently he is the chairman of Yong Fon Bank. Kung-wha Ding was appointed as Chairman of Financial Supervisory Commission for Tsai

Ing-wen's administration in May 2016. Both of them reviewed Taiwan's economic situation and proposed new strategies on how to further develop Taiwan's financial and economic industries. In addition, we had four panel sections that discussed foreign trade, financial markets, fintech industry, and how to upgrade Taiwan's hi-tech industry. In addition, I also made a keynote speech, reviewing my involvement of academic and economic policy in Taiwan and China. I also gave some suggestions to the new government.

Chapter

16

Contributions to Taiwan's Management Education

I have contributed in many ways to the management education in Taiwan. Apart from teaching and lecturing at universities, I also delivered short courses for industry practioners, and assisted in the founding of the Chinese Financial Association (currently the Taiwanese Finance Association). I also organized two international financial conferences on academic, practical, and policy research in Taiwan.

My first teaching experience was in 1965 when I received my master's degree from the Graduate Institute of Economics, National Taiwan University (NTU). I taught statistics at Tang-Shui Technology and Business College (currently Aletheia University). The course was scheduled on Saturday afternoons, so I could teach after work. I was very excited about this since it was my first formal teaching job.

Upon the invitation of Chairman Ting-shen Lin in 1979, I came back to Taiwan and taught Corporate Financial Management at Tatung Institute of Technology. It was my first teaching job at a Taiwanese college since I left Taiwan to study abroad. There were more than 30 students in my class and the outcome was quite marvelous. In the summer of 1987, Chairman Yu-tsung Lin of the Department of Finance, NTU, invited me to teach International Financial Management at NTU and at National Chengchi University. This time there were more than 30 students in my classes. Prof. Gili Yen, Prof. Ching-liang Hsu, Prof. Yung-cheng Su, Prof. Hsien-hsin Liao, and Prof. Shih-fang Hu sat in my class as well. When I served as Distinguished Research Professor at the Management College, NTU in spring 1998, I taught special seminar classes for four months for the doctoral students at the school.

Additionally, I taught on-the-job training classes for managers. In January 1988, Mr. Ching-yi Wang, CPA, invited me to Arthur Andersen in Taiwan to give a course on stock analysis for 20 of the firm's managers. This was the beginning of my teaching for enterprises. Afterwards, I taught at the Banking Institute of the Republic of China (BIROC) for mid- and high-level banking managers in 1992, 1996, and 1998.

Between August 17 and 28, 1992, I taught a short course on banking management and analysis at BIROC. In this intense 10-day course, we had classes for five hours every day. The course content was based on my newly published books, *Corporate Finance: Theory, Method, and Applications* and *Security Analysis and Portfolio Management*. I also invited a few of my former Ph.D. students, Prof. Yun Lin and Prof. Dar-yeh Huang, to teach banking risk management alongside me. We not only discussed banking management and analysis, but also the reasons why capital accounts should be liberalized. We also analyzed the political risks in investing in Mainland China and suggested our government draft relevant policies to reduce the risks.

Every student was required to make an analysis of the banking risk management of his/her own bank based on its financial balance sheet for a take-home assignment. Later, from my discussions with students, I found that there was an immense difference between the current banking business and that of 1963–1968 when I worked at ICBC. Through the discussions with these experienced banking managers, I learned a great deal of new information about Taiwan's banking business.

There were 51 students in my class, including representatives from almost all of the banks in Taiwan. Now, all of these students hold important positions at their banks. I am really proud of them and believe that they will make more contributions to Taiwan's banking system in the future.

In May 1996, when I returned to Taiwan to participate in the inauguration of President Lee Teng-hui, I held another symposium at the BIROC. I hosted the symposium on risk management and analysis on financial derivatives for three days. The symposium focused on the approaches of banking risk management and its new theories. At that time, the Ministry of Finance was researching the accounting management principles for risk management. I asked one of my previous students, Prof. David M. Chen, to lecture for two hours on the accounting methods in dealing with futures and options.

In the spring of 1998, when I taught at the Management School of NTU, I held another symposium at the BIROC on June 18. My lecture was about financial crisis and banking risk management and included topics related to the ban of NDF trading by domestic institutions. Prof. Chih-ming Cheng and Prof. Ying-kan Wen also assisted and lectured at the symposium. I took this opportunity to defend the Central Bank's policy in forbidding domestic institutions to trade NDF. I was very glad to have these three opportunities to be involved in training mid- and high-level banking managers in Taiwan.

To promote the financial management education in Taiwan, I lectured many times at Taiwanese universities, such as National Taiwan University (NTU), Tamkang University (TKU), National Chengchi University (NCCU), National Cheng Kung University (NCKU), National Central University (NCU), National Dong Hwa University (NDHU), Yuan Ze University (YZU), Feng Chia University (FCU), and Chaoyang University of Technology (CYUT).

My teaching experience at TKU was the beginning of my lecturing at Taiwanese universities. In 1979, I accepted an invitation from President Clement C.P. Chang to teach a special one-week short course, "Financial Analysis, Planning, and Prediction." In 1986, upon the invitation from Dean Hsin-fu Tsai, I taught another one-week course, "The Systematic Analysis of Financial Theories." The content of these two short courses was published in a special book. In April 1994, Chairman Liu of the Department of Finance invited me to a conference held by TKU to deliver the keynote speech, "Teaching and Researching Interrelationship among Finance, Accounting, Economics, and Accounting." In May 1995, Prof. Liu invited me to give a lecture to their faculty and students.

Upon the invitation of Chairman Tsun-siou Lee in July 1990, I taught short courses at my alma mater's (NTU) Department of Finance, delivered a keynote speech and presented a paper at the Conference on Financial Markets held by the Department of Finance, NTU. My speech addressed the development of stock markets in Taiwan, while the paper I presented was entitled "Theories and Real Cases of Dividend Policy." Prof. Gili Yen arranged for me to give a lecture on the research relationship between finance and economics in the Department of Economics, NTU in spring 1992. NTU is the school I visit most frequently to teach seminars or give a speech.

In addition to lecturing at schools, I have been invited to deliver speeches regarding financial management and investment in Mainland China to different companies all the time. In the summer of 1979, I taught "Banking Management" at the International Commercial Bank of China. In the summer of 1986, my high school classmate, Mr. Yen-cheng Huang, invited me to Yuen Foong Yu Paper Manufacturing Company to speak about the economic development and investment outlook of Mainland China. Chairman Shen-hai Kuo also invited me to Madou Township of Tainan County to lecture on the investment opportunities in Mainland China. In the meantime, Prof. Yu-tsung Lin invited me to Taipei Chungshan Hall to lecture on stock analysis. In the summer of 1987, I gave a speech on the prospects of stock markets in Taiwan at China Times Plaza. In 1991, the Far Eastern Group invited me to lecture on financial analysis and management. In June 1997, I delivered the speech "The Outlook of Asian Markets after the Financial Crisis" at China Development Industrial Bank, and in August 1999, I addressed the Pacific Basin markets and policies after the financial crisis at the Taiwan Stock Exchange Corporation.

To promote the financial research in Taiwan, Chairman Yung-san Lee, Dean Gili Yen and I initiated the Chinese Financial Association (CFA) in the office of the 2nd Division of Taiwan Institute of Economic Research, in April 1992. Chairman Yung-san Lee was elected as the first president; Prof. Gili Yen, the secretary-in-general; and Prof. Tai Ma, the editor of the *Journal of Chinese Finance*. CFA has played an important role in the promotion of financial research in Taiwan since then.

I am also very proud of my students who finished their studies in the U.S. and have been very successful in their own careers in Taiwan.

Dr. Son-nan Chen, professor and chairman of the Department of Money and Banking, NCCU, was my postdoctoral student at the University of Georgia at Athens (UGA, 1974–1976). Dr. Chen received his Ph.D. from the Department of Accounting, UGA and worked on his postdoctoral research with me. Under my advising, he completed his postdoctoral paper, "Statistics Distribution of Investment Return Index," and coauthored three other papers with me. Two of them were published in *Management Science* while the other two were in the *Journal of Economics & Businesses* and the *Quarterly Review of Economics & Business*. Before coming back to Taiwan, Prof. Chen taught at Virginia State University (VSU) and University of Maryland. He is probably one of the most experienced finance professors with the most published financial papers in Taiwan now. Prof. Tai Ma of the National Sun Yat-sen University (NSYSU) was his student at VSU.

Dr. Gili Yen, dean of the Management School, CYUT, was my one of my schoolmates at NTU. We became acquainted with each other through Prof. Da-ho Lin, chairman of the Department of Economics, NTU, in 1986. Although he was not one of my students, he did sit in my class on international financial management, which I taught when I returned to Taiwan in the summer of 1987. We worked together and coauthored three papers. He, Mr. Yung-san Lee, and I initiated the Chinese Financial Association. He also assisted me in the organization of the 3rd Conference on Pacific Basin Finance, Economics and Accounting held in Taipei on August 8 and 9, 1995. In the spring of 1992, he invited me to lecture on financial issues at NCU and NTU as a distinguished professor of the National Science Council. He also participated in the debut of the Conference on Financial Economics and Accounting which I organized in August 1990 at Rutgers University and attended the PBFEA conference many times. His paper collection entitled "Empirical Studies on Business Finance and Government Policy in Taiwan" was published in 1996 by the Pacific Basin Business,

Economics, and Finance Research Center, which I chaired. Now, he is the associate editor of the *Review of Pacific Basin Financial Markets and Policies* and also a member of the editorial board of the annual journal *Advances in Pacific Basin Business, Economics and Finance*.

Dr. David M. Chen, Accounting Professor of Fu Jen Catholic University (FJCU), was one of my students at UIUC. While at UIUC, he had taken two of my courses and was my research assistant. I also participated in his dissertation committee. Prof. Chen served as director of the Institute of Finance, FJCU, and was the director of the Institute of Accounting, National Chung Cheng University. He is very knowledgeable in accounting and in new financial products. He specializes in the accounting methods used to deal with new financial products. He was the associate editor of the *Review of Pacific Basin Financial Markets and Policies*.

Dr. Yun Lin, professor and chairperson of the Department of Finance at NTU, was one of my research assistants at UIUC. Her dissertation was titled "Financial Futures Products and Banking Risk Management" and she coauthored two published papers with me. In spring 1998, she invited me to NTU as a distinguished research professor to teach Ph.D. students. She also invited me to participate in the 4th NTU International Conference on Finance, which she organized and was held in January 2000. She was a member of the editorial board of the annual journal *Advances in Investment Analysis and Portfolio Management*.

Dr. Chau-chen Yang, professor of the Department of Finance, NTU, was another one of my research assistants at UIUC. He helped me a lot with data and materials collection for my books, *Corporate Finance: Theory, Method, and Applications* and *Statistics for Business and Financial Economics*. He completed his dissertation on stock dividend policies under my advising and coauthored papers with me regarding stock dividend policies and Taiwan's stock markets. He was my assistant in the Foundation of Pacific Basin Financial Research and Development and also one of the associate editors of *Review of Pacific Basin Financial Markets and Policies*.

Dr. Chin-wen Hsin, chairperson of the Department of Finance and director of the International Financial Research Center, YZU, finished her dissertation regarding futures options at UIUC. We coauthored two papers on futures options, and she invited me to participate in the Conference on Financial Crisis and Economic Policies, which she organized and was held at YZU in March 2000.

Dr. Dar-yeh Hwang, professor of the Department of Finance, NTU, was my student at Rutgers University. Under my advising, he completed his dissertation, "Empirical Analysis and Theory of the Insurance Rate of Bank Deposit." He also published a related paper with me.

Dr. Hsien-hsing Liao, professor of the Department of Finance, NTU, was my research assistant and took my real estate financial analysis course at Rutgers University. He helped me a lot with the data analysis of the first version of my statistics book, *Statistics for Business and Financial Economics*.

Dr. Ahyee Lee, professor and chairman of the Department of Economics, FJCU, took my course at Rutgers University and also published two papers with me. He took part in writing the problem-solving manual for *Statistics for Business and Financial Economics* and coauthored with Ron Moy the students' supplementary materials for *Statistics for Business and Financial Economics*.

Dr. Chin-chen Chien, professor and chairman of the Department of Finance, NCKU, was another one of my students at Rutgers University. He completed his dissertation, "Relationship between Corporate Profits and Stock Prices," under my advising and we also coauthored three papers. He is also the associate editor of the *Review of Pacific Basin Financial Markets and Policies*.

Dr. Rong-jen Wu, associate professor and acting chairman of the Department of Finance, National Yunlin University of Science and Technology (NYUST), took my courses at UIUC. He was writing his dissertation regarding dividend policies under my advising when I left UIUC for Rutgers. Due to my departure, he changed his advisor and finished his dissertation on financial markets and policies in conjunction with the empirical data analysis of Taiwan's financial markets.

Dr. Chien-chung Neih, professor of the Department of Finance, TKU, was my student at Rutgers University. Under my advising,

Chien-chung completed his dissertation regarding the forecast of foreign currency exchange rate, which focused on foreign currency exchange theories and empirical data analysis. He also helped me a lot with organizing two international conferences at Rutgers University.

Dr. Ching-fu Chang, associate professor of the Department of Accounting, National Cheng Chi University, was one of my Ph.D. students at Rutgers University as well. I knew him through Prof. Gili Yen, who was Ching-fu's advisor for his master's thesis. Prof. Gili Yen, Ching-fu, and I coauthored a paper, "The Effect of Chinese New Year Holidays to Stock Prices." I advised Ching-fu on his accounting dissertation titled "Corporate Capital Structure and the Wage Problem of High-Level Managers." He was my assistant and helped me a great deal in the data analysis of the second version of *Statistics for Business and Financial Economics*.

My other students who are working in Taiwan include Professors Mei-hwa Lin, Yung-cheng Su, Jeng-Bau Lin, Chiung-liang Chen, and Wen-chuan Lee. Prof. Mei-hwa Lin took my financial course at UIUC; Prof. Yung-cheng Su took my course on international financial management in the summer of 1987; Prof. Jeng-Bau Lin was my postdoctoral student at Rutgers University for one year; Prof. Wen-chuan Lee worked as my research assistant at Rutgers, and I was one of the dissertation committee members for Prof. Chiung-liang Chen at Rutgers. My master's degree students include Tzu-chiang Yang, Kun-hsien Lin, and Chia-hung Kuo of UIUC; Cho-kun Hsu, Tsang-An Kuo, Yu-ming Chen, Su-tien Chen, and Cheng-tao Yu of Rutgers University. Tzu-chiang Yang and Kun-hsien Lin worked at China Development Industrial Bank; Chia-hung Kuo works at Taipei Branch of Bankers Trust Co., U.S.; Cho-kun Hsu, Tsang-An Kuo, and Yu-ming Chen work at the Central Bank of China, R.O.C.; Su-tien Chen at the Bank of Taiwan; and Cheng-tao Yu is a member of the Legislative Yuan. I am very proud of all their achievements.

Finally, I must mention Prof. Sheng-syan Chen, distinguished professor of finance, National Taiwan University. Although I did not advise Prof. Chen directly, he did have a very close relationship with me. Right after he received his Ph.D. from SUNY-Buffalo in 1995, I invited him to Rutgers University as a visiting professor for one semester to conduct research with me. In fall 1995, Prof. Chen accepted an offer from Nanyang Technological University in Singapore (NTU, Singapore) and taught there. In the summers of 1996 and 1997, I served as Visiting Distinguished Professor for two months at NTU, Singapore. Each summer while I was there, Prof. Chen and I continued our research and coadvised Ph.D. students. Until now, we still continue our cooperation in research and have published 12 papers together; two of them were in *The Financial Review* and other papers were published in the *Journal of Banking and Finance*, *Financial Management*, *Journal of Future Markets*, *Quarterly Review of Economics and Finance*, and others.

Under a dedicated arrangement planned by Professors Chien-chung Neih, Jeng-Bau Lin, and Gili Yen, my previous students and friends held a party to celebrate my 60th birthday at the Regent Hotel in Taipei on June 12, 1999. My wife, Schwinne, was invited too. At the birthday party, I reviewed my 26 years in teaching and thanked all my students for preparing the party. My previous students happily chatted with each other about their experience with my teaching.

Many of my students joked and told stories that I gave them a hard time. Some who graduated from UIUC said, "Usually, when Prof. Lee was happy, he would speak in Taiwanese; when he was mad, English; in between, he would speak in Mandarin." They threw me a very enjoyable birthday party. After the banquet, they presented me with a gift and took pictures to record these memorable moments.

Those who attended my birthday included Professors Yun Lin, Chau-chen Yang, Dar-yeh Hwang, and Hsien-hsing Liao of NTU; Prof. Chien-chung Neih of TKU; Professors David M. Chen and Ahyee Lee of FJCU; Prof. Mei-hwa Lin of NCCU; Professors Chin-wen Hsin and Sheng-syan Chen of YZU; Prof. Jeng-Bau Lin of National Chung Hsing University; Professors Chiung-liang Chen and Wen-chuan Lee of FCU; Prof. Rong-jen Wu of NYUST; Senior Specialists Cho-kun Hsu and Tsang-An Kuo of the Central Bank; Member of the Legislative Yuan, Mr. Cheng-tao Yu; and Senior Specialist Wan-jiun Chiou of Shanghai Commercial & Savings Bank; and Chairman M.S. Lin of MEGIC Corporation.

To promote the research on finance, economics, and accounting in Taiwan, I held the 3rd and 7th Annual Conferences on Pacific Basin Finance, Economics and Accounting in Taiwan, in August 1995 and May 1999, respectively. I also invited Minister Paul C.H. Chiu, Governor Fai-nan Perng, Prof. Son-nan Chen, Prof. Gili Yen, Prof. Chau-chen Yang, Prof. David M. Chen, and Prof. Chin-chen Chien as the associate editors of the *Review of Pacific Basin Financial Markets and Policies* to gain more international recognition for Taiwanese officials and scholars.

I also used other ways to help encourage Taiwanese scholars to conduct more research. For instance, in 1979 I suggested to President Clement C.P. Chang of TKU that he promote the faculty's research by giving cash awards. I also recommended that President Wei-jao Chen and Dean Hong-chang Chang require higher quality publications when evaluating faculty promotion in the Management School, NTU.

When I served as Visiting Distinguished Professor at NTU between April and July 1998, I was honored to join a three-day external evaluation meeting for the Management School. The evaluation committee included Prof. Shih-chun Hsu, Prof. Chih-wen Lee, Prof. Robert Hamada, dean of the Management School of Chicago University, Prof. Paul Danos, dean of Dartmouth College, Prof. Li-te Lee, Yale University, and myself. All of the committee members agreed that Dean Hong-chang Chang had contributed a great deal in enhancing the quality of the Management School and his efforts also helped spur on the teaching staff of other management colleges in Taiwan to do more quality research.

As far as I know, the departments of finance, economics, and accounting in Taiwan may boast the highest number of faculty members with Ph.D. degrees in Asia Pacific. However, only by raising the research quality, will Taiwan become one of the leaders in business education in Asia Pacific and cultivate more finance and economics professionals, who would support the development of Taipei as a regional financial center.

During the last 20 years (1996–2016), I frequently go back to Taiwan to give seminars and teach short courses at different universities. I most frequently give seminars at National Taiwan University and

National Chiao Tung University. Since 2008 I have helped National Chiao Tung University organize international finance conferences. NCTU International Finance Conference was just held in January 2016. As I mentioned in a previous chapter, one of my well-known international conferences, "Conference on Pacific Basin Finance, Economics, Accounting, and Management," has been held six times in Taiwan. The first conference was held in 1995 and was then held again in 1999, 2003, 2006, and 2011. The most recent conference, the 24th PFEA conference, was held on June 11 and 12, 2016 at National Chiao Tung University.

Finally, I would like to give two suggestions on business education in Taiwan. First, we should teach students in English to help them improve their English. In Hong Kong and Singapore, teachers in management schools teach in English, thus their students' English was much better than ours. Teaching our students in English would give them an advantage in the international stage as far as language is concerned. Second, doctoral students should be required to complete their dissertation in English. This will allow them to have opportunities to compete in the international markets. I sincerely hope that domestic scholars and experts can take my suggestions seriously and put them into action, although by this moment Taiwan's scholars and experts have taken most of my suggestions into account.

Chapter 17

Forty Three Years of a Challenging and Rewarding Academic Career

Since I have contributed a lot in both academics and policy to my home country, which have been discussed in previous chapters, professors, students, businessmen, and government officials decided to celebrate my 40-year teaching career. On January 10, 2014, National Chiao Tung University (NCTU) held an international conference to celebrate my teaching career. The celebration was held in conjunction with the 7th NCTU International Finance Conference at National Chiao Tung University, Taiwan. The title for this conference was "7th NCTU International Finance Conference and Celebration for Professor Cheng-Few Lee's 40-year Teaching Career." I gave a speech[1] entitled, "40 Years of a Challenging and Rewarding Academic Career." This chapter is based upon my speech and also includes a brief report of that conference. In addition, I will also describe my activities from 2013 to 2016.

I was really honored to have this conference to celebrate my 40-year teaching career, which was made possible only by my hard work and by

[1] This speech only briefly described my academic activities, which includes teaching, service, research, journal editing, conference organizing, and textbook writing. More detailed information about these activities can be found in the previous chapters.

the help of my friends, colleagues, teachers, students and others.

To begin with, I appreciate the opportunity I had to earn my high school degree from Chien Kuo High School (1952–1958), which is the best high school in Taiwan, and my bachelor's degree in economics from National Taiwan University (1958–1962), which is the best university in Taiwan. After one year of military service and five years of service at the Bank of China (1963–1968), I left Taiwan to earn my master's degree in statistics from West Virginia University and then went to SUNY-Buffalo to earn my Ph.D. in economics and finance.

Since I earned my Ph.D. in economics from SUNY-Buffalo, I have taught at the University of Georgia (1973–1976), the University of Illinois at Urbana-Champaign (1976–1988), and Rutgers University (1988–present). In August of 2013, I completed four decades of my academic career. During this 40-year period, I have experienced many challenging and rewarding academic activities. These activities can be classified into teaching, research, and service.

In 1973, the Department of Banking and Finance at the University of Georgia hired me as an assistant professor of finance. During this period, I received a lot of support in both teaching and research from UGA. In addition, my chairman, Bob Dince, gave me a lot of support in my work; therefore, I performed very well in teaching and research. My wife Schwinne Lee also earned her master's degree in accounting at the University of Georgia.

In 1976, the University of Illinois at Urbana-Champaign hired me as an associate professor without tenure; I earned my tenure in 1977 and was promoted to full professor in 1978. In the same year, I was invited to be associate editor of *Journal of Finance and Quantitative Analysis*. They gave me IBE chair professor in 1982. When the University of Illinois hired me, they gave me three missions. First, they expected me to upgrade the quality of the Department of Finance. They especially wanted me to convert a relatively qualitative type of program to a more quantitative type of program. Second, they expected me to create a high quality interdisciplinary Ph.D. program among finance, accounting, and economics. Third, they expected me to improve the quality of the faculty in the Ph.D. program.

From 1978 to 1988, I was Ph.D. director, where I was in charge of the departmental seminar, Ph.D. preliminary exam, and recruiting faculty. During this period, I invited Professor Merton Miller from the University of Chicago, Prof. Larry Summers and other well-known faculty to give a seminar at the University of Illinois. In 1982, Prof. Merton Miller came to Illinois to deliver his seminar, and when I introduced him I predicted that Merton would earn a Nobel Prize in Economics in the future. In 2013, Merton earned his Nobel Prize in Economics with Harry Markowitz and William Sharpe. Merton wrote me a "thank you" card and said, "CF, your prediction, it turned true."

In addition, I initiated a master's degree in finance in 1979. The Department of Accounting at the University of Illinois was the first university to have a Ph.D. program in accounting. The College of Business at the University of Illinois set up their Department of Finance in 1964. This might have been the first university in the United States to create a separate finance department. During my 12-year period at UIUC, I performed very well in teaching, research, and service. Overall, I was able to carry out the mission, which the University of Illinois expected me to accomplish.

In 1987, my son, John C. Lee, earned his B.A. in economics and my daughter, Alice C. Lee, earned her B.S. in electrical engineering. They graduated on the same day. President David Ikenberry told me that my family broke the University of Illinois' record, since both of my children studied at Illinois and graduated on the same day. I liked University of Illinois very much; however, once my children graduated and moved to other cities, my wife asked me to move to a bigger city too.

In 1988, I received an endowed chair professorship from SUNY-Buffalo, University of Oklahoma, and University of Memphis. In addition, Rutgers University offered me a special Professor II (Distinguished Professor) to match the offers from the other three universities. Rutgers University also offered me the highest salary among the faculty of the business schools and departments of economics. In addition, Rutgers University gave me financial resources to do research, edit journals, and organize conferences. I decided to accept the job offer at Rutgers University.

Based upon the above-mentioned experience in research, teaching, and service I would like to further explore my four-decade experience in academic activities.

Research Activity

My research activity can be classified into academic papers and publications, journal editing, and paper presentation.

A. Academic Journal and Publications

In the past 43 years, I have published more than 225 papers in more than 20 different journals in finance, accounting, economics, statistics, and management. In addition, I have published 26 books from 1973 to 2016, which has been discussed in Chapter 12. I was ranked the most published finance professor in the world from 1953–2008. Some important journals (which I have published) in different subject areas are presented as follows:

1. Finance journals: *Journal of Finance*, *Journal of Financial and Quantitative Analysis*, *Financial Management*, *Journal of Corporate Finance*, *Journal of Banking Finance*, and others.
2. Accounting journals: *The Accounting Review*, *Journal of Accounting Research*, *Review of Accounting Studies* and others.
3. Economics journals: *Review of Economics and Statistics*, *Regional Science*, *Urban Study*, *Journal of Econometrics*, and others.
4. Statistics journals: *Journal of Business and Economics Statistics*, *Journal of American Statistical Association*, and others.
5. Management journals: *Management Science* and others.

B. Journal Editing

Besides being an associated editor of the *Journal of Financial and Quantitative Analysis* (1977–1983) and other academic journals, I have been an editor for *Financial Review* (1986–1991) and *Quarterly Review of Economics and Finance* (1987–1990). I established the *Review of*

Pacific Basin Financial Markets and Policies and *Review of Quantitative Finance and Accounting*. In addition, I also established *Advances in Financial Planning and Forecasting, Advances in Quantitative Finance,* and *Accounting and Advances in Investment Analysis and Portfolio Management* and *Advances in Pacific Basin Business, Economics and Finance.* In Chapter 12, I have discussed these activities in detail.

C. Paper Presentation

In the last 43 years, I have presented papers at prestigious associations such as: American Financial Association, Western Financial Association, American Statistical Association, Financial Management Association, and other prestigious academic conferences.

I have been invited to present papers and consult academic programs internationally in Great Britain, Sweden, Israel, Spain, Hong Kong, Singapore, China, Japan, Taiwan, Thailand, Vietnam, and Australia and other countries.

Service Activity

My service activity includes administration, development of courses, and organizing conferences.

1. Administration Activities
   a. I was the Ph.D. director at the University of Illinois at Urbana Champaign from 1978 to 1988.
   b. Rutgers University hired me in 1988 to set up a department of finance at the New Brunswick campus.
   c. I initiated and started a master's program on quantitative finance with Ivan Brick in 2001.

2. Conference Activities
   I established the following well-known academic conferences:
   a. Conference on Financial Economics and Accounting: This conference was established in 1990 at Rutgers University and currently this conference is a consortium of Rutgers University, New York University, University of Texas at Austin, Indiana

University, Maryland University, Georgia State University, University of Toronto, Temple University and Turlane University. This conference has been recognized as the best conference in the interdisciplinary area of finance and accounting.

b. Conference on Pacific Basin Finance, Economics, Accounting and Management: This conference was established at Rutgers University in 1993. This conference was held at Rutgers University (1993, 1996, 2001, 2005, 2012), Hong Kong (1994, 1998), Taiwan (1995, 1999, 2003, 2006, 2011, 2016), Singapore (1997, 2002), Thailand (2000, 2004, 2009), Vietnam (2007, 2015), Australia (2008, 2013), China (2010), and Japan (2014). This conference is one of the three most important conferences in the area of finance and economics in the Pacific Basin area.

3. Course Development
I have developed new finance courses for the University of Illinois at Urbana-Champaign, Rutgers University, and National Chiao Tung University. These courses are Corporate Finance, Investment Analysis, Asset Pricing and Portfolio Management, Financial Planning and Forecasting, and Futures and Options.

4. Service Activity
I have chaired Ph.D. dissertations for the University of Georgia, University of Illinois at Urbana-Champaign, Rutgers University, and National Chiao Tung University.

During the last 43 years, I have been involved with more than 100 Ph.D. dissertations. These Ph.D. students performed exceptionally well and they teach at the Wharton School, University of Michigan, University of Southern California, University of Washington, State University of New York at Buffalo, University of Oklahoma, Indiana University, University of Georgia, Memphis University, Notre Dame University, Arizona State University, University of Dayton, Miami University, University of Houston, Hong Kong Science and Technology University, National Taiwan University, National Chiao Tung University, National Central

University, National Cheng Kung University, and others.

Many of my previous Ph.D. students hold chair professorships at different prestigious universities: S.P. Baginski (University of Georgia), Randy P. Beatty (University of Southern California), Victor L. Bernard (University of Michigan) who had passed away in 1995, Carl R. Chen (University at Dayton), C.W. Chen (Hong Kong University of Science and Technology), Chen-Chin Chu (Memphis University), Scott E. Harrington (Wharton School), Frank H. Page (Indiana University), Thomas F. Schaefer (Notre Dame University), Calvin Sealey (University of North Carolina at Charlotte), S.E. Sefcik II (University of Washington), David B. Smith (University of Nebraska), Duane Stock (University of Oklahoma), John K. Wei (Hong Kong University of Science and Technology), and Chunchi Wu (State University of New York at Buffalo).

Besides these 15 students mentioned above, I was either chairman or a committee member for more than 100 other Ph.D. students' dissertations at University of Georgia, University of Illinois, Ohio State University, National Chiao Tung University, and Rutgers University. All of these students are currently teaching at prestigious universities in the United States, Taiwan, Korea, Hong Kong, Singapore, Tunisia, and China.

During the past 43 years, I have had a very rewarding academic experience. I am one of the lucky first generation foreign scholars to have the opportunity to do academic service at University of Georgia, University of Illinois at Urbana-Champaign, and Rutgers University at New Brunswick. I have delivered the expectations, which these three universities expected me to complete. I hope I can serve 10 more years in academia and deliver more contributions to Rutgers University, the academic profession, and business consultation. In addition, I hope I can continue to be involved in economics, finance and policy, and business consulting in Taiwan and other Asian countries.

In the 7th NCTU International Finance Conference there were three keynote speeches, three discussion panels, and eight academic sessions. At this conference I gave a welcome remark and then President Chang and Dean Chang gave a short speech to welcome the participants. I gave the first keynote speech, "Four Decades of a Challenging and Rewarding Academic Career." Chun-yen Chang was the chairperson of the first keynote speech. The second keynote speech, "The Real Effect of the Initial Enforcement of Insider Trading Laws," was delivered by Professor Jon Wei, chair professor of finance at the Hong Kong University of Science and Technology, and chaired by Sheng-syan Chen. Professor Jon Wei graduated from the University of Illinois Urbana-Champaign in 1984 and I was his dissertation advisor. Professor Joshua Ronen, who is the chair professor at NYU, delivered the final keynote speech entitled, "Did the 'Fair Values' Required under GAAP and IFRS Deepen the Recent Financial Crisis?" Min-teh Yu chaired this keynote speech.

The first discussion panel on bank risk management included Sheng-cheng Hu, Yung-kang Ching, and Chairperson Yeh-ning Chen as panelists. Min-teh Yu was the chairperson for this discussion panel. Sheng-cheng Hu, Cheng-mount Cheng, Show-ling Jang, and Jiunn-rong Chiou led the second panel entitled, "The Cross-Strait Agreement on Trade in Services' Impact on Financial Markets," and Rong-yi Wu, president of Taiwan Brain Trust, was the chairperson. Dean Chao-hsi Huang, Professor Eric S. Lin, and I myself led the last discussion panel on the contribution of Professors Eugene Fama, Lars P. Hansen and Robert J. Shiller. Wen-liang Hsieh of National Chiao Tung University was the chairperson for the final discussion panel.

There were eight academic sessions and they were as follows: Corporate Finance and Real Estate, Microstructure, Credit Risk and Risk Management, Corporate Finance, Financial Accounting and Auditing, Option Pricing, Assets Pricing and Corporate Finance, and Investment Analysis.

In sum, I have a challenge and rewarding academic career during 1973 to 2016. Based upon my experience in academia, practice, and policy, I would like to give some advice to students and young faculties as follows.

Undergraduate and master's students:

1). Patiently learn basic theories, methodologies, and tools.

2). Apply these tools to real world scenarios by keeping updated with world and financial news.

3). Ask questions because you don't know what you don't know.
4). Integrate finance knowledge with other subject areas throughout your education.
5). In order to be a successful future manager, try to improve your analytical, writing, and presentation skills.

Ph.D. students:

1). Ph.D. programs generally accept students from various majors including business, economics, statistics, and mathematics; therefore, you should try to make sure to have basic knowledge of finance, economics and accounting.
2). Command good research, you should learn as much theory, methodology, and writing skills as you can.
3). Choose a dissertation topic as early as possible. You should not fear talking to your Ph.D. advisors about your research topic. Ph.D. advisors and Ph.D. student can learn simultaneously from each other.
4). Learn how to write a research paper as soon as possible. You should note that writing a paper could better prepare you for future research in finance topics.

Young faculty members:

1). It is well known that most research universities require faculty to publish academic papers (the so-called "publish or perish"); therefore, you have a lot of pressure to publish. You need to maintain a balance between your teaching, research, and service.
2). Young faculty members frequently become unmotivated to continue their dissertations. You should know that your

dissertation is one of the important sources for you to publish. You should not easily give up on your dissertation and in fact should work to improve it.

3). Young faculty members should realize that research papers should not only be published in top journals. After a couple of tries of submitting to a top journal, you should consider submitting to a second-tier journal in order to get it published. You should know that having a paper published in a second-tier journal would still earn you academic credit. It is possible to use the paper published in a second-tier journal as a base and improve the quality of your research so you can eventually submit to a higher-tier journal. In a famous Chinese book entitled *Art of War*, the message is to tell the general that they should not discourage their soldiers even if they fear the war. In other words, generals should tell their soldiers to regroup and win the war again.

Chapter

18

Life Begins at 70

When I was in senior high school, the late president of the Control Yuan of R.O.C., Mr. Yu Yeo-jen quoted the old saying, "Life begins at the age of 70," to describe his own life. Most people thought of his words as the tales of One Thousand and One Nights. However, as I know, there was a story as to why he said that.

When he reached 70 years old, Mr. Yu's health was not well. He usually needed his nurse to help him to go to the bathroom. One day, someone asked him, "When will you retire?" He replied, "President Chiang (Kai-shek) is older than I and he has not yet retired. How can I talk about retirement?"

Just after my 60th birthday, I thought over the essence of Mr. Yu's saying again and encouraged myself by thinking, "life begins at the age of 60." I expected myself to aggressively walk toward the next stage of my own life. Now I am 77 and lucky to be healthy enough to play an active role in teaching, service, and research.

In this autobiography, I have discussed and reviewed my childhood, my education, my work experience, and my achievements in my academic career. I am always optimistic. I understand the essence of the universal saying, "You must work hard to succeed."

Starting from the first year of the elementary school to the age of 77, the past years of my life can be divided into the following stages:

- Beginning: The six years of elementary school (1946–1952)
- Awakening: The six years of high school (1952–1958)
- Maturing: Undergraduate years, the years studying for a master's degree at NTU and working at the Bank of China, currently ICBC (1958–1968)
- Being revitalized: Studying overseas (1968–1973)
- Promotion: Assistant professor to professor (1973–1978)
- Gaining recognition: Promoted from professor to IBE Chair Professor (1978–1982)
- Becoming world-renown: Starting at Rutgers University to current (1988–present)
- Five-year perspective: In the next five years, I am planning to publish four books and 15–20 papers.

In the "beginning" stage I didn't know the world at all. Studying and minding my own business were the best ways to protect myself. Although I lived in a well-to-do family, the farmers' life wasn't rich at all. In fact, at that time Taiwan's social and political environment was very complicated. I always thought, "I can reach certain goals, and I must really work hard to reach them; although my life is not as good as the rich, mine is surely better than those who are worse than me." Thus, I lived a simple but happy life. And fortunately, among my friends and classmates it was rare that any of them were wealthy, so I was never jealous and kept a healthy attitude.

When the junior section of Chien Kuo High School accepted me, I felt more confident in myself. Although my life became a little bit harder, I had help from my grandparents, parents, aunt and uncle, and friends. They always kept me confident and in high spirits. When I was studying in senior high, my thoughts were gradually maturing. However, because of the heavy load of homework and studying, I didn't have time to care about the outside world, which was full of turmoil. Therefore, I was able to set myself clear goals and plans for my future. I called this the period of awakening.

Entering college, I gradually started to experience the real world by way of moonlighting. I began to doubt the dictatorship ruled by the Chiang Kai-shek, but dared not say anything. After one year of R.O.C military service, I gained admission to the Graduate Institute of Economics, NTU and also got a job at the Bank of China. When I became more confident in myself, I also understood more about the country and the world. My view was widening. Having worked for a while, I was really upset with the environment in Taiwan and decided to go abroad to search for new life. That was the end of my "maturing" stage.

After arriving in the United States, I studied in the economics Ph.D. program at West Virginia University. One year later, I changed my field to statistics and got a master's degree. During this period, I was well trained in quantitative analysis, which helped me a lot when I studied for my economics and finance Ph.D. degree at SUNY-Buffalo. During my years at SUNY-Buffalo, with help from my advisor, Murray Brown, Frank C. Jen, and other professors, I worked hard for the interdisciplinary study of economics, finance, and statistics and got my economics and finance Ph.D. degree in three years. To my best knowledge, I was part of the first groups of econometricians to study finance in the United States. Since then, I built up my foundation for future research. I recognized this as the end of the stage of "being revitalized" and beginning of "promotion."

In August 1973, I taught at the University of Georgia as an assistant professor and then transferred to UIUC in August 1976. In 1978, I was promoted to full professorship. Within these five years, I devoted myself entirely to teaching and researching and saw brilliant results. In this stage, I charged forward into an optimistic career. In 1977, I served as associate editor for the *Journal of Financial and Quantitative Analysis*, which ranked second among the financial journals in the United States at that time. The "promotion" stage ended when I was promoted to be a full professor in 1978.

After I became a full professor, I continued my research and paid more attention to helping my Ph.D. students. In 1982, I was promoted to distinguished professorship at UIUC. Before I left for Rutgers University in 1988, I was conducting research, teaching, and helping Ph.D. students. I had also published the famous textbook *Financial Analysis and Planning: Theory and Application* in 1985, served as editor of the annual *Advances in Financial Planning and Forecasting* (1982 to present), served as co-editor of *The Financial Review* (1986–1991), and served as editor of the annual *Advances in Quantitative Analysis of Finance and Accounting* (1986 to present). In addition, I was appointed co-editor of *Quarterly Review of Economics and Finance*. Meanwhile, I was working on my other three books: *Corporate Finance: Theory, Method, and Applications*, *Security Analysis and Portfolio Management*, and *Statistics for Business and Financial Economics*. During this period, I served as Ph.D. director and seminar coordinator. What I learned before had fully blossomed in this recognition stage.

In 1988, Rutgers University invited me to set up a department of finance at its New Brunswick campus and to be a distinguished professor of finance. My career stepped into a new era during my 27 years (1988–2015) at Rutgers, which was when I became world-renowned. I worked hard in teaching and doing research and also got involved heavily in administrative jobs. In addition, I published *Corporate Finance: Theory, Method, and Applications* (with Joseph E. Finnerty), *Security Analysis and Portfolio Management* (with Joseph E. Finnerty and Donald H. Wort), the first edition of *Statistics for Business and Financial Economics* (with John C. Lee and Alice C. Lee), *Foundations of Financial Management* (with Joseph E. Finnerty and Edgar A. Norton), and the second and third editions of *Statistics for Business and Financial Economics* (with John C. Lee and Alice C. Lee), a total of five books. I also founded two quarterly journals, *Review of Quantitative Finance and Accounting* and *Review of Pacific Basin Financial Markets and Policies*. I also served as editor of three annual journals, *Advances in Investment Analysis and Portfolio Management*, *Advances in Pacific Basin Business*, and *Economics and Finance and Advances in Financial Planning and Forecasting.*

During my time at Rutgers University, I have initiated two

important international conferences. The first conference, "Conference in Financial Economics and Accounting," started in 1990. Currently, this conference is a nine-university consortium and consists of Rutgers University, NYU, University of Texas at Austin, Indiana University, University of Maryland, University of Toronto, Georgia State University, Temple University, and Tulane University. The second conference is the "Conference on Pacific Basin Finance, Economic, Accounting and Management."

At present, I am editor of two quarterly journals, four annuals, and chairman of two conferences. Meanwhile, I also participate in the policy research of "Taiwanese Financial Market and Policies" and provide my opinions to government officials, academic institutions, and the industry all the time. While I am extremely busy, my name is also becoming even more popular. At this moment, I can clearly see what I'm going to do for the next five years. I'm going to continue to edit my journals and teach classes. I also expect to publish 15–20 papers and four books. I can only hope my health will allow me to accomplish my plan for the next five years.

When I think back on my academic life, I can't help but think how not only have I benefited from a successful career, but how my students have benefited as well. An old saying goes that the fame of a general is built up upon tens of thousands of dried bones; however, the reputation of a professor also benefits the tens of thousands of his students. We can conclude by borrowing a Chinese proverb

"一將成名萬骨枯，一師成名萬生輝。"

Appendix I

Chronology of Events

1939	In January, Cheng-Few Lee was born in Lung-Si Tang, Wu Chuan Village, Ta Yuan Township, Tao Yuan County, Taiwan.
1946	CF Lee entered Pu-shin Elementary School.
1952	CF Lee graduated from the elementary school and passed the entrance examination to the Junior Section of Chien Kuo (C.K.) High School, Taipei.
1955	CF Lee graduated from the Junior Section and was granted to study in the Senior Section of C.K. High without taking an entrance exam.
1957	The incident of Liu Tzu-jan happened and anti-U.S. emotions swept across Taiwan.
1958	CF Lee graduated from the senior high school and got the admission into the Department of Economics, National Taiwan University (NTU).
1960	CF Lee took the summer R.O.C. military training.
1962	CF Lee graduated from the Department of Economics, NTU.
	CF Lee served as an officer of the R.O.C. military in Tainan (Southern Taiwan).

1963 CF Lee passed the entrance examination and studied in the Graduate Institute of Economics, NTU.

Passed a special entrance examination and worked for Bank of China (currently International Commercial Bank of China – ICBC).

1965 CF Lee married Miss Schwinne C. Tseng of Fengyuan Township, Taichung (central Taiwan).

1966 John C. Lee, the son of CF Lee, was born.

1967 CF Lee got the master's degree in economics from NTU.

1968 CF Lee was awarded scholarship from West Virginia University (WVU) and went abroad to the U.S. to study for Ph.D. in economics.

Alice C. Lee, the daughter of CF Lee, was born.

1969 CF Lee changed his major to the master's program in statistics.

1970 CF Lee got the master's degree in statistics from WVU.

CF Lee was awarded scholarship and went to study for the economics Ph.D. program in the State University of New York at Buffalo (SUNY-Buffalo).

1971 Taiwan was out of the United Nations in October.

CF Lee was President of the local section of Taiwanese Association of America (TAA) at Buffalo.

1973 Chiang Ching-kuo declared the Ten Big Construction Plans.

Taiwan government abolished the system of "fertilizers exchange with rice."

CF Lee got his Ph.D. in economics from SUNY-Buffalo.

CF Lee taught in the Department of Finance, University of Georgia at Athens (UGA).

1976 Mao Zedong died in September and the "Gang of Four" was arrested right after.

CF Lee started teaching in the University of Illinois at Urbana-Champaign (UIUC).

CF Lee published more than 10 academic papers.

1977 CF Lee honorably served as associate editor of the *Journal of Financial and Quantitative Analysis.*

"Chung-Li Incident" happened.

1978 CF Lee was promoted to full professor.

Chiang Ching-kuo inaugurated as President of the Republic of China.

Lee Teng-hui took office as Taipei City Mayor.

CF Lee had published more than 20 academic papers.

1979 The United States ended formal diplomatic relationship with Taiwan in January.

Chinese Communists confirmed Deng Xiaoping's reform plan.

The Congress of the United States passed the Taiwan Relations Act (TRA).

CF Lee came back to Taiwan for the first time after 11 years since he left for the U.S. in 1968. He taught in Tatung Institute of Technology and Tamkang University, Taipei, in July and August.

Formosa Incident (Kaohsiung Incident) happened in December.

In December, CF Lee hosted Linda Gail Arrigo's speech regarding the Formosa Incident in UIUC.

1980 CF Lee published *Readings in Investment Analysis* (with Jack C. Francis and D. E. Farrar). McGraw-Hill Book Company.

CF Lee had published more than 30 academic papers.

Many people arrested for the Formosa Incident were tried in military courts and sentenced.

1981 CF Lee published *Financial Analysis and Planning: A Linear Programming and Simulations Equation*. Tamkang University Press, Taiwan.

Lee Teng-hui took office as the Governor of Taiwan Province.

1982 CF Lee served as the editor of the annual journal, *Advances in Financial Planning and Forecasting.*

CF Lee was promoted to the IBE Distinguished Professor of Finance in UIUC.

CF Lee delivered short courses in Wuhan University, Mainland China.

CF Lee delivererd a speech in Tokyo University.

CF Lee had published more than 40 academic papers.

1983 CF Lee published *Financial Analysis and Planning: Theory and Application, A Book of Readings*. Addison-Wesley Publishing.

1985 CF Lee published the textbook, *Financial Analysis and Planning: Theory and Application*. Addison-Wesley Publishing.

CF Lee served as co-editor of *The Financial Review*.

1986 CF Lee served as editor of the annual of *Advances in Quantitative Analysis of Finance and Accounting*.

CF Lee delivered short courses in Tamkang University, Taipei.

CF Lee had published more than 60 academic papers.

1987 CF Lee served as co-editor of the *Quarterly Review of Economics and Business*.

CF Lee published *Theoretical Framework of Financial Analysis and Application* (in Chinese).

CF Lee opened the course, "International Financial Management," for the graduate students in National Taiwan University and National Chengchi University, Taipei.

1988 CF Lee started to teach in Rutgers University as Distinguished Professor as well as Chair of the Department of Finance.

Lee Teng-hui inaugurated as President of the Republic of China.

CF Lee had published more than 80 academic papers.

1989 CF Lee served as editor of the annual *Advances in Investment Analysis and Portfolio Management*.

1990 CF Lee initiated and organized the first annual Conference on Financial Economics and Accounting in Rutgers University.

CF Lee addressed the keynote speech in the Conference of Financial Markets, held by National Taiwan University.

CF Lee published *Corporate Finance: Theory, Method, and Applications* (with Joseph E. Finnerty). Harcourt Brace Jovanovich Publishers.

CF Lee published *Security Analysis and Portfolio Management* (with Joseph E. Finnerty and Donald H. Wort). Scott, Foresman and Company.

Dr. Harry M. Markowitz, Dr. Merton H. Miller, and Dr. William F. Sharpe were awarded the Nobel Prize in Economics.

In May, Lee Teng-hui was inaugurated as the 8th President of the Republic of China.

CF Lee organized the 1st FEA Conference at Rutgers University, October 19 and 20.

1991 CF Lee served as editor of the *Review of Quantitative Finance and Accounting.*

CF Lee had published more than 100 academic papers.

Coordinator of the 2nd FEA Conference that was held at SUNY-Buffalo on September 12 and 13.

1992 CF Lee delivered the keynote speech in the China Economic Association.

CF Lee delivered the keynote speech at University of Pennsylvania for the 2nd Generation Program of Taiwanese American Conference.

CF Lee addressed the keynote speech in the Summer Camp of Midwest Taiwanese Americans.

CF Lee taught Banking Management and Analysis in Banking Institute of the Republic of China (BIROC).

Coordinator of the 3rd FEA Conference that was held at New York University on November 6 and 7.

1993 CF Lee served as editor of the *Review of Pacific Basin Financial Markets and Policies.*

CF Lee published *Statistics for Business and Financial Economics*. D.C. Heath.

CF Lee organized the first annual Conference on Pacific Basin Business, Economics and Finance in Rutgers University.

CF Lee delivered the keynote speech in the Conference on Finance, held by Tamkang University, Taipei.

CF Lee served as Distinguished Professor in The Chinese University of Hong Kong.

CF Lee's classmates from Department of Economics, NTU, held a grand reunion in Los Angeles for the anniversary of 30 years after graduation.

Coordinator of the 4th FEA Conference that was held at Washington University in St. Louis on October 1 and 2.

1994 CF Lee organized the 2nd Annual Conference on Pacific Basin Business, Economics and Finance in The Chinese University of Hong Kong and co-edited the paper collection with Prof. Chao-ping Chiang.

CF Lee came back to Taiwan in summer to lead the research on the plan of "Developing Taipei into a Regional Financial Center" and proposed the development policy of "industry is the root, while finance the leaf."

Coordinator of the 5th FEA Conference that was held at the University of Michigan on October 21 and 22.

1995 CF Lee organized the 3rd Annual Conference on Pacific Basin Business, Economics and Finance in August; Taipei collaborated with the Institute of Taiwan Economics and Research.

The Executive Yuan of the Republic of China started to promote the plan, "Asia Pacific Operation Center."

Coordinator of the 6th FEA Conference that was held at the University of Maryland on November 11 and 12.

1996 CF Lee served as Distinguished Professor in Nanyang Technological University, Singapore, in summer.

CF Lee organized the 4th Annual Conference on Pacific Basin Business, Economics and Finance in Rutgers University.

Lee Teng-hui won the first democratic presidential elections. CF Lee came back to Taiwan to join the inauguration ceremony.

CF Lee hosted the Symposium on Risk Management and Analysis on Financial Derivatives in Banking Institute of the Republic of China (BIROC).

CF Lee organized the 7th FEA Conference at Rutgers University on November 8 and 9.

1997 CF Lee served as Distinguished Professor in Nanyang Technological University, Singapore, in summer.

CF Lee organized the 5th Annual Conference on Pacific Basin Finance, Economics and Accounting in Singapore, Nanyang Technological University.

Hong Kong was returned to China on July 1.

CF Lee published *Foundations of Financial Management* (with Joseph E. Finnerty and Edgar A. Norton). West Publishing Company.

Michael Lee, CF Lee's grandson, was born.

Coordinator of the 8th FEA Conference that was held at SUNY–Buffalo on November 7 and 8.

1998 CF Lee served as editor of the *Review of Pacific Basin Financial Markets and Policies.*

CF Lee served as Distinguished Research Professor in the Management School of National Taiwan University.

CF Lee organized the 6th Annual Conference on Pacific Basin Finance, Economics and Accounting at Hong Kong Polytechnic University, Hong Kong.

The Asian Financial Crisis occurred.

CF Lee hosted the Symposium on Financial Crisis and Banking Risk Management in BIROC.

Coordinator of the 9th FEA Conference that was held at New York University on November 6 and 7, 1998.

1999 CF Lee organized the 7th Annual Conference on Pacific Basin Finance, Economics and Accounting in Taipei, National Taiwan University, President Lee Teng-hui was the honored guest speaker.

CF Lee chaired the Foundation of Pacific Basin Financial Research and Development.

CF Lee, John Lee, and Alice Lee published the second edition of *Statistics for Business and Financial Economics.* World Scientific Publishing.

In December, CF Lee and Hong-Chang Chang co-edited the *Collected Papers of Pacific Basin Financial Markets and Policies.*

In December, *Autobiography of Cheng-Few Lee: With Discussions on the Future of Taiwan and Pacific Basin Countries* (in Chinese) was published by Hwatai Publishing Company.

CF Lee had published more than 150 academic papers.

Coordinator of the 10th FEA Conference that was held at the University of Texas-Austin on October 29 and 30.

2000 In September CF Lee gave important advice to President Chen Shui-bian, about how to effectively utilize Taiwanese foreign exchange reserve.

CF Lee co-organized the 8th Conference on PBFEA that was held in Chulalongkorn University Bangkok, Thailand on May 25 and 26.

CF Lee published *Statistics for Business and Financial Economics*, Second Edition. World Scientific Publishing.

Coordinator of the 11th FEA Conference on "Financial Economics and Accounting and the 7th Mitsui Life Symposium on Global Financial Markets" that was held at the University of Michigan, School of Business Administration on November 3 and 4.

2001 Co-organizer of the Economic and Financial Summit in Taipei, January 2001.

CF Lee was the program director of the 9th PBFEA Conference held at Rutgers University on September 21 and 22.

CF Lee organized the 12th FEA Conference at Rutgers University on September 21 and 22.

2002 CF Lee co-organized the 10th PBFEA Conference held in Singapore on August 7 and 8, at the Nanyang Technological University, Singapore.

Coordinator of the 13th FEA Conference that was held at the University of Maryland, College of Business and Management on November 15 and 16.

2003 CF Lee was the program director of the 11th PBFEA Conference, held on May 30 and 31, in Taiwan at National Chiao Tung University, Hsinchu.

Coordinator of the 14th FEA Conference that was held at Indiana University, Kelley School of Business, on October 31 and November 1.

2004 CF Lee coordinated the 12th PBFEA Conference, held in the Consortium of Thai Universities, Bangkok, Thailand.

Coordinator of the 15th FEA Conference that was held at the University of Southern California, Marshall School of Business and Leventhal School of Accounting, on November 19 and 20, 2004.

2005 CF Lee was the program director of the 13th PBFEA Conference held at Rutgers University on June 10 and 11.

	Coordinator of the 16th FEA Conference that was held at the University of North Carolina, Kenan-Flagler Business School, on November 18 and 19.
2006	CF Lee was the co-organizer of the 14th PBFEA Conference, held at the Foundation of Pacific Basin Financial Research and Development, Taiwan.
	CF Lee published *Encyclopedia of Finance,* edited with Alice C. Lee. Springer.
	Coordinator of the 17th FEA Conference that was held at Georgia State University, on November 17 and 18.
2007	CF Lee co-organized the 15th PBFEA Conference that was held at Ho Chi Minh City University of Technology, Ho Chi Minh City, Vietnam on July 20 and 21.
	Coordinator of the 18th FEA Conference that was held at New York University, Stern School of Business, on October 26 and 27.
2008	CF Lee coordinated the 16th PBFEA Conference that was held in Australia for the first time, at Queensland University of Technology, Brisbane, Queensland.
	Lecture at University of Zaragoza, Zaragoza, Spain.
	Coordinator of the 19th FEA Conference that was held at Georgia State University, on November 14, Andres Almazan.
2009	CF Lee was appointed as a member of the Board of Policy Advisors at the Research Center on Fictitious Economy and Data Science, Chinese Academy of Science in China.

CF Lee co-organized the 17th PBFEA Conference held at the University of the Thai Chamber of Commerce, Bangkok, Thailand.

CF Lee co-directed the 3rd International Conference on Business in Asia (iCBA).

CF Lee published *Financial Analysis Planning & Forecasting: Theory and Application*, Second Edition. World Scientific Publishing.

CF Lee organized the 20th FEA Conference, held at Rutgers University on November 13 and 14; a lot of Lee's former Ph.D. students came to this conference to celebrate his 70th birthday.

CF Lee was recognized in Jean L. Heck and Philip L. Cooley's "Most Prolific Authors in the Finance Literature: 1959–2008" as the most published finance professor from 1953 to 2008.

2010 CF Lee gave a keynote speech entitled "Dividend Policy: Theory and Empirical Evidence" at the 18th PBFEA Conference held at the Graduate University of Chinese Academy of Sciences Beijing, China.

CF Lee published *Handbook of Quantitative Finance and Risk Management* with Alice C. Lee and John Lee. Springer.

Coordinator of the 21st FEA Conference that was held at University of Maryland, Robert H. Smith School of Business, on November 12 and 13.

2011 CF Lee was the program director of the 19th PBFEA Conference held on July 8 and 9, at the Foundation of Pacific Basin Financial Research and Development, Taiwan.

Coordinator of the 22nd FEA Conference that was held at Indiana University on November 18 and 19.

2012 CF Lee directed the 20th PBFEA Conference held at Rutgers University on September 8 and 9.

Coordinator of the 23rd FEA Conference that was held at USC on November 16 and 17.

2013 CF Lee delivered a keynote speech and received the Siwei Cheng Award in Quantitative Management at the International Academy of Information Technology and Quantitative Management (IAITQM) in April.

CF Lee was on the committee for the 21st PBFEA Conference held at Deakin University in Melbourne Australia on July 4 and 5.

CF Lee published *Statistics for Business and Financial Economics,* Third Edition, with John C. Lee and Alice C. Lee. Springer.

CF Lee published *Encyclopedia of Finance,* Second Edition, edited with Alice C. Lee. Springer.

CF Lee published *Security Analysis, Portfolio Management, and Financial Derivatives* with Joseph Finnerty, John Lee, Alice C. Lee and Donald Wort. World Scientific Publishing.

Coordinator of the 24th FEA Conference that was held at University of North Carolina Chapel Hill on November 15 and 16.

2014 CF Lee received the Dean's Meritorious Award for Research from Rutgers University in October 2014 for the 2013–2014 academic year. This award recognized CF Lee's long career in research, his work with doctoral students, his capabilities of organizing conferences and editing journals, and his overall contribution to the Rutgers Business School.

The 22nd Annual Conference on Pacific Basin Finance, Economics, Accounting, and Management was held on September 4 and 5 in Aichi University, Nagoya, Japan.

Coordinator of the 25th FEA Conference that was held at Georgia State University on November 14 and 15.

2015 CF Lee published *Handbook of Financial Econometrics and Statistics* with John C. Lee. Springer Reference.

The 23rd Annual Conference on Pacific Basin Finance, Economics, Accounting, and Management was held on July 16 and 17 in Saigon Technology University, Ho Chi Minh City, Vietnam.

CF Lee organized the 26th FEA Conference at Rutgers University on November 6 and 7. In this conference, he invited two other founding members, Professor Frank C. Jen and Marty Gruber, to celebrate the sixth anniversary. All three received a plaque from Rutgers Business School.

2016 CF Lee published *Financial Analysis Planning & Forecasting: Theory and Application,* Third Edition, with John C. Lee. World Scientific Publishing.

CF Lee published *Essentials of Excel, Excel VBA, SAS and MINITAB for Statistical and Financial Analyses*, with John C. Lee, Jow-Ran Chang, and Tzu Tai. Springer.

CF Lee organized the 24th Annual Conference on Pacific

Basin Finance, Economics, Accounting, and Management that was held in National Chiao Tung University, Taiwan on June 11 and 12.

Coordinator of the 27th FEA Conference that was held at University of Toronto on September 30 and October 1.

Appendix II

List of Important Books Authored and Coauthored by Cheng-Few Lee

In this appendix, we will list a number of important books (some with tables of contents) written by Cheng-Few Lee and others.

(1) *Security Analysis, Portfolio Management, and Financial Derivatives*

(2) *Statistics for Business and Financial Economics,* Third Edition

(3) *Financial Analysis, Planning and Forecasting: Theory and Application,* Third Edition

(4) *Essentials of Microsoft Excel, Excel VBA, SAS and MINITAB for Statistical and Financial Analyses*

(5) *Financial Econometrics and Statistics*

(6) *Intermediate Futures and Options*

(1) *Security Analysis, Portfolio Management, and Financial Derivatives.* Published by World Scientific, 2013
By Cheng-Few Lee, Joseph E. Finnerty, John Lee, Alice C. Lee, and Donald H. Wort
For more information about this book, please go to http://www.worldscientific.com/worldscibooks/10.1142/8116.

(2) *Statistics for Business and Financial Economics,* Third Edition. Published by Springer, 2013
By Cheng-Few Lee, John C. Lee, and Alice C. Lee
For more information about this book, please go to http://link.springer.com/book/10.1007%2F978-1-4614-5897-5.

(3) ***Financial Analysis, Planning and Forecasting: Theory and Application*, Third Edition. Published by World Scientific, 2016**
By Cheng-Few Lee and John C. Lee
For more information about this book, please go to
http://www.worldscientific.com/worldscibooks/10.1142/9810.

(4) ***Essentials of Microsoft Excel, Excel VBA, SAS and MINITAB for Statistical and Financial Analyses*. Published by Springer, 2016**
By Cheng-Few Lee, John C. Lee, Jow-Ran Chang, and Tzu Tai

Contents

2.6 Charting JPM's data using Excel's Chart Wizard
2.7 Read Data into SAS and Create Chart Graph
2.8 JPM's Financial Statements
2.9 Retrieving Stock Prices from Google Finance
2.10 Retrieving Stock Prices from Quandl
2.11 Statistical Summary

Chapter 3 Histograms and the Rate of Returns of Johnson & Johnson (JNJ)

3.1 Introduction
3.2 Calculating the Rate of Return of JPM
3.3 Frequency Histograms in EXCEL
3.4 EXCEL's Data Analysis Tool — Histograms
3.5 Histogram of JNJ's Return using SAS
3.6 Statistical Summary

Chapter 4 Numerical Summary Measures on Rate of Returns of Amazon, Walmart and the S&P 500

4.1 Introduction
4.2 Retrieving Stock Prices from Quandl.com
4.3 Numeric Measures of the S&P 500, Amazon and Walmart
4.4 Arithmetic Mean (Average)
4.5 Median
4.6 Standard Deviation
4.7 Variance
4.8 Coefficient of Variation
4.9 Minimum, Maximum and Range
4.10 Quartiles
4.11 EXCEL MACRO — BoxPlot
4.12 Z Score
4.13 Z Score in EXCEL
4.14 Skewness
4.15 Skewness in EXCEL
4.16 Coefficient of Correlation

Chapter 5 Probability Concepts and Their Analysis

Chapter 6 Discrete Random Variables and Probability Distributions

Chapter 7 The Normal and Lognormal Distributions

Chapter 8 Sampling Distributions and Central Limit Theorem

Chapter 19 Index Numbers and Stock Market Indexes

Chapter 20 Sampling Surveys: Methods and Applications

Chapter 21 Statistical Decision Theory: Methods and Applications

Part B Advanced Applications of Microsoft Excel Programs in Financial Analysis

Chapter 22 Introduction to EXCEL Programming

Chapter 23 Introduction to VBA Programming

Chapter 24 Professional Techniques Used in EXCEL and EXCEL VBA Techniques

24.1 Introduction

24.2 Finding the Range of a Table — Current Region Property

24.3 Offset Property of the Range Object

24.4 Resize Property of the Range Object

24.5 Used Range Property of the Range Object

24.6 Go To Special Dialog Box of EXCEL

24.7 Importing Column Data into Arrays

24.8 Importing Row Data into an Array

24.9 Transferring Data From an Array to a Range

24.10 Workbook Names

24.11 Dynamic Ranges

24.12 Global versus Local Workbook Names

24.13 Dynamic Charting

24.14 Listing All File in a Directory and Subdirectory

Chapter 25 Binomial Option Pricing Model Decision Tree Approach

25.1 Introduction

25.2 Call and Put Options

25.3 Option Pricing — One Period

25.4 Put Option Pricing — One Period

25.5 Option Pricing — Two Period

25.6 Option Pricing — Four Period

25.7 Using Microsoft Excel to Create the Binomial Option Call Trees

25.8 SAS Programming Code Instructions to Implement the Binomial Option Trees

25.9 American Options

25.10 Alternative Tree Methods

25.11 Retrieving Option prices from Yahoo Finance

25.12 Summary

Appendix 25.1 EXCEL Code — Binomial Option Pricing Model

Chapter 26 Using Microsoft Excel to Estimate Alternative Option Pricing Models

26.1 Introduction
26.2 Option Model for Individual Stock
26.3 Option Model for Stock Indices
26.4 Option for Currencies
26.5 Future Option
26.6 SAS Programming Code Instructions and Examples
26.7 Using Bivariate Normal Distribution Approach to Calculate American Call Options
26.8 Black's Approximation Method for American Option with One Dividend Payment
26.9 American Call Option when Dividend Yield is Known
26.10 Summary

Chapter 27 Alternative Methods to Estimate Implied Variance

27.1 Introduction
27.2 Excel Program to Estimate Implied Variance with Black–Scholes Option Pricing Model
27.3 Excel Program to Estimate Implied Variance with CEV Model
27.4 WEBSERVICE EXCEL Function
27.5 Retrieving a Stock Price for a Specific Date
27.6 Calculated Holiday List
27.7 Calculating Historical Volatility
27.8 Summary

Appendix 1 Application of CEV Model to Forecasting Implied Volatilities for Options on Index Futures

Chapter 28 Greek Letters and Portfolio Insurance

28.1 Delta
28.2 Theta
28.3 Gamma
28.4 Vega
28.5 Rho
28.6 Formula of Sensitivity for Stock Options with Respect to Exercise Price
28.7 Relationship Between Delta, Theta, and Gamma
28.8 Portfolio Insurance
28.9 Summary

Chapter 29 Portfolio Analysis and Option Strategies

29.1 Introduction
29.2 Three Alternative Methods to Solve Simultaneous Equations
29.3 Markowitz Model
29.4 Sharpe Performance Measure
29.5 Option Strategies
29.6 Summary

Chapter 30 Simulation and its Application

30.1 Introduction
30.2 Monte Carlo Simulation
30.3 Antithetic Variates
30.4 Quasi-Monte Carlo Simulation
30.5 Applications
30.6 Summary

Part C Applications of SAS Programs to Financial Analysis

Chapter 31 Application of Simultaneous Equation in Finance Research: Methods and Empirical Results

31.1 Introduction
31.2 Two-stage Least Squares Estimation
31.3 Three-stage Least Squares Estimation

(5) *Financial Econometrics and Statistics*. To be published by Springer, 2017

By Cheng-Few Lee, Hong-Yi Chen, and John Lee

Contents

Chapter 10: Simultaneous Equation Models
Chapter 11: Application of Simultaneous Equation in Finance Research

Part B Financial Statistics

Chapter 12: The Binomial and Multi-nomial Distributions
Chapter 13: The Relationship between Binomial Distribution and Option Pricing
Chapter 14: The Normal and Lognormal Distributions
Chapter 15: Copula, Correlated Defaults, and Credit VaR
Chapter 16: Multivariate Analysis: Discriminant Analysis and Factor Analysis
Chapter 17: Stochastic Volatility Option Pricing Models
Chapter: 18 Alternative Method to Estimate Implied Variance
Chapter 19: Numerical Valuation of Asian Options with High Moments in the Underlying Distribution
Chapter 20: Ito's Calculus: Derivation of the Black–Scholes Option Pricing Model

Part C Derivations of Option Pricing Model and Other Topics

Chapter 21: Alternative Methods to Derive Option Pricing Models
Chapter 22: Constant Elasticity of Variance Option Pricing Model: Integration and Detailed Derivation
Chapter 23: Option Pricing and Hedging Performance under Stochastic Volatility and Stochastic Interest Rates
Chapter 24: Option Bounds: A Review and Comparison

(6) *Intermediate Futures and Options*. To be published by World Scientific Publishing, 2018

By Cheng-Few Lee and John Lee

Contents

Part A Introduction

Chapter 1: Introduction
Chapter 2: Financial Market and Financial Instruments

Chapter 3: Futures, Options and Swap: An Overview
Chapter 4: Introduction to Valuation Theories

Part B Futures and Hedging

Chapter 5: Futures Valuation and Hedging
Chapter 6: Commodity Futures, Financial Futures, and Stock-Index Futures

Part C Option Strategies, Option Pricing Models, and Their Applications

Chapter 7: Options and Option Strategies
Chapter 8: Option Pricing Theory and Firm Valuation
Chapter 9: Decision Tree and Microsoft Excel Approach for Option Pricing Model
Chapter 10: Normal, Log-Normal Distribution, and Option Pricing Model
Chapter 11: Index Option and Currency Option and Interest Rate Option
Chapter 12: Comparative Static Analysis of the Option Pricing Models
Chapter 13: Implied Variance, Implied Distribution, and Volatility Smiles
Chapter 14: Portfolio Insurance and Synthetic Options
Chapter 15: Noncentral Chi-Square and Constant Elasticity Volatility Option Pricing Model
Chapter 16: Exotic Options
Chapter 17: Real Options
Chapter 18: Ito Calculus: Derivation of the Black–Scholes Option Pricing Model

Part D Other Related Topics

Chapter 19: Swaps and Bond Portfolios: Management and Strategy
Chapter 20: Warrants and Convertible Bonds Valuation
Chapter 21: Credit Risk and Value at Risk
Chapter 22: "Options Strategy, Option Valuation, Implied Variance and Hedging Strategy: Company A vs. Company B"

Appendix III

Additional Materials

The following items can be found in the Supplementary page of this autobiography's website (http://www.worldscientific.com/worldscibooks/10.1142/10182):

1. Faculty and staff who taught at the U.S. Chinese Center from 1983 to 1984

2. "Rutgers Professor Played a Role in China's Economic History"

3. Message to the 3rd Conference on Pacific Basin Business, Economics and Finance, by Lee Teng-hui, President, Republic of China, on August 8, 1995

4. President Lee's address for the 7th Conference on PBFEA at 9 a.m., May 28, 1999 (the original speech was in Chinese)

5. Appendices 9B, 9C, and 9D
   (a) Appendix 9B: Syllabus for Futures and Options
   (b) Appendix 9C: Syllabus for Asset Pricing and Portfolio Analysis
   (c) Appendix 9D: Syllabus for Corporate Finance

6. List of the attendants at the opening party and friends who sent flower baskets for congratulations on the setting-up of the Foundation of Pacific Basin Financial Research and Development

7. Cheng-Few Lee's mission and teaching activities at Rutgers University

8. References of the interviews in newspapers and magazines

9. CV of CF Lee

10. "Old Friends, Exceptional Scholars"

11. List of host universities, program chairs, keynote speakers of past conferences on financial economics and accounting

12. List of conferences on Pacific Basin Finance, Economics, Accounting, and Management from 2000 to 2016

13. "Annual Conference on Pacific Basin Finance, Economics and Management Held in Taiwan"

14. Additional photos of Cheng-Few Lee's activities